EXTRAORDINARILY BADASS AGILE COACHING

Robert Galen

RGCG LLC
Cary, NC

Many of the designations used by manufacturers and sellers to distinguish their products are claimed as trademarks. Where those designations appear in this book, and the publisher was aware of the trademark claim, the designations have been printed with initial capital letters or all capitals.

The author and publisher have taken care in the preparation of this book, but make no expressed or implied warranty of any kind and assume no responsibility for errors of omission. No liability is assumed for incidental or consequential damages in connection with or arising out of the use of the information contained herein.

Copyright © 2022 Robert Galen and RGCG, LLC
All rights reserved.

No part of this publication may be reproduced, stored in a retrieval system, or transmitted in any form or by any means, electronic, mechanical, photocopying, recoding, scanning, or otherwise except as permitted under Sections 107 or 108 of the 1976 United States Copyright Act, without the prior written permission of the publisher—RGCG, LLC.

ISBN: **978-0-9885026-5-9**

Printed in the United States.

Contents

Forewords   iii

Acknowledgments   ix

1   Introduction to Badassery in Agile Coaching   1

I • Agile Coaching Basics   17

2   The Mindset of the Badass Agile Coach   19
3   Agile Coaching Frameworks   35
4   Badass Agile Coaching Agreements   49
5   The Badass Agile Coaching Arc   69
6   The Badass Agile Coaching Operating System   87

II • Agile Coaching Models and Practice   105

7   The Agile Coaching Growth Wheel   107
8   An Agile Coaching Story, Part 1   127
9   An Agile Coaching Story, Part 2   149
10   Badass Metaskills for the Agile Coaching Growth Wheelm179
11   The Badass Agile Coach's Guide to Coaching UP   193

III • Nuanced Agile Coaching   215

12   Badass Agile Coaching in the Language of the Client   217
13   Badass Pair-Coaching   229
14   Badass Role-Based Coaching   241
15   Badass Context-Based Coaching   261
16   Situational Awareness as a Badass Agile Coach   275

IV • Continuous Learning   291

17   The Badass Agile Coach's Guide to Starting Your Day   293
18   Dojo Practice for the Badass Agile Coach   307
19   Setting Up a Badass Agile Coaching Community of Practice   319
20   Sharpening Your Badass Saw   329

Afterword   343

About the Author   347

Index   348

Foreword by Don MacIntyre

When I received an email from Bob Galen early one morning asking if I'd consider writing a foreword for his new coaching book, I immediately agreed. I found the fact that we were both in email at 5:45 on a Saturday morning amusing and yet another thing we appear to have in common. Bob and I were both early adopters of agile and focused on helping others adopt agile likely before the term "agile coach" was coined.

I don't recall exactly when I met Bob. I suspect it was at a Scrum Alliance conference or retreat, as we're both Certified Enterprise Coaches (CEC) and Certified Agile Leadership Educators (CALe). What I do remember is that every time we'd run into each other, talking about one agile topic or another, we'd always seem to be on the same page. In the years since, we've found opportunities to coach, teach, and present together. So, when asked to consider this book, I had no doubt that I'd enjoy it.

Bob has been a force in the agile coaching community for many years now. I've been in awe of the time and energy he has put into developing our community over the years. He is constantly sharing his experience, thoughts, and opinions in his writings, blogs, podcasts, and presentations.

Many long time agilists tend to gravitate toward just teaching classes after establishing a name for themselves. Not Bob. He's a coach. A coach's coach. A badass coach. He's passionate about agile coaching and passionate about helping others coach. He is constantly helping out coaches with mentoring, coaching retreats, dojos, coach camps, coaching clinics, etc. Bob is well known in the coaching community from all the contributions he has made. And this book is yet another item in his long list of contributions.

In *Extraordinarily Badass Agile Coaching*, Bob and friends have provided the agile coaching community with an exceptional toolbox of agile coaching patterns that will benefit agile coaches of all levels.

In the Agile Coaching Basics section, Bob introduces the reader to various agile coaching frameworks, introduces a number of tools, and helps to define what an agile coach is and what it isn't. I really enjoyed the way Bob called out the contrast between agile coaching, personal coaching, and professional coaching. This is an important distinction to consider, since some in our community appear to want to be personal life coaches while others want to simply coach the process and not the people. At the next agile conference, if you ask 10 "agile coaches" what an agile coach does, you'd likely get 10 different answers. Defining what an agile coach is and is not, is important. As a community, we should really align on our job descriptions so we can help our customers better understand the role.

While discussing the various coaching stances, I enjoyed how Bob provocatively shared why the common Coaching stance should not be at the heart of our coaching model. Coaches should take this to heart. With the Agile Coaching Agreements Canvas and Coaching Arc, Bob provides us with tools to help us define our relationship with our clients, better prepare ourselves for how we show up, and in general take a more mindful approach to our coaching plan. Bob then ties it all together with the Badass Agile Coaching Operating System formed around mindsets, the agile coaching stances, and the client's experience.

In the Agile Coaching Models and Practice section, Bob and friends share another powerful tool for the coaching community. The Agile Coaching Growth Wheel provides a fantastic visual of what it means to be and grow as an agile coach. I had come across the Wheel after a coaching retreat a few years ago, but it was not until reading this book that I took a close look at the matured product. I was so impressed with what the Agile Coaching Growth Wheel has become that I immediately introduced it to the agile coaching practice I am currently leading at Pfizer. The Wheel is something that all agile coaches should become familiar with.

The coaching stories included in the section on the Wheel do an excellent job of pulling the concepts that have been shared together in a familiar fashion. Coaches will easily relate to the fictional settings and situations described in the stories, as they include the typical situations that we tend to run into.

Bob also provides metaskills for us to consider beyond the Wheel in important areas such as the realm of leadership. Engaging with leaders is something agile coaches do on a daily basis. It is imperative that we include agile leadership and the ability to coach leaders in our coaching toolbox.

In the Nuanced Agile Coaching section, Bob focuses on the importance of language, the value of pairing with other coaches, coaching for specific roles and contexts, situational awareness, and diversity. Coach pairing as a practice is highly underutilized. Some of the more successful agile consulting companies actually do this as a norm—and not just for mentoring those new to coaching. Having two sets of eyes and ears and two sets of experiences can greatly increase the value of agile coaching for all involved—and can even make it more fun!

To close out the book, Bob reminds us of the value of coaching dojos, setting up a community of practice, and the importance of continuous learning, and suggests practices that will help you take a mindful approach to starting your day as an agile coach.

That's a lot of stuff. But the field we have chosen is a complex one. It does not matter if you are new to agile coaching or a seasoned veteran who is awake and doing email at 5:45 a.m., this book will help you learn how much more rewarding it could be, for both you and your clients, to be a more well-rounded coach with many more tools in your toolbox.

You've opened the toolbox. Now get to work helping us advance the practice of agile coaching.

Foreword by Paddy Corry

Reflecting on what I take away from reading *Extraordinarily Badass Agile Coaching,* three things really resonate with me.

The first is about community, and how important it is to the evolution of the agile coaching profession. Our agile coaching "trade" is evolving in real time through discourse and dialogue, experience, and experimentation. Many perspectives have helped to mold it and bring it to the version we see today. Even the Agile Coaching Growth Wheel itself, described by Mark Summers in section II of this book, has evolved and taken shape with participation and involvement from many agile coaches in community settings. We all stand on the shoulders of giants.

To tell the story of Extraordinarily Badass Agile Coaching and what it could be, Bob has also assembled a capable community of writers, a team of diverse voices. This team is walking their talk, demonstrating how the evolution and professionalization of agile coaching depends on community, while telling their own stories as a collective.

Agile coaching can feel like a fuzzy and solitary profession at times. The way the book is written reminds me in quite real terms that we are all part of a professional community, and that feels great. It's also a vivid demonstration of how we can achieve more when working together. To me, that is definitely badass.

The second point that has stayed with me from this wonderful book is the sheer wealth of experience so deftly conveyed. There is a lightness of touch to the way it is shared, and that makes the book very accessible. There is an explicitly stated intention to "go wide" in terms of experience rather than to "go deep" into details on any individual topic.

Chapter by chapter, this creates a lovely pace for the reader, with hard-earned knowledge lightly offered, and steadily accumulating into the wisdom coaches need, right as we watch. I would be willing to bet that even very experienced agile coaches will discover something new, useful, and practical to take away from this book. It is full of experience and solid ideas. That is also badass.

The third thing that has stayed with me is the choice of title, the playful invitation or gentle challenge to agile coaches out there to reflect on how we practice.

The word "badass" is not common in Dublin, where I am from. There are local words that mean the same thing, but they might not export quite as well! However, by putting the word *badass* in the title, Bob is inviting you, as a coach of coaches, to think about how you can work as an agile coach more on the front foot.

From my own experience, as someone with more naturally introverted tendencies, I started out my Scrum Master career with Servant Leadership as a default stance or way of being, and I don't believe that always served me well. In addition, there is danger in sticking too rigidly to a Coaching stance: It's just not always appropriate. Reflecting on a more badass approach to agile coaching described within these pages, I can consciously work on practicing alternative stances when appropriate, and reflect on how to be effective with them in an authentic and congruous way. I mean, come on, that is badass!

I hope that you will experience this sense of community, this breadth of experience so deftly shared, and the invitation to reflect on your practice throughout the pages of this book. You're in safe hands with Bob as your wise guide.

I wish you an enjoyable and extraordinarily badass agile coaching journey!

Acknowledgments

First, I want to acknowledge those who have come before me in this agile coaching journey. The first person that comes to mind is Lyssa Adkins. Yes, that Lyssa. She literally wrote the book on agile coaching. But beyond that, she has been a beacon of leadership in this space for well over a decade and I must thank her for her ideas, energy, and spirit.

Next, I want to thank Paddy Corry and Don MacIntyre for taking the time to read early drafts of the book and for writing such thoughtful forewords. I approached both of them because I wanted practicing, in-the-trenches agile coaches to write the forewords instead of fellow consultants, authors, or pundits. I thought it would serve to ground the pragmatic intent of the book. It means the world to me that they found value in the book's contents and shared their honest thoughts and reactions.

I also want to thank all of the agile coaches I've collaborated with on my CEC journey. One of the things I really value is the sense of community that the Scrum Alliance has fostered. Lyssa Adkins, Roger Brown, Pete Behrens, Don MacIntyre, and Michael Sahota were early role models for me, whether they realize it or not and I'm forever in their debt.

Next, I want to thank the group that co-created this work with me: Mark Summers, Rhiannon Galen-Personick, and Jennifer Fields. You all have been a joy to work with and made me (and the book) so much better because of our collaboration. Thank you for sharing your ideas.

Stuart Young has provided the fantastic sketch artistry for the book. You can see his work at the beginning of each chapter and on the cover. Stuart has added not only the sketches, but inspired my writing as well. I can't thank Stuart enough for his work. Beyond the pure creativity of each sketch, he and his sketches have inspired so much of the flow of ideas within the book.

Kimberly Andrikaitis helped me bring consistency, order, and creativity to many of the figures in the book. I've worked with Kim before and she's a creative wizard when it comes to PowerPoint. I leveraged that wizardry and she exceeded my expectations. And the book is better for it.

I found a wonderful group of technical reviewers for the book that I'm incredibly thankful to. They included Joel Bancroft-Connors, Paddy Corry, Peter Fischbach, Michael Huynh, Dana Pylayeva, Art Pittman, Mauricio Robles, and Leon Sabarsky. They all provided ongoing insights, comments, and suggestions that helped me to better refine, focus, and organize the book's ideas.

I particularly want to call out Paddy for also helping me experiment with some of the book's tools and techniques with his Dublin DNA coaching group.

DeAnna Burghart has edited several of my books and is a joy to work with. She is incredibly skilled, passionate, meticulous, experienced, and kind. I can't think of another person that I'd rather co-create a book with than DeAnna. I can't recommend her highly enough nor thank her enough for her contributions to and advice for the book. And, it was a fun journey too!

I also want to thank the Scrum Alliance for the tireless work they have done in the coaching certification space. If you've followed my writing, you know that I sometimes get frustrated with what they haven't done. But that doesn't mean I'm not thankful for all of their progress. And this includes the many volunteers who've helped in the certification efforts.

As an extension to this, for several years I was a volunteer in the Scrum Alliance for their coaching retreats. This is where I met many coaches, met Mark Summers, was initially exposed to the Wheel work, and was inspired to offer focus and help to the world of agile coaching. That inspiration has led me to continue my community involvement in coaching camps, dojos, and retreats. But it's also led to my passion to write and share this book.

I've saved the most important thank you till last. I want to thank my wife, Diane, for her ongoing and constant support of my consulting, coaching, and writing. Writing takes a time away from ourselves and our family, and her patience and support makes it all possible. Thank you, my love!

And yes, to my dogs, past and present: Foster, Bentley, Zoe, and Woody, thanks for adding joy, energy, and excitement to my life. I don't know where I would be without the influence of my beasts.

If I've forgotten anyone, and I'm sure I have, please hear my thanks for the role you've played in my journey, my work, and this book.

I'm incredibly grateful to all of you. Thank you!

1

Introduction to Badassery in Agile Coaching

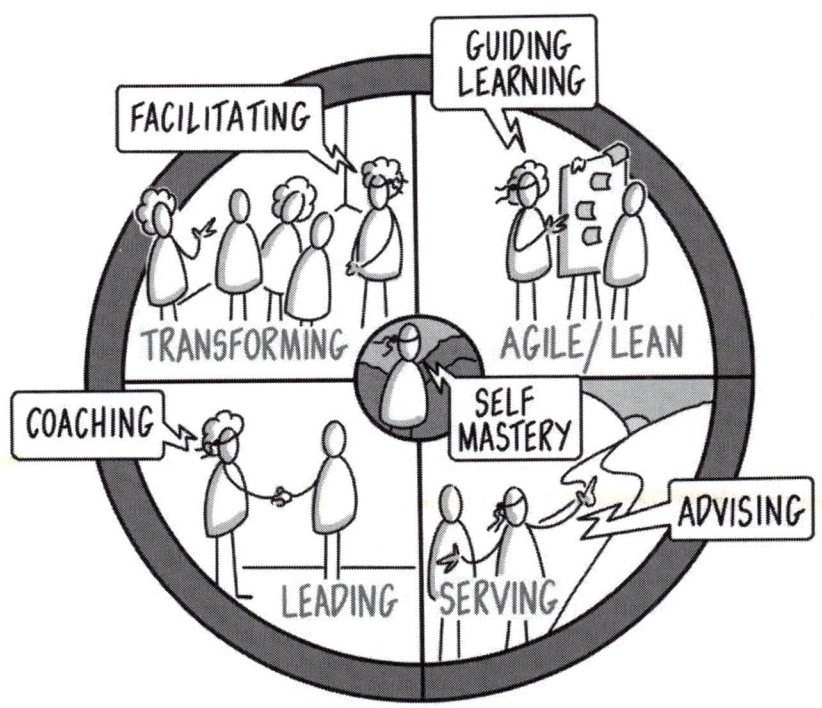

First of all, welcome to our book. It's an honor to meet you and a privilege to help guide your agile coaching journey.

We hope this book sets the stage for badassery in your coaching journey and inspires you to pursue excellence in that worthwhile endeavor. We also hope that it establishes a baseline for what can be an incredibly fuzzy role in agile contexts by answering some crucial questions: What is an agile coach? What in the world do they do? And how do you become great at this role?

An Invitation

Dear agile coach,

You are focused on helping individuals and organizations rethink their way of working. This is an incredibly challenging job, but a beautiful one. You help your clients grow and learn as individuals, as teams, and as organizations.

You will rarely have any formal authority. But as an agile coach, you have informal authority, and you decide how you will wield it.

Will you influence people by being genuinely interested in them, connecting with them, helping them reflect, and finding their next steps in accordance with agile principles?

Are you open to rethinking your way of working? Are you coachable?

Do you have a genuine interest in people? If you care, your clients will care.

You help them stay open, withhold judgment, and overcome their assumptions, cognitive biases, and overconfidence cycles. This will require that you yourself withhold judgment, and be open to learning from everybody.

I invite you into this book. Please enter with an open mind and heart. We'll be sharing tools, tactics, strategies, approaches, stories, and experience that have worked for us; you will need to perform the situational heavy lifting of making it work for you and your clients.

Are you open to this challenge? Are you willing to change, learn, and grow?

Well, then, welcome to the path of becoming an Extraordinarily Badass Agile Coach.

We're glad you're here!

Why Extraordinarily Badass?

I asked a well-known agile consultant, author, and coach to write a foreword for me. He said no, and the primary reason he gave was that he was uncomfortable with my use of the word badass. He even quoted some online definitions of the term in his reply. As I read them, I clearly saw his point. None were very complimentary or positive indicators of the competencies and skills I envision for an *Extraordinarily Badass Agile Coach*.

I'm not dwelling on that reply here, but it did inspire me to further explain my choice of words. While I can't change global definitions or individual reactions to the term *badass*, I can explain what being badass means to me, and my intent behind using the word in this book.

First, I use badass as an adjective. The online thesaurus Wordhippo says this implies "displaying outstanding skill, knowledge, and experience in a given field," and provides a long list of synonyms, including:

> expert, skilled, masterly, adept, proficient, adroit, accomplished, practiced, consummate, dexterous, deft, crackerjack, complete, artful, wicked good, formidable, nimble, agile, distinguished, top-notch, masterful, world-class, effective, admirable, dazzling, finished, exceptional, elite, marvelous, seasoned, well-versed, professional, outstanding, stellar, clever, gifted, competent.

I want to complement those adjectives with a few of my own:

> humble, resilient, reflective, curious, artful, playful, exuberant, joyous, dedicated, courageous, dogged, open-minded.

I realize I just inundated you with words, but I want to give you a broad and deep sense of my use and interpretation of *badass*. Each of these words indicates how I'm thinking about my coaching attitude and posture in relationship to my — and hopefully your — badass agile coaching journey.

Based on feedback from my colleagues and others, I seriously considered changing the title. But on deeper reflection, I decided that the *badass* theme throughout the book fully represents my vision and aspirations for you as a reader and a practicing agile coach.

You see, agile coaching isn't easy, nor is it for the faint of heart. It's full of frustrations, misinformation, bias, and pure change resistance. It's full of high client expectations that are often based on a fundamental misunderstanding of what coaching is (and isn't). It's also full of hubris and imposters who are coaches in name only, looking more for money, title, and prestige than to serve their clients. In a word, agile coaching is *challenging*, because it deals with people, and people are often messy.

It's hard to stand out amid these challenges—to set yourself apart, to be an example.

I believe that only by being badass can you do that successfully. By being broadly skilled and well-balanced in your use of those skills, a craftsperson who looks at agile coaching as a lifelong journey of learning, growth, and client impact.

So, to all of you dedicated agile coaches and aspiring badasses, please read on, as I hope this book helps to grow your badassery. And the world, agile and otherwise, certainly needs more Badass Agile Coaches.

To all others, thank you for considering this journey. Now may be a good time to exit the aircraft.

Why Us?

The first question I want to answer for you is why you should trust my advice and that of my coauthors.

First, experience. We all have decades of real-world experience coaching real people (individuals, teams, groups, roles, organizations) in agile contexts. If you're looking for a lot of academic studies and references, unfortunately you'll have to look elsewhere. Here, we're sharing tried and true experience.

We'll focus on what has worked for us—models, canvases, tools, techniques, stances, approaches, mindsets, and learning modes. We'll share all of that with you with a stance of humble camaraderie in the hope you will join our community of Badass Agile Coaches.

I've been an agile coach for about 20 years and a Certified Enterprise Coach (CEC) with the Scrum Alliance since 2012. It's a select group; as of this writing there are only about 140 of us around the world. I focus on being approachable and creating opportunities for fellow coaches to ask me for help, and I've usually been able to provide that help when they ask. I've been privileged to coach, train, and mentor so many agile coaches over the years that I often describe myself as a coach of coaches.

I also consider myself a well-rounded coach. One difference I bring to the table is experience in relatively senior leadership roles, which has given me insights into how to coach down, sideways, and importantly, up, to leadership.

But enough about me. Since this is a joint effort, let me share some background on the other key contributors.

Contributors

Multiple contributors have helped create this book for you. I'm grateful and honored to have the opportunity to work with such talented people on this project.

Jennifer Fields

www.linkedin.com/in/jennifer-fields-0b40aa4/

Jennifer began her agile journey as a developer and never looked back. Along the way she added to her agile toolbox by working in a variety of roles—project manager, Scrum Master, product owner, and agile leader—each helping to solidify and strengthen her agile mindset and coaching chops. Her wide-ranging experience and time spent at the senior leadership table give her a keen ability to work with folks across organizations, meeting them where they are to help them get to where they long to be.

Dedication: Thanks to Bob for investing in and supporting my journey.

Rhiannon Galen-Personick

www.linkedin.com/in/rhiannon-she-her-galen-personick-13aa99a/

Rhiannon comes from a different perspective, having spent the past 18 years as a social worker supporting child welfare. Rhiannon has worked both directly with clients and in a leadership role in several organizations. In her most recent role as a director of practice and professional development, she has worked alongside senior leadership and middle managers, supporting their growth through coaching and by being the energetic cheerleader we all need at times.

Rhiannon has worked extensively in the areas of diversity and race, creating curricula and training social workers on race consciousness, and helping many white social workers work toward a conscious acknowledgment of white privilege. Rhiannon has a deep passion for LGBTQIA+ advocacy, and assists her organization in developing workers who use inclusive practices.

Dedication: I would like to dedicate this book to my family—my amazing partner, Ben, and our two children, Vara and Mika—and to the amazing team of people who have helped shape me—Perquida, Katie, Jo, and Chantel!

Mark Summers

www.linkedin.com/in/markwsummers/

Mark Summers believes happiness always comes first. He has learned through experience that if people are having fun, then anything is possible.

Mark was one of the UK's first agile coaches and today is a leading figure in the ongoing story of agile coaching, a speaker at conferences, a leader of retreats, and a coach who never stops reflecting and evolving. If you're an agent of change, he believes you have to be on a continuous learning journey yourself.

Uncompromisingly honest with himself, energizing and thought-provoking as a coach, Mark is committed to helping people succeed by becoming happier, more open, and more autonomous as individuals and as teams.

Dedication: For my wife, Melanie, and our children, Lewis and Norah.

Mark contributed chapters 7, 8, and 9. He shared his direct experience co-creating the Agile Coaching Growth Wheel and several wonderfully detailed and nuanced coaching conversations to show you how to navigate the various stances within the Wheel.

Jennifer contributed chapters 14 and 15. She added even more coaching conversations, leveraging this book's Coaching Arc metaphor for her contextual coaching examples. You can *feel* her coaching presence and experience in the conversations.

Finally, Rhiannon contributed chapter 16, which is dedicated to situational and contextual thinking about diversity within and around your clients. I'm so thankful to include her unique perspective.

Each of these authors has added so much to the project and to the story we're trying to tell. Without them, this book would not provide the rich guide we hope we've created.

Goals for the Book

This book has four target audiences:

1. **Aspiring coaches**—folks who want to break into agile coaching and are looking for ways to develop, learn, and grow. I would

put Scrum Masters in this category, as coaching capabilities are an inherent part of excelling in that role.
2. **Practicing coaches**—folks who are looking to broaden their skills and competencies. I would put anyone who is looking to achieve the Scrum Alliance of CTC (Certified Team Coach) and CEC (Certified Enterprise Coach) in this category, and those pursuing similar coaching paths, particularly because these are well-rounded certifications with a focus on practiced skill.
3. **Master coaches**—folks who realize that the journey never ends and there is always something new to learn. This includes anyone who has the curiosity to look inside themselves, increasing their self-awareness, and the humility to keep growing and developing their coaching chops.
4. **Clients**—yes, clients! Since agile coaching is inherently confusing for those practicing it, imagine what it's like for our clients. This includes clients who are trying to hire or engage agile coaches and clients who don't know what to look for or how coaching works.

I know. That's a broad set of goals for a relatively short book. Which leads to one of the other goals for the book.

In any book, the author needs to make some early and fundamental decisions. Will the book be narrow or broad in coverage? Will it be shallow or deep in exploration? This, while also considering the overall length and approachability of the book.

I've decided to cast a broad net in this book, addressing every aspect of professional agile coaching that I think is relevant for achieving extraordinary badassery. Given that, I have chosen breadth over depth, and this book will not take many deeper dives in content. We'll leave that for you to pursue when you wish. At the end of each chapter, we'll share some relevant exploration points—books, articles, videos, and podcasts you can use to continue your journey.

Now, let's explore our understanding of what professional agile coaching is.

What Is Agile Coaching?

Please note that you will see the word *coach* or *coaching* a lot in this book. When you see either, we recommend you think *agile coaching*, simply because that's what the book is about. If we want you to think about, for example, *professional coaching* or the *professional coaching skills* instead, we have endeavored to use those words. So as a general rule, please assume we mean *agile coaching* unless we specifically say otherwise.

Now, let me start by establishing what agile coaching isn't. Professional badass agile coaching isn't:

- Family coaching
- Business coaching
- Personal coaching
- Therapy of any sort
- Just professional coaching
- Just consulting
- A place to complain or vent
- Sports coaching

Instead, it is a multivariate and multiskilled activity that includes some of the above but is unique in the coaching universe. That's probably why it's so confusing and so hard to define for so many.

An agile coach is a bit of a unicorn that is incredibly situational. As needed, they might choose to adopt the following *stances* with their clients:

- Mentor
- Teacher
- Consultant or advisor
- Modeler or exemplar
- Coach (in the professional coaching sense)
- Facilitator
- Evangelist (motivating or inspiring the client)

An agile coach will often switch between a few of these stances in a single coaching session. This is one of the most important distinctions between an agile coach and a professional coach. A professional coach will largely stay within the coaching stance, while the agile coach is more situationally aware and able to switch stances to better meet the client's goals.

In that way, there is a sense-and-respond nature to the craft of agile coaching. Perhaps this story will help explain the difference. I was coaching a VP at a client not long ago. While I'd met this person several times, this was our first coaching session. I started by asking questions. The VP stopped me after a few minutes, appearing a bit frustrated, and said,

> My last agile coach only asked me questions. That's all they ever did over the course of six months of coaching. They never helped me with a challenge, never provided advice, never explored options with me, never helped me to better understand agility and the role I needed to play. It was simply question after question after question!
>
> Are you going to do that too?
>
> If so, I don't think this is going to work out. I engaged you because I need help. Your help. We're struggling here to successfully implement agile. Really struggling! And I understand that I need to be engaged and solving my own problems but, dammit, you're the expert in this space.
>
> So, I've got a question for you: Can you help me?

This is incredibly common. You might think this is a "problem client" or a leader who is looking for easy answers, but this is not a client problem. This is a coaching problem. Obviously, the previous agile coach had a single tool (or stance) in their toolbox—professional coaching. In that stance, they focused on client inquiry via powerful questions and client discovery of solutions, approaches, or alternatives.

If that is your only stance, then I'd argue that you're leaving clients like this one in your wake—clients you didn't serve well, didn't meet where they were, and didn't help. And I firmly believe that we need to and can do better than that!

But there's even more nuance to this unique form of coaching. The professional agile coach must also have broad and deep knowledge of lean practices, agile practices, tools, techniques, scaling models, and organizational models, among many other things.

Sounds challenging, doesn't it? Well, it is. That is, if you want to do it well. And just being good at it isn't the goal of this book. Instead, our goal is for you to become an

Extraordinarily Badass Agile Coach!

There, we said it. If we're going to do something, let's be badass at it.

Internal vs. External Coach

This book tries to stay focused on the art and craft of agile coaching independent of your role or title or whether you're a consultant, contractor, or employee operating as an agile coach.

But there are *huge* situational differences between coaching from the inside as an employee and coaching from the outside as a consulting coach. I want to acknowledge these differences.

One obvious difference is what I'll call *skin in the game*—internal coaches usually have more of it. And with this personal investment comes awareness of the political and power situations within their organizational cultures as they navigate the nuance of agile coaching. They also have to live with the outcomes of their coaching for far longer than most external coaches.

Another difference between internal and external coaches is in the privilege of the coach. You've all heard the story of an internal coach who has been making the same recommendation for six months to a year without their clients taking them seriously. Then one day an external consulting coach visits, makes the same recommendation, and everyone thinks it's the best idea on the planet.

The point I'm trying to make here is to stay aware of your organizational position (internal vs. external) when reading this book and applying the learning. What an external coach might try in two weeks, an internal coach might decide to slow-play over the course of a year. Those situational, strategic coaching decisions are yours to make—unapologetically—based on your own *organizational contexts*.[1]

Certainly, I want you to become an Extraordinarily Badass Agile Coach, but I also want you to be aware of your contexts, role, privilege, risks, and rewards. In other words, I want you to stay safe too.

The Client

Another definition that's important is who is being coached. Depending on who that is, their role, the situation, and the context, the coaching can be quite different. Figure 1 defines my I's of client awareness for agile coaching—what I, as an agile coach, need the client to understand and support as part of our coaching relationship.

Establishing role clarity around the client and the coach is an important step in establishing the coaching relationship.

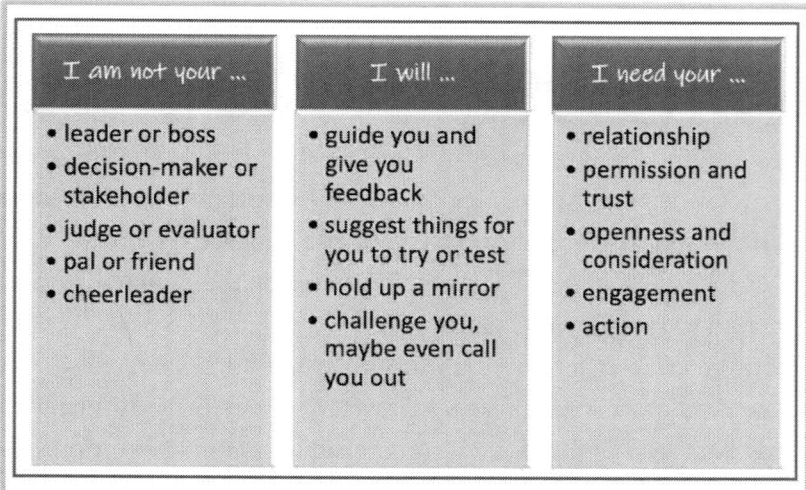

FIGURE 1. The I's of Client Awareness for Agile Coaching

---

[1]. There's a more thorough treatment of all of the aspects for internal versus external coach roles in the Badass Agile Coaching Repo (registration link in the afterword).

Throughout the book we're going use the term *client* to refer to the person or group being coached. It could imply

- an individual,
- a team,
- a group,
- an organizational silo or function,
- the entire leadership team,
- a specific role (Scrum Master, leader, stakeholder, product manager, etc.),
- your sponsor, or
- anyone you are serving.

Professional agile coaching can apply to individuals or groups. Again, we want to be directionally aware of the roles and adjust our approaches and stances accordingly, but we need the nimbleness to respond quickly to a wide variety of client contexts.

Badassery as an Agile Coach

Another driver for writing the book is our fundamental belief that there is far too much mediocrity in the world of agile coaching. One way to measure this is the sheer number of agile coaches popping up every day. It seems as if all it takes to hang out your coaching shingle is a couple of classes and a series of certification letters after your name. If anything, the problem is increasing over time as more and more people want to cash in on the agile wave.

Someone told me just the other day that they did a LinkedIn search for the term *agile coach* and got 240,000 matches—nearly a quarter of a million potential coaches.

I'd argue that very few are badasses.

One of the major enablers for this trend is the lack of a clear definition of agile coaching. We hope to provide some of that missing clarity by using the Agile Coaching Growth Wheel as a central model in this book. We'll explore it much more in section II. But we'll also emphasize the breadth of skill required across all aspects of the Wheel, with an emphasis on what deepening your skills within each stance might entail.

A final driver for this book is establishing a higher bar for what *good* looks like—badassery, if you will—in professional agile coaching. For example, I don't think it's good enough to be accomplished or expert at just one or two stances. You have to work hard to be broad, balanced, and skilled as a badass coach, with an emphasis on breadth.

To paint an image of badassery for you, here are a few key attributes we think of in professional Extraordinarily Badass Agile Coaches:

- We walk our talk, even under pressure or when no one is looking.
- We meet our clients with a mindset of respect, service, and gratitude for the opportunity.
- We have the courage to speak truth to power (even if that power pays us).
- We continuously strive to learn and grow as coaches, adding competency across *all* of the coaching stances.
- We are coachable (and have at least one ongoing coach).
- We are mentored and we mentor, and we fundamentally understand the value of mentoring.
- We strive to continuously improve our communication capabilities—including our storytelling.
- We have or align with a code of ethics and we hold to those ethics in all aspects of our coaching journey.
- We realize that professional coaching, while incredibly valuable, is only one stance to be used when appropriate in specific contexts.
- We respect the client and meet them where they are, not where we want them to be.
- We respect leaders and leadership, not falling into the common agile anti-pattern of judging up and blaming up.
- We not only coach individuals, we endeavor to be systems thinkers and system aware, and to coach the system wherever appropriate.

- We approach coaching as an inside-out endeavor, first focusing on our own self-awareness and behavior before looking (and coaching) outward.
- We maintain our humility, easily show our vulnerability, and realize that we need to serve.
- We make and take the time for personal reflection and self-care.
- We are intensely curious and powerful listeners, even to what is unsaid.

Does that list resonate with you? Excite you? We sure hope so. You'll explore all of those ideas and many more throughout this book. We encourage you to keep this image of badassery in the back of your mind as you read

A Badass Character

I also want to introduce you to an important character in the book (see figure 2). You'll see them in the sketches throughout the text. They can surface as ninja or sensei in the sketches (look for the headband), indicating they are operating as Extraordinarily Badass Agile Coaches.

I want them to be a continuous visual reminder (and motivator) of how you can develop mastery and badassery in agile coaching.

FIGURE 2. Our badass coaching character

Suggested Reading Flow

There are four primary sections in the book:

    I. Agile Coaching Basics
    II. Agile Coaching Models and Practice
    III. Nuanced Agile Coaching
    IV. Continuous Learning

If you're an **aspiring coach**, we recommend that you read the book as presented, from beginning to end. You'll probably find the most value in that order.

If you're a **practicing coach**, we recommend beginning with chapter 2, on mindset, and then perhaps going right to section II. We also recommend that you do a detailed skills assessment using the Comparative Agility Agile Coaching Personal Improvement (PI) survey to determine your balance across the Wheel and craft your journey based on the skill gaps you find. There's more information and an access link in the afterword.

If you're a **master coach**, we recommend first surveying the table of contents and looking for ideas that pique your interest. You might also try reading the headings within each chapter, as they give you a good idea of the focus within each. And we'd certainly recommend reviewing the materials on the Wheel, the coaching dojo, and the arc of a coaching conversation. But keep in mind that although you might think of yourself as a master, we all have something to learn in our journey toward being an Extraordinarily Badass Agile Coach.

Finally, if you're a curious **client**, we recommend reading chapters 3, 4, 5, 12, and 18. This should give you a solid sense of the important role that you play in your coaching and what excellence looks like in your agile coaches.

Stay agile and stay badass, my friends.

Bob Galen, Jennifer Fields, Rhiannon Galen-Personick,
and Mark Summers
November 2021

I • Agile Coaching Basics

The Mindset of the Badass Agile Coach

Agile Coaching Frameworks

Badass Agile Coaching Agreements

The Badass Agile Coaching Arc

The Badass Agile Coaching Operating System

2

The Mindset of the Badass Agile Coach

Agile coaches often talk about DevOps, frameworks, Agility, Business Agility, and agile transformations as being all about mindset. Well, I have some news for you. Agile coaching is all about mindset as well. And we need to be more aware of ours, staying reflective and becoming more self-aware about our own areas of improvement.

A huge part of that mindset is focused inwardly toward humility, client service, curiosity, and discovery. We also need to realize that we're all role models and that everything we do or say matters.

So, being humble, present, and intentional is inherent to badass agile coaching.

Introduction

Many agile coaches say they have the right mindset, but saying it doesn't make it so. The only true measure of your mindset is your behavior—whether you continuously walk your talk.

In this chapter, I want to explore some specific aspects of an effective agile coaching mindset. The premise here is that you are aware of these aspects, exhibit them, and are continuously honing, refining, and improving them.

In Service of the Client

The first and perhaps most important element of the agile coaching mindset is whether you view yourself in service of and to your clients. In this case, *client* refers to any individual, team, group, or organization you might be coaching.

In other words, this is the notion of approaching your coaching as a servant leader, entering each coaching context with a mindset of service. I think a big part of this is letting go of your baggage—your previous client-specific experiences, assumptions, mental clutter, and biases.

I have an exercise that I go through before engaging with a client for the first time and right before each coaching session. It goes like this:

- I close my eyes.
- I imagine myself in service to the client and needing to release my biases before our session.
- I hold my arms out and imagine holding a briefcase (or suitcase, depending on the amount of baggage) in each hand.
- Then I start filling the bags, clearing my mind so that I can enter the client's space with minimal baggage.
- When they are full, I drop the bags, letting go of everything.
- Finally, I open my eyes and enter the space.

I've found that this exercise helps me meet the client with a service-oriented mindset. I've also found that it creates better client outcomes, because I'm less cluttered and more present and focused.

Clients Don't Need Fixing

Let me share a poem that captures the essence of this section of the book.

A Fixer

A fixer has the illusion of being casual.
A server knows he or she is being used
in the service of something greater,
essentially unknown.

We fix something specific.
We serve always the something:
wholeness and the mystery of life.

Fixing and helping are the work of ego.
Serving is the work of the soul.
When you help, you see life as weak.
When you fix, you see life as broken.
When you serve, you see life as whole.

Fixing and helping may cure.
Serving Heals.

When I help, I feel satisfaction.
When I serve, I feel gratitude.

Fixing is a form of judgment.
Serving is a form of connection.[2]

[handwritten margin note: "im not sure if I agree"]

I have a confession to make. My name is Bob Galen and I'm a (hopefully) recovering fixer. I've been a fixer as a software developer, as a

---

2. This anonymous poem is widely circulated in the agile community. It is based on "In the Service of Life" by Rachel Naomi Remen, published in *Noetic Sciences Review*, Spring 1996.

manager and leader, as a project manager, and now as an agile coach. My natural tendency is to enter any coaching or consultative engagement thinking

- you have many problems and I can fix them for you;
- you don't fully understand agile, so I need to tell you and teach you;
- you are not leading your team in an agile way and I can help you to stop doing that;
- you ...

You get the picture.

Now, don't get me wrong. My heart is in the right place. I always want to help my clients and serve them. But I've learned that I'm not helping them, or at least not creating sustained learning and growth, if I solve everything for them.

I've also learned that this approach is disrespectful. When I do this, my perspective in engaging with the client is

- you are broken or don't know or don't have the skill, and
- I am all-skilled, all-knowing, and know how to fix, modify, or correct you.

How presumptuous, self-centered, and obnoxious is that?

As Badass Agile Coaches, we need to drop our inner fixer as much as possible. Sure, you can occasionally let that little rascal out, but do it as thoughtfully and infrequently as possible.

I believe our egos play a strong part in our fixer mentalities, so a part of playing the includes becoming humbler and more egoless in our approach to coaching, leadership, and life. The servant leadership work of Robert K. Greenleaf can be a helpful guide and compass for your journey here. (See the links at the end of this chapter for more information.)

The Prime Directive of Agile Coaching

I'd like you to approach every client contact point with the mindset described here. According to the International Coaching Federation, coaching

> honors the client as the expert in his/her life and work, and believes that every client is creative, resourceful, and whole. Standing on this foundation, the coach's responsibility is to:
>
> - Discover, clarify, and align with what the client wants to achieve
> - Encourage client self-discovery
> - Elicit client-generated solutions and strategies
> - Hold the client responsible and accountable[3]

Keep in mind that central premise: the assumption that "every client (individual, team, group, organization) is creative, resourceful, and whole."

Say it with me five times.

Now believe it.

And now, behave like you believe it.

That's the Prime Directive for our mindset as an agile coach, which I'd like you to hold tightly throughout the book.

Mindfulness and Staying Present

You can't discuss mindset without talking about the notions of mindfulness and presence.

I view mindfulness as first settling one's own mind. That is, not being focused on the past (mistakes, problems, personal issues) or the future (expectations, goals, aspirations) but on the present. Staying within each moment, being present, and paying full attention to *now*

---

3. https://icfhoustoncoaches.org/What_is_Coaching_.

in all aspects of our coaching—the now within ourselves and the now within our client.

Investigate — I'll discuss my ORSC[4] (Organization and Relationship Systems Coaching) training throughout the book, mostly because it made such a deep impression on me. ORSC is focused on coaching the system—which could be a small to large group, a team, or an organization—rather than coaching the individual.

One of my takeaways from ORSC was something they called *dancing in the moment* with your coaching. Dancing is being mindful and staying fully present, reacting to the conversation flow or journey and going wherever it takes you.

A part of your dancing is listening to all the communication channels available to us: the verbal and the nonverbal. Another part is trusting your experience as you flow—becoming comfortable with the ambiguity of not necessarily knowing where you are going, and letting the coaching emerge.

Your Presence and Privilege

Next, I want to discuss two aspects of your agile coaching: your presence and your privilege. You could use many words to describe your presence as an agile coach:

- Confidence
- Charisma
- Gravitas
- Aura
- Personality
- Mystique
- Commitment

I'll simply call it your *presence*. You not only want to be aware of your presence, you want to be intentional about bringing it into each client coaching session. This is the *professional* part of being a Badass

---

4. www.crrglobalusa.com/welcome.html.

Agile Coach, and you need to intentionally develop it as you would any other skill. Your clients will perceive and expect a certain level of this presence as part of your coaching.

But along with your presence should come an awareness of your *privilege*. Meaning, you need to show care when operating as an agile coach and always understand the privileges you have that your clients don't.

For example, I've often been asked about coaching up. As an agile coach, how do you provide coaching to leaders who are potentially not behaving well in their agile contexts? I'll often challenge these coaches. I'll speak about courage and the responsibility they have to speak truth to power. I'll tell a story or two about how I approached and challenged a CEO or a CTO to stand down a bit when micromanaging their teams.

To be honest, I often make it sound far too easy. And then I simply wave my hands and tell them to do the same thing next time they encounter a similar situation.

The problem is, my mindset when offering that coaching doesn't acknowledge my privileges:

- Being a skilled and experienced coach.
- Being an outside consultant.
- Being viewed as an expert by these clients.
- Being paid significant rates to be that expert.
- Being safe to express myself honestly with these clients.

Point being, I had privileges that the coaches I was talking to didn't have, and I should have been more aware of it when coaching them. I should have understood that gap and met them where they were versus where I was.

Your presence and privilege are something you have, not something you can directly control. So, my point in bringing them up is to increase your awareness of them and encourage you to step out in your coaching with that understanding in mind.

Metaskills

One of my most powerful takeaways from ORSC training is the notion of metaskills, which may have its origins in the book of the same name by Amy Mindell.

Definition

Here's the definition from the ORSC Dojo Workbook:

> A MetaSkill™ is the attitude, stance, philosophy or "come from" place that the coach stands in when coaching.[5]

I also align it or include it within my mindset as a coach. Putting on the mind of, or putting on the hat of, my metaskills.

Examples

Here are the seven base metaskills that are defined by and core to the ORSC model:

1. Commitment
2. Heart—entering with compassion
3. Deep Democracy—holding a space so that *all* voices are heard
4. Playfulness
5. Respect
6. Collaboration
7. Inquiry/Awareness—showing curiosity, then saying attentive to what happens next

All of these are largely self-explanatory.

One metaskill that I probably overuse a bit is playfulness. I try to bring lightheartedness and playfulness to all of my coaching. It complements my personality to a degree, in that I often use humor to establish rapport or defuse resistance and conflict.

---

5. www.crrglobalusa.com/store/p7/ORSC-Dojo-Workbook.html.

Applying Metaskills in My Agile Coaching

I've become much more intentional in how I enter each agile coaching situation, stopping to take a bit of time to prepare first.

One thing I do to prepare is consider the metaskills I should bring to the coaching system. That is, of the myriad of metaskills that I can leverage, both from the ORSC core list and from my own awareness and experience, which do I plan to use? Here are a handful that I often find myself using:

- Curiosity—childlike mind.
- Deep Democracy—all voices, including the voice of the system.
- Courage / Lion's Roar.
- Playfulness—self-deprecation, joking, lightheartedness.
- Mirror—reflecting back.

I usually focus on one or two metaskills that I will emphasize in my mind before and during the coaching session. I've discovered that trying to take on too many metaskills decreases my effectiveness in leveraging them.

The wonderful thing I've observed is that how I enter the system (my mindset, my intentions, my metaskills) affects the client or system itself. That is, the system often starts to mirror those metaskills back to me. If I enter a group retrospective with the metaskills of curiosity and playfulness, then the entire team seems to be more curious and playful in their exploration of continuous improvement opportunities. And all of this without me really "doing anything" but putting on those two metaskills.

Or, when I enter a coaching session with a small group of executives, I usually put on the metaskills of courage, curiosity, and challenger. Quite often they are looking for me to provide answers to them (Advising stance) and quite often I'll challenge them on this idea—trying to engage them in the solutioning, ownership, and partnership. But this can be a challenge to actually *do*, so the metaskills help my focus.

Additional Considerations

When using metaskills, two things are incredibly important. First, you need to meet your client (the system) where it is. There's nothing more frustrating for your client than, say, meeting them with playfulness when nobody is in a playful mood because they're in the middle of a nasty corporate merger.

You also need to consider what the system needs. Sometimes, you may make a courageous decision to show up with a metaskill that might not be embraced or welcome, but is nonetheless needed. Trusting yourself is important here; courage and persistence are also essential. But don't get stuck in a metaskill that is obviously not serving your client.

Finally, consider the degree of your metaskills. You can be all-out zany playful or just a bit playful. Keep the system's temperature (emotional field—discussed later in this chapter) in mind and adjust your metaskills accordingly.

Inside-Out Curiosity – Journaling and Personal Reflection

Extending the idea of reflection, I'm a fanatic about journaling as a tool for agilists who are looking to learn and grow. In journaling, you capture the essence of your journey. I consider part of the journal to essentially be a travelogue of sorts. You're keeping notes around your travels, learnings, observations, experiments, results, ideas, and discoveries. There's almost nothing too small to include in your journal, and this log becomes a rich landscape for you to uncover things.

For example, I've written a blog post about the richest communication being what is not said. How can you listen to nothing? Well, you can't if you're not observing and capturing conversations. But if you are, then you can go back and mine those conversations for hints that might help you reduce your blind spots.

Capturing Your Value

Another important aspect of your journaling is capturing the value you have provided in your coaching. Think in terms of what value you provided today, this week, this month or quarter, and in the longer term. This is more for you to reflect on personally than it is to use as a marketing or status reporting tool—to generate some positivity around yourself and your successes along the way.

You see, we often look forward too much at the challenges ahead of us and we fail to look back at the impacts we have had. Since coaching can be so challenging at times, it's important to take time to reflect on your successes; journaling is a time to do just that. Take the time to appreciate yourself, your impact, your learning, and your value.

Developing your curiosity, leveraging all available sources of information, should become an important part of your agile mindset. Which leads into your emotional intelligence. *[handwritten: in Trello share wins?]*

Emotional Intelligence (EQ)

Daniel Goleman identifies the following five key elements of emotional intelligence:

1. Self-awareness
2. Self-regulation
3. Motivation
4. Empathy
5. Social skills

[handwritten: which am I least skilled at?]

While these are more general in nature, I'll explore each in turn from a skill or focus perspective as an agile coach.[6]

Self-Awareness

Self-awareness means being aware of how you feel and your emotions as well as how those around you are feeling. It also means that you're

---

6. Using this as a reference: www.mindtools.com/pages/article/newLDR_45.htm.

aware of your strengths and weaknesses and that you have humility.

Ways of strengthening your self-awareness might include journaling, reflection, and practicing mindfulness. I'd also add gaining feedback, both direct and anonymous, via surveys of your clients and colleagues.

Self-Regulation

Self-regulation is all about staying in control. You'll rarely trigger on something or verbally attack someone—losing your temper, if you will. You also won't stereotype people or make rushed, emotional decisions. You maintain a level of personal accountability.

Ways of strengthening your self-regulation might include establishing and focusing on your core values, holding yourself more accountable, and practicing remaining calm. How you handle stress and the mechanisms you employ in doing so are important parts of your self-regulation capabilities. *Core values as a coach exercise*

Motivation

Self-motivation is a key here. Learning what drives you and establishing goals and a vision for yourself is critical, as is revisiting those goals often. In agile circles, we often talk about establishing your *why* at various levels—individually, at a team level, at an organizational level, and at a leadership level. Finding your why is probably your first self-motivation step.

Ways of strengthening your motivation include realigning to your why, establishing clear goals, reflecting on your current situation, and staying hopeful and optimistic about your future.

Empathy

Empathy is not sympathy. It's putting yourself in others' shoes and looking at the world from their perspective. To do this effectively, you need to understand their world by exploring it with them and listening effectively. Another part of empathy is a focus on developing others, which may require you to challenge them.

Ways of strengthening your empathy include being aware of and responding to others' emotions and feelings, paying close attention to body language, becoming a more powerful and active listener, and amplifying your curiosity when it comes to better understanding others.

Social Skills

Social skills are focused on how you interact with others. One key is communication skill and capabilities. Are you equally skilled at giving and receiving good and bad news? How do you handle conflict and emotional issues? Are you a role model and able to motivate others?

It's not about introversion versus extroversion, although that is a factor. Rather, given your innate ability, how socially aware are you?

Ways of strengthening your social skills initially focus on the quality of your communication skills in one-on-one situations, in small groups, and in large groups. While oral communication is a key, because of its multichannel nature, written communication is also important. I would say practice is crucial here.

The Emotional Field

In my ORSC training, we explored the notion of the emotional field in our coaching conversations. The perspective was focused on being aware of it in our coaching—staying present and listening to the emotional field as another channel of information about the system.

Before ORSC, I simply coached. Emotions were there at times, but I often ignored them or tried to coach through them. To be honest, emotions are often difficult for me and generally make me uncomfortable. Because of this training, my coaching mindset has shifted to become much more aware of the emotional field—not just of individuals, but of the entire system.

For example, let's say I'm coaching a small group of leaders and one of them angrily reacts to a problem they're ignoring. I've learned to

- not be triggered by the outburst or ignore it;
- acknowledge and normalize that individual's anger;
- most importantly, observe everyone else (the emotional field) to see how the outburst is impacting the system; and
- finally, call it out to the system to see how everyone is handling the outburst.

Calling It Out or Naming It

Beyond noticing what's going on in the emotional field, a powerful aspect of coaching with it is simply naming it. For example, I might ask questions of the group just described:

- I notice that everyone quieted down after Bill's outburst.
- What are you all feeling right now?
- How could we change the emotional field right now?
- Is there something we can do to return to where we were?

As a coach, I'm not reacting directly to the emotional field. I'm simply staying attuned to it and making the system aware of it as it changes.

And remember, you as the coach are part of the system and part of the emotional field. So, observing it also implies staying tuned into yourself and how you are showing up, reacting, and shifting within the emotional field.

Reframing

The final aspect of the agile coach's mindset that I want to explore in this chapter is what I'll call *reframing*.

One of the best examples of reframing I can think of is from Dale

Emory's article "Resistance as a Resource,"[7] which explored how we—not just coaches but anyone—can reframe terms to change the entire way we view things.

In his article, Emory used *resistance* as the trigger word. From an agile coaching perspective, we often refer to others as "resisting" the excellence of the agile transformation we're offering them, which frames that word negatively. Often, we think of resistance as synonymous with blocked, closed-minded, passive-aggressive, and uncooperative.

Since we're thinking of resistance in these negative terms, the folks we're coaching will sense that from us, which will create resistance—even if it wasn't there in the first place. But, if we reframe our views of resistance, perhaps view it as simply data or valuable information, then it changes the entire context of our coaching.

I've used reframing on resistance as an example, but you should use this tactic as a means of changing your views and biases on anything that strongly triggers you, while generally changing your coaching mindset.

---

7. Here's the source on Dale's website: https://dhemery.com/articles/resistance_as_a_resource/. And here's a presentation on the Agile Alliance website: www.agilealliance.org/wp-content/uploads/2016/01/Resistance-as-a-Resource-presentation.pdf.

Further Reading

This InfoQ article explores the agile mindset in more detail: www.infoq.com/articles/what-agile-mindset/.

I'd also recommend a *very* thorough reading of the Agile Manifesto—not only the Manifesto proper but also the 12 principles and the history behind these documents. All can be found here: https://agilemanifesto.org/.

A deep exploration of the work of Robert Greenleaf might also be a worthwhile exercise. You can find general information on his website. (Start here: www.greenleaf.org/what-is-servant-leadership/.)

I have two recommendations to explore surrounding better understanding your privilege as a coach:

- This is a blog post about it: www.agile-moose.com/blog/2020/12/19/the-privilege-of-my-agile-coaching.
- And this is a Meta-cast podcast that explores it: https://player.captivate.fm/episode/65b0368d-a8fa-4bd3-baa4-8461e534a97b.

This is an article focused on how to get started in your journaling. As with many things, it takes time to make it a habit, but it's a habit worth developing: www.agile-moose.com/blog/2019/6/23/journaling-how-to-get-started.

3

Agile Coaching Frameworks

Any profession or craft needs a clear baseline for true mastery. In the agile coaching community, we've shied away from clearly defining our profession, perhaps as something too prescriptive for this free-flowing and situational activity. But that has opened the door to incredible variability in the understanding of what an agile coach does.

Not only has this diluted the craft, allowing for mediocrity and one-tool or one-stance coaches, it has also made it hard for our clients to understand what an agile coach is and does and what value they offer.

Just as the timber frame of a building shows tremendous craft and precision, to the point of beauty, so should professional badass agile coaching display the precision, clarity, and beauty of our wonderfully nuanced craft so that we all understand the value proposition.

Introduction

It seems to me that nobody has wanted to define an agile coaching framework or place a stake in the ground saying yes, *this* encapsulates all of the aspects of agile coaching. Capturing the craft, if you will, and reinforcing what *good* looks like.

Sure, folks have alluded to it; for example, the Agile Coaching Institute's Agile Coaching Competency Framework. But frameworks have not been tied strongly enough to agile coaching and the requisite competencies.

One of the themes of this book, and this chapter, is to go on record to declare that professional badass agile coaching needs to support and model a multivariate framework that supports all aspects (stances) of our craft. The anchor we propose is the Agile Coaching Growth Wheel model. We'll be doing a deep dive into it in chapter 7 and providing examples of the Wheel in use across chapters 8 and 9.

But first we'll explore several existing frameworks, both to expand your thinking around frameworks in general and to set the stage for the Agile Coaching Growth Wheel. Specifically, this chapter will discuss:

- Examples of coaching models or frameworks
- Ways an agile coach might use frameworks
- The evolution in agile mindset and model thinking

Now, let's explore some frameworks.

The Baseline Coaching Model

The notion of *roles* or *stances* is inherent to any coaching model or framework. Figure 3 illustrates a model that includes nine coaching roles. These are a collection of roles that an agile coach typically adopts across a variety of coaching situations.

I think of the counselor, facilitator, and coaching roles as being the least prescriptive. They are soft and exploratory, and leverage the client's experience to help them through problem-solving or self-improvement. From another perspective, these are "stickier" stances because they inspire the client to change from the inside out.

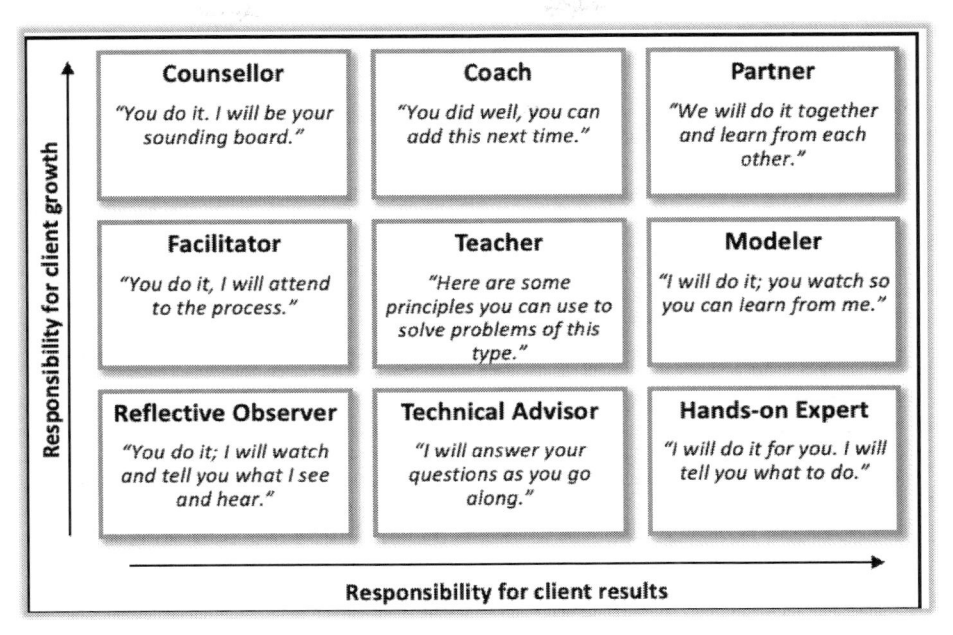

Counsellor "You do it. I will be your sounding board."	**Coach** "You did well, you can add this next time."	**Partner** "We will do it together and learn from each other."
Facilitator "You do it, I will attend to the process."	**Teacher** "Here are some principles you can use to solve problems of this type."	**Modeler** "I will do it; you watch so you can learn from me."
Reflective Observer "You do it; I will watch and tell you what I see and hear."	**Technical Advisor** "I will answer your questions as you go along."	**Hands-on Expert** "I will do it for you. I will tell you what to do."

Vertical axis: Responsibility for client growth
Horizontal axis: Responsibility for client results

FIGURE 3. Nine coaching roles. *Source*: www.growingagile.co.za/2016/03/the-9-coaching-roles/ by Esther Derby and Don Gray; originally from "Choosing a Consulting Role" by Douglas Champion, Davie Kiel, and Jean McLendon.

The technical advisor (think of it as an expert agile/lean practitioner), the modeler, and the hands-on expert stances are the most prescriptive roles. In these, the coach leans into their own expertise and provides more consultative guidance. These stances are probably the least sticky, because the client is largely being told what to do.

I often use reflective observer as an adjunct to my coach stance, as it helps me in staying present, observing, and sharing what I'm observing with the client system. The partner stance is another adjunct for me, because it combines nicely with all of the stances. One of my favorite coaching metaskills is adopting the mindset of partnering with the client—envisioning that we're in it together.

I like that the teacher stance is central to this model. For me, it's my default or baseline stance, especially since I enjoy teaching my clients as a way of serving them.

Using the Baseline Model for Coaching Arc Planning and Pivoting

I use this nine-square model all the time in my coaching. I find it useful when preparing and planning my client Coaching Arcs (explored in more detail in chapter 5). I'll often scribble down stances I envision adopting for a particular coaching conversation just to center my mind on what might be needed. Figure 4 shows a sample of that scribbling as I apply it to a Coaching Arc.

Coaching Arc

Opening Moves	Middle Game	Endgame
Coaching – Questions, with Curiosity	Teaching and Modeling	Advising – Coaching – Closing Questions

FIGURE 4. Sample Coaching Arc flow through the chess metaphor

Of course, I don't stay stuck in the plan; I'm sensing and responding all along the way. So, in the middle game, I might pivot from teaching and modeling to perhaps continue the coaching from the opening moves.

The point is that leveraging this model helps me clarify how I'm showing up and focus on being present in that stance. It also helps me clearly envision potential stance switches so that they're clean and clear within each arc.

Agile Coaching Frameworks   39

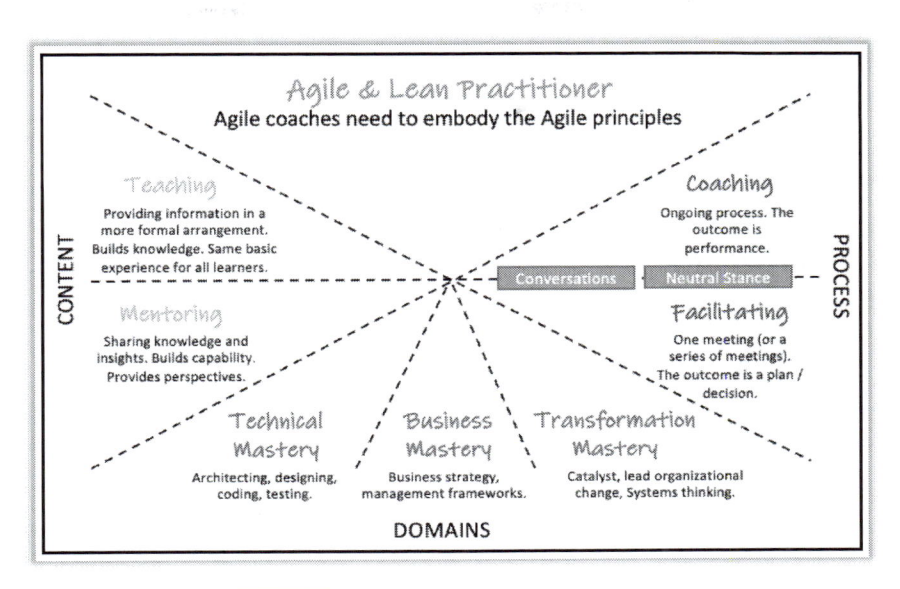

```
                    Agile & Lean Practitioner
         Agile coaches need to embody the Agile principles

         Teaching                              Coaching
         Providing information in a            Ongoing process. The
         more formal arrangement.              outcome is
         Builds knowledge. Same basic          performance.
  CONTENT experience for all learners.                              PROCESS
         - - - - - - - - - - - - [Conversations] [Neutral Stance] - -
         Mentoring                             Facilitating
         Sharing knowledge and                 One meeting (or a
         insights. Builds capability.          series of meetings).
         Provides perspectives.                The outcome is a plan /
                                               decision.

              Technical     Business    Transformation
              Mastery       Mastery     Mastery
              Architecting, designing,  Business strategy,   Catalyst, lead organizational
              coding, testing.          management frameworks.  change, Systems thinking.

                              DOMAINS
```

FIGURE 5. Agile Coaching Competency Framework. *Source*: The ACCF was created by the Agile Coaching Institute, and released under a Creative Commons license. This figure is a derivation of the framework.

Agile Coaching Competency Framework

The Agile Coaching Competency Framework (ACCF), shown in figure 5, is the grandfather of all agile coaching frameworks and is still the most widely known and used. It was created by the Agile Coaching Institute (ACI), which was founded by Lyssa Adkins and Michael Spayd in 2010. I've also heard it called the X-wing model because of its unique shape and because of how well *Star Wars* references resonate with our agile clients.

There are four primary quadrant areas within the ACCF:

1. Agile & Lean Practitioner skill competencies
2. Content (teaching and mentoring) competencies
3. Process (professional coaching and facilitating) competencies
4. Domain (technical, business, and transformation mastery) competencies

I think of the practitioner and domain areas as representing our experience outside the realm of direct agile coaching skills. These reflect the agile knowledge and our domain-journey knowledge acquired during our careers.

For example, I've been a senior leader and an agile evangelist and coach many times during my professional journey. My leadership experience maps well to the business transformation mastery competency areas. It also makes me a better coach and facilitator to senior leaders in the process competencies.

A Focus on Well Roundedness

The ACCF implies that agile coaching

- is a **multifaceted** discipline,
- which includes **professional coaching** as a subset competency,
- while also requiring **agile/lean expertise,**
- with **broad professional expertise** across the technology and business segments,
- and requiring **transformation mastery** (change artistry, change management, change champion, change models) as a domain-level competency.

One of the primary intents of the model is to encourage every agile coach to conduct self-assessment and self-reflection as to their strengths and weakness across each of the competency areas. That reflection should not be to arbitrarily grade your skills, but as motivation to create a continuous improvement plan that strives to fill in missing competencies so that your coaching becomes more well-rounded.

What Might Be Missing?

While the ACCF is a solid model that has been used for over 10 years, you can make an argument that some things are missing from it. I want to explore a few of those omissions next.

The Coach as an Individual

The first area that comes to mind is a focus on the individual coach — that is, an inside-out view that includes self-care, self-assessment, and self-improvement. Areas that come to mind include:

- Assessing yourself against a model.
- Finding your gaps and developing a personal development plan.
- Journaling and personal reflection.
- Personal mentoring and finding a coach.
- Being coachable, more self-aware, and emotionally intelligent.
- Community involvement.
- Practicing your craft through coaching, coaching, and more coaching.

I believe any good agile coaching framework should have a strong emphasis on taking care of yourself and growing yourself.

But the coach as an individual isn't the only gap, I see in the ACCF, and others have been motivated to extend the model too.

More Agile & Lean Practitioner Clarity

Jonathan Kessel-Fell suggested several extensions to the ACCF in a 2019 LinkedIn article (see figure 6).[8] First, he expanded the Agile & Lean Practitioner area to include three new areas:

1. **Agile & Lean.** This area maps directly to the original intent, focusing on direct skill and experience with agile and lean approaches.
2. **Mindset & Behaviors.** Here, Jonathan emphasizes that the agile coach needs to be an exemplar by walking the talk of the agile mindset and exhibiting consistent behaviors supporting it. A significant part of this is modeling positivity and the art of the possible—not in an artificial cheerleader fashion, but as a genuine extension of your mindset. This extension also stresses that how we show up each day as coaches makes a difference.
3. **People & Influence.** One of the things I've always felt was

---

8. www.linkedin.com/pulse/new-perspective-agile-coaching-competency-framework-kessel-fell/.

missing from some of the prominent coaching models was the coach's role as an evangelist, with attributes like passion, enthusiasm, or our drive to champion and inspire. Agile transformations are a change and changing is hard. The energy that a coach gives their clients can make a huge difference in how they navigate their journey. Jonathan gets that.

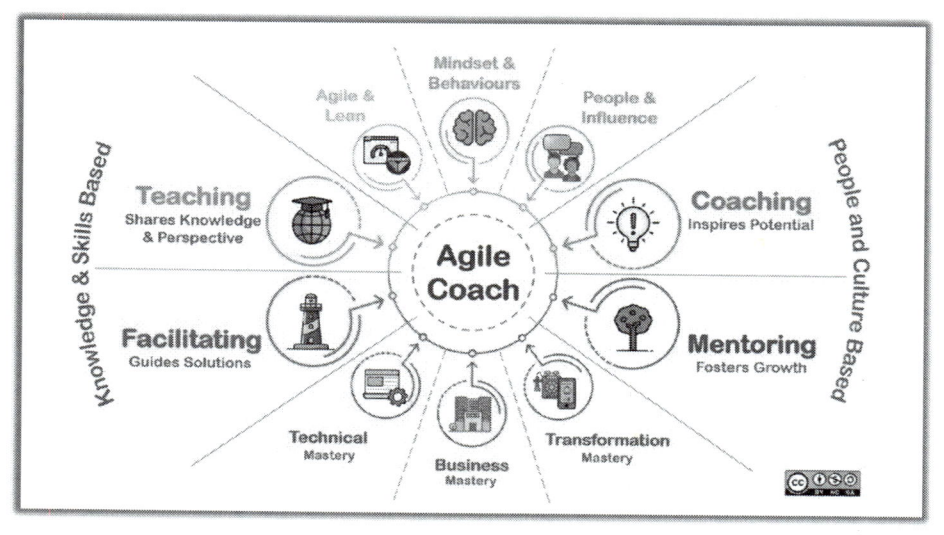

FIGURE 6. Kessel-Fell's adjustments to the ACCF. *www.linkedin.com/pulse/new-perspective-agile-coaching-competency-framework-kessel-fell/*. Used by permission.

Here's a wonderful quote from Jonathan's article on the People & Influence responsibility:

> It does not matter how much knowledge or experience you have in the world of Agile and Lean if you cannot share this information in a way that energizes people to grow and transform. Agile Coaches need to be amazing at what are called "soft skills," they need to know how to talk with people, how to listen intently and when to shut up and let people try things out themselves. It is only through these skills that you can truly influence people/situations and bring about lasting change.

Jonathan also swapped around facilitation and mentoring, grouping People & Culture Based activity on the right side of the model. In general, I like Jonathan's people- and culture-centric adjustments to the overall model. His version emphasizes the aspects that I feel are more important than others.

Where Is the Heart of Your Model?

Jake Calabrese is a Colorado-based agile coach who has a strong agile and professional coaching background. He and I often have a different take on the ACCF, as you can see in his three-part series of posts (links are provided at the end of the chapter).

Jake's view is that the ACCF is still a relevant and useful tool as is. That's not necessarily wrong. He argued in his blog series that if anyone perceives gaps in the ACCF it's because of a lack of understanding and depth in their interpretation of the model.

With due respect to Jake, I think there are some real gaps in the ACCF which, while not devaluing it, encourage others to clarify or extend the model, much as Jonathan Kessel-Fell did.

The one major point of disagreement I have is where Jake alludes to the coaching stance as being the central one in the model. Here's a quote from part one of his series:

> The coaching stance is what ACI refers to as "the heart" of ACI's Agile Coaching Competency Framework. The coaching stance is supposed to be the place you start from and return to. The elements highlighted (in the whitepaper) are maintaining neutrality, serving the client's agenda, reducing client dependence, not colluding, and signature presence. Signature presence is similar to "bring yourself" ... I have thought about the coaching stance like a "coaching home" where you can check-in to ground yourself.

I'm using Jake's perspective to make a more global point about my thinking around "the heart" of any agile coaching competency framework.

I strongly disagree that the coaching stance should be the heart of your model as an agile coach. Why? Because I think it's too passive of a stance and I've seen far too many coaches stay there or leverage the stance far too much.

I do believe that the coaching stance is incredibly useful. And, as you'll see later in this book, I think it's a wonderful way to begin and end your Coaching Arcs. But that being said, I believe a consulting/advising stance should be the heart of your coaching mindset.

For me, the central question is whether I better serve the client as professional Badass Agile Coach using the coaching stance or the consulting/advising stance. I believe the latter is more proactive, engaged, and willing to switch to other stances as appropriate. There is more of a sense-and-respond nature to it.

My biggest complaint with the coaching stance is that, by definition, it's not designed to switch to other stances. It's sort of stuck in asking questions and challenging the client to come up with their own direction and solutions. That's great if you're a professional coach, but far too limiting for an agile coach.

Mindset Models

To wrap up this chapter, I thought I'd change direction a bit and explore a couple of what I'll call mindset models. While they're not directly related to agile coaching, they do represent different perspectives for the agile mindset. They highlight how we need to keep the mindset "in mind" as we're coaching, which is one of the important distinctions between agile coaching and professional coaching.

I've chosen three models to explore in turn:

1. The Heart of Agile, by Alistair Cockburn
2. Kanban's Change Management Principles, by David Anderson
3. Modern Agile, by Joshua Kerievsky

Each of these models has some interesting ideas for us to consider as agile coaches.

The Heart of Agile

Alistair Cockburn's Heart of Agile returns to the Agile Manifesto and the basics of the mindset it tried to establish. It reminds us as coaches to look for opportunities to grow ourselves and our clients in the four areas it highlights:

1. **Deliver.** This quadrant reminds me to remind my coaching clients that everything in agile aligns with delivering customer value. If they lose sight of this, then everything else we focus on is moot. Agile is about our customers. You can also extrapolate this to our profession of agile coaching, which is all about our clients—serving them, meeting them where they are, and helping them to improve.
2. **Collaborate.** One of the things I try to emphasize in my coaching is establishing a partnership with each and every client. This might fly in the face of the professional coaching stance in that we want to maintain a distance of sorts from our clients, being more of a questioner or a mirror for them. And while I understand and agree with maintaining some degree of separation, I also feel that adopting a partner stance can be incredibly powerful for the client. It makes them feel like they're not alone in their journey. Again, it's a subtle balancing act.
3. **Reflect.** Can we say (and do) reflection, retrospection, introspection, and reviews often enough? I'd say no. Reflection is one of those things that is central to experimentation, learning, and continuous improvement. From an agile coaching perspective, I think self-reflection and system-reflection should be developed into one of your superpowers.
4. **Improve.** Tightly coupled to *reflect*, this is the area where we take the tactical learnings and do something with them. We act. From an agile coaching perspective, it applies to our own investment in sharpening our own saws. That's why I invested in an entire chapter (chapter 20) on improving our craft of professional badass agile coaching. Heck, it's why this book exists!

Kanban's Change Management Principles

For the past few years, I've been trying to merge a handful of Kanban principles into my coaching mindset. Here are the three I've been focusing on and why:

1. **Start with what you do now.** In other words, meet the client where they are. This is helpful for me because I have a tendency to sometimes meet the client where I want them to be, which is incredibly presumptuous and not very helpful to the client. Sure, my heart is in the right place, but it should never be about my agenda.
2. **Encourage acts of leadership at every level.** We often think of leadership as being hierarchical, connected to your title, role, or place within the organizational structure. But that's not where leadership really is. My experience is that it's an emergent property and that nearly anyone can be a "leader" wherever they are in the organization. As an agile coach, we can help to show, inspire, and encourage leadership everywhere with our clients.
3. **Agree to pursue improvement through evolutionary change.** As in the inspect and adapt principle within Scrum, this reminds me of the power of reflection, adaptation, and experimentation leading to truly evolutionary change. Remember, this isn't incremental change or baby-steps change. Instead, as agile coaches we're looking to empower and inspire everyone in the organization to see things in new ways, and helping to create the safety required for these experiments.

I'll bet you hadn't thought of Kanban as a mindset model before this. Well, please consider changing that view and internalizing much of what it has to offer.

Modern Agile

The final model I want to share is Joshua Kerievsky's Modern Agile Wheel.[9] He introduced it in 2016. I believe the intent was to inspire a

---

9. Here's an InfoQ article introducing Modern Agile: www.infoq.com/articles/modern-agile-intro/.

community-driven movement to "get back to basics" in our agile mindsets and approaches. While this model has become popular among experienced agilists, I'm not sure it's had a strong impact on our broader community, which is unfortunate.

I want to again put on an agile coaching hat and view the model through that lens.

1. **Make People Awesome**. Of course, we need to begin here. It's all about the people, and this lands squarely in our sights for all of our client coaching. I want to emphasize here that this means all people and not just the teams. As agile coaches, we need to be activating the awesomeness in everyone.
2. **Make Safety a Prerequisite**. To me, this is tightly coupled to making people awesome. That is, you can't make people awesome if it's not safe to experiment, learn, and grow.
3. **Experiment & Learn Rapidly**. There's a wonderful video by Richard Sheridan of Menlo Innovations where he talks about wanting to get "bad news" as quickly as possible so he can learn, adapt or pivot, and respond as a leader.[10] He couples safety with this notion of sharing bad news. I couple it with the notions of experimentation and learning.
4. **Deliver Value Continuously**. I'll connect this back to the *deliver* focus in the Heart of Agile. The same client-focused reactions apply here: We as coaches exist to serve and provide value to our clients.

I hope you see the connection between these three mindset models and your agile coaching mindset. While agile coaching is incredibly broad and nuanced with regard to stances, perspectives, and skills, it's still very much about developing and growing an agile mindset.

---

10. https://youtu.be/Oe8VTi3m8U8.

Further Reading

This is the original whitepaper, circa 2011, where the ACI reviewed the individual competency areas of ACCF: https://agilecoachinginstitute.com/agile-competency-whitepaper/.

The ACI also provides incredibly useful resource lists for self-directed learning in each of the competency areas: https://agilecoachinginstitute.com/agile-coaching-resources/.

This is Jake Calabrese's three-blog series on the ACCF. There's a lot of good stuff in here about how to interpret, act on, and create a deeper understanding of the model:

- https://jakecalabrese.com/understanding-acis-agile-coach-competency-framework/
- https://jakecalabrese.com/learning-from-acis-agile-coach-competency-framework/
- https://jakecalabrese.com/agile-coaching-framework-visual-walk-through/

This is a nice article contrasting The Heart of Agile with Modern Agile: https://medium.com/agile-insights/heart-of-agile-vs-modern-agile-3c47d34e8c6.

This video by Todd Little explains the Kanban Mindset: https://youtu.be/AtPlUrTaivk.

4

Badass Agile Coaching Agreements

You're an agile coach in a highly charged at-scale transformation effort. Teams, individuals, senior leaders, and key stakeholders are coming to you daily looking for pithy, valuable coaching advice, in real time and with a sense of urgency.

It's incredibly tempting to just dive in, react, and begin "coaching" in the flow of each day. A similar notion would be to give delivery dates to everyone who asks you for advice without proper planning. Don't do it!

It's often counterintuitive, but you need to slow down and establish agreements before you coach anyone. A coaching agreement establishes your scope boundaries and provides guardrails for how you and your client will approach the coaching. It also sets expectations of the coach and client roles, which is crucial. My point being: never, ever coach without establishing an agreement.

Introduction

When I was taking my ORSC coaching training, I remember one of my trainers talking about running through a day of coaching. She would set up one-hour coaching sessions for six or so straight hours without a break. Keep in mind, this was a very experienced professional (not agile) coach.

I couldn't help but think to myself that she had reserved no time between the sessions for preparation and wrap-up activity. How the heck could she maintain continuity between her clients' contexts? So, I asked the question.

Her answer, essentially, was:

- She was highly experienced, having been a coach for more than 10 years.
- She had worked with these clients before.
- And since the clients were accountable for their results, there was little that she "owned" in the coaching relationship.

That approach seemed to work for this coach, but it doesn't necessarily work for me. And I highly recommend that you avoid this approach yourself, no matter how much experience you have.

As an alternative to her strategy, this chapter is focused on establishing coaching agreements. That includes setting up the conditions of coaching, preparing for your coaching, and closing your coaching. That is, we will move from the initial agreement to a "closed loop," if you will, of preparation, note-taking, closing thoughts, and preparation for the next session.

Professional Coaching Agreements

One of the fundamental aspects of professional coaching is establishing a coaching agreement with your client before you begin. I think this practice carries over nicely into the realm of agile coaching. Being consistent and rigorous in establishing and maintaining your agreements is an important part of becoming a Badass Agile Coach.

Agreements as a Core Competency

Establishing your coaching agreement is one of the International Coaching Federation (ICF) core competencies—the first in their Co-Creating the Relationship competencies—and here is how they define it on their website (as of October 2021):

> Partners with the client and relevant stakeholders to create clear agreements about the coaching relationship, process, plans and goals. Establishes agreements for the overall coaching engagement as well as those for each coaching session.

Expanding on the ICF definition by considering aspects particular to agile coaching, your coaching agreement could include:

- Establishing your role as a coach—what's in play or in scope for you and what's not.
- Establishing goals for your coaching and the partnership relationship you'll be adopting with the client.
- Explaining the variety of coaching stances (see chapter 3) that you'll be using as a coach.
- Exploring tactical dynamics—how often you'll meet, when, and for how long.
- And of course, if you're an independent coach, such mundane topics as your rate, billing, and turnaround dynamics.

ORSC – Designed Coaching Alliance

My ORSC training introduced me to the notion of creating a designed coaching alliance (DCA) or designed coaching partnership (DCP).

Your first step as a coach should be establishing (designing) your coaching partnership with your client(s) or the system, which includes defining, exploring, and understanding your client's agenda so that you can serve it and them. You should do this at the beginning of your overall coaching relationship and then at the beginning of each coaching session. I know this sounds restrictive, but the entire notion of DCAs is about establishing a working agreement and developing clarity around the system and its relationship to your coaching. So, it's important to begin well.

These agreements are based on asking your client a fairly prescriptive set of questions. For example, at the outset of the coaching relationship you might ask, What overall outcomes are you trying to achieve with our coaching, or What are your overall goals?

Then, during each coaching session you might follow up with questions like, What would you like to work on today? What outcomes are you looking for? How will you know when we have met those outcomes?

At the end of each session, you might ask, Did we meet the outcomes you were looking for? And at the end of your final coaching session, you might ask, Did we meet the outcomes you were looking for?

The key idea with both the DCA and DCP is to design your alliance with your client. It's a collaborative, conversational, and co-creative process. The questions are intended to be open-ended, to encourage the client to think more deeply about their goals and aspirations for your coaching.

The process shouldn't be rushed or shortened. And don't forget, while the entire purpose of establishing your DCA or DCP is to inspire a conversation, you should capture the essence of the agreement—writing it down and confirming the understanding between yourself and your client.

Extending or Changing Your Agreement

Your coaching agreement is not a static thing, certainly not like a business contract. It's probably going to morph as you and your clients grow, learn, and evolve in their journey. So, it's important to check in with the contract fairly often. I wouldn't necessarily do it at every coaching session, but when you accomplish major goals, or when the client changes existing goals or adds new goals, those are perfect times to revisit your agreement.

I like to use the term *circling back* when we're revisiting our goals. It implies an informal but regular cadence. I recommend that you err on the side of circling back often with your client, particularly in the early stages of your coaching relationship, because most goals evolve and change as the client gains additional clarity with your coaching.

Explaining and Personalizing the Coaching Experience

As I mentioned previously in this chapter, a big part of establishing your client agreement is explaining what coaching is. Not what a book says it is, or what the ICF says it is, but what it is for you:

- How do you view your role as a professional Badass Agile Coach?
- What coaching stances will you be using?
- When or under what circumstances will you be switching stances?
- What ethics will be governing your coaching, and how? (We'll explore this in more detail later in the chapter.)

And you might want to weave in a bit of the badassery aspects when you're explaining all of this.

I sometimes share with my clients a personal story about why I got into coaching or why I'm so energized about agility in the first place. I'm not trying to make it about me, impress them, or take up a lot of time. I'm simply trying to personalize the coaching experience. Usually, I do this as part of agreement-setting in our first coaching session. It generates discussion around my style and approach as an agile coach. It is not uncommon for the client to have an aha moment, which is when I hear things like this:

- I didn't realize *that's* what a coach did!
- I wanted you to solve all of my problems, but you don't do that, do you?

- I have to be far more engaged in this partnership than I realized, don't I?
- I never realized why you were coaching. Your journey to get to this point is compelling, and I understand your intentions much better now.
- Wow, I *really* don't want to be coached by you. It's not personal, but we really aren't aligned, are we?
- Thank you for sharing, but I wanted someone to do things for me (a minion) and you're not that …

You get it. The agreement process is about clarity and alignment between the client and coach, and establishing an agreement on the outcomes for the coaching. Skip it at your own peril. (But please, don't skip it.)

Establishing and Defining Outcomes

Probably the most important part of any coaching agreement is establishing goals and outcomes that the client envisions for themselves. While these need to come from the client, as a coach, I'll often help them narrow and clarify their goals.

One of the things I've borrowed from my agile experience is using the user story notion of *acceptance criteria* here. For example, consider this client goal: *Establish more safety within teams and with the leaders reporting to them.* How would we measure or accept that? The following might be initial indicators:

- The client detaches from more meetings, trusting their direct reports.
- The client senses more risks being taken (failures) in their team's work—demonstrated in the sprint reviews.
- The client also detects more critical feedback / radical candor being shared with them from team members and direct reports.

Agile Coaching Agreement Canvas

The intent of the Canvas is to inspire conversations between the client and coach to gain clarity around how you'll show up together to establish your coaching ecosystem & partnership.

Client:	Last updated:
Client Goals & Outcomes *Try to keep it to 1 overarching goal and 2-3 supporting goals.*	

Agreements & Coaching Stances – Style *Clarity for how are we showing up together, your style, and stances as you dance around the Wheel.*	**Acceptance Criteria** *How will we determine that each outcome has been met?*
Role Clarity: Coach *Describe the Coach role in detail (expectations, boundaries).*	**Role Clarity: Client** *Describe the Client role in detail (expectations, boundaries).*
Plans, Overall Coaching Arc, Individual Arcs *Aligning your plans and Arcs to achieve the client's goals. This section evolves.*	**Special Agreements** *Special needs, notes for particular activities/stances. Also, space for coach's observations.*

This work is licensed under CC BY-NC 4.0

FIGURE 7. Agile Coaching Agreement Canvas, v1.0

As we're coaching, our discussions and explorations are (somewhat) bounded by the goal and the acceptance criteria. But again, this is simply an example. Meeting the goal can also be as simple and soft as the client wanting to move on for now—declaring that the goal, in their mind, has been met.

Agile Coaching Agreement Canvas

Figure 7 shows a canvas I've developed that can be useful when establishing agreements with your clients. It's not intended to share with the client; it's more to help in your planning for your agreement discussion. It will help you capture your thoughts and plans around how you'll operate with the client, and it will remind you of what needs to be said or established in your coaching agreement.

It's also a useful artifact to return to before you begin each coaching session—reminding you of the agreements, plans, and goals that have been established.

The Plan, or the Art of Planning

Following naturally from agreements is establishing a clear plan for your coaching. One of the things I like about planning is that the coach needs to think about how to describe strategy and flow to the client in order to share how their coaching will help the client achieve their goals. Done properly, planning sets expectations for the overall Coaching Arc flow, interim conversational arcs, possible coaching activities or approaches, and the strategy to achieve the client's goals.

The planning conversation should not just be the coach presenting a fully developed plan. While you may present a conceptual plan, your client should be a partner in co-creating it. The plan should be a baseline shared vision between the coach and client. It can then serve as a guide for executing the plan or for capturing any changes or pivots discovered over time.

Journaling as a Planning Device

Some of my best planning doesn't emerge directly from planning. Planning includes:

- Considering what's going on and the client context.
- Thinking about what I want to do next.
- Consideration of the most effective metaskills to leverage.
- Reflecting on past coaching sessions.
- Brainstorming on future flow possibilities.

These things emerge as I walk around, travel, coach others, read a book, and just go about my life. Client ideas and plans emerge constantly. It's part of the creative process of being a Badass Agile Coach.

I highly recommend that you take up journaling as an ongoing practice in your coaching. This is the place where you capture those creative thoughts in real time. I also use my journal for game planning and for ideating about Coaching Arcs.

Agile Coaching Arc Example for Agreement Conversation

I thought I'd share an Agile Coaching Arc example for what that initial, agreement-focused conversation might look like. Here's a somewhat challenging situation, where the outcomes are highly dependent on establishing a solid beginning. (Agile Coaching Arcs are discussed in more detail in the next chapter.)

The Situation

This is a coaching conversation with a team lead on one of the teams you're shepherding. The lead is overly protective of their knowledge and experience and is unwilling to work well with the team. In other words, they're incredibly dominant.

Their boss has asked you to coach the lead and basically told the lead to be coached by you. Which isn't the best way to begin your coaching relationship.

You want to "go softly" in this initial introduction, trying to establish some rapport, trust, and a relationship. But somehow, you need to get their behavior into the equation. The resulting arc is shown in figure 8.

Opening Moves
- Set metaskills before the session: courage, clarity, and empathy.
- Complete the canvas with some pre-meeting coaching goals.
- Enter in Teaching stance.
- Introduce the client to agile coaching (definition, stances, your role, their role) and the importance of establishing a coaching agreement.
- Switch to Coaching stance.
- Establish the goal for this coaching session: Why are we here?

Middle Game
- Largely *stay* in Coaching stance.
- Explore:
  - Client context—build empathy and understanding;
  - Client self-awareness around behaviors with the team;
  - Potential goal(s) for the client's coaching.
- Begin converging on an overarching shared goal for the coaching:
  - Establish session goals for the next two or three coaching sessions and goal acceptance criteria.

Endgame
- Oscillate between Coaching stance and Consulting/Advising stances to firm up ownership and responsibility.
- Review the goals and outcomes that emerged; agree on them.
- Agree on clear acceptance criteria for the early goals.
- End positively, acknowledging the efforts the client made in a prescriptive situation.

FIGURE 8. Example Coaching Arc for Agreements

Post-Arc Analysis

Based on the situation, the entire first coaching session arc was focused on gaining shared clarity, establishing measurable goals, and then gaining agreement to focus on those goals. Another big focus was establishing a coaching relationship, given the nonvoluntary nature of the coaching.

In the real world you might gain agreement much faster than this, but I'm trying to create space for doing it well. The effectiveness of the coaching is often improved by having a solid foundation.

And keep in mind that, in this case, your coaching was not voluntary. It was prescribed. This can create a tense and emotionally charged beginning. It's important to try and defuse that by going more slowly and co-creating the relationship.

Knowing When It's Over

All good things must come to an end, and that includes each of your coaching relationships and agreements. The trick is to know when you've successfully met the client's goals or outcomes. Establishing the agreement is a first step in determining when you are done.

For example, if you review the client's goals and see they've all been met, it might be time to close. Or if the client feels as if everything they were looking for is accomplished. Normally, closure is self-evident if you're paying attention to your coaching relationship. When in doubt, ask your client what they think.

I think of these as more positive closure events or discussions, but there are certainly times when things aren't so positive.

Non-Positive Closure

Agile coaching, and professional coaching in general, isn't for everyone. That's perfectly normal. Another way of thinking about it is that we're often unaligned in our expectations of roles, responsibilities, actions, and outcomes. That includes the coach *and* the client.

Here are a few examples of what I'll call non-positive closure revelations:

- Realization that there is a style, expectation, ethical, or practice gap between the client and coach.
- Realization that the client isn't seriously taking ownership of/for their goals and outcomes.
- Realization that the coach's skills are lacking in a stance that is strongly needed by the client to achieve their goals.
- Realization that there is a personality gap or conflict between the coach and client; little or no relationship or alignment.
- Realization by the coach that they've been coaching with the client for too long and that they've become pickled.[11]

But the reality is that coaching engagements are not all positive when you're looking through the lens of serving the client. Don't be reluctant to close your coaching when your Spider-Sense is tingling. That could happen before you ever begin coaching, or at any time during your coaching. Sometimes, the best thing you can do is not coach until there is alignment and agreement between you and your client.

Notion of Coach Entry

While you as a coach have a responsibility to establish agreements with your coaching clients, there is another often overlooked responsibility for the people bringing you in to coach.

I refer to it as *entering* you as a coach into the team and/or organization. Usually, I expect the stakeholder or sponsor for your coaching to kick off the introduction.

What usually happens is that a leader or sponsor decides to bring in an internal or external coach. They'll meet with the coach, give them a charter or focus, and then tell them to, well, *go coach*. There is no

---

11. I'm referring here to Prescott's Pickle Principle from Gerald Weinberg's The Secrets of Consulting: "Cucumbers get more pickled than brine gets cucumbered." Think about it ...

organizational introduction, no explanation around why the coach is there, and no explanation of the expected focus or outcomes.

The coach is expected to enter themselves and explain what they're doing and why they're doing it. While they often can do this, it's not best. Those being coached often perceive that they have no say in the matter, and they don't understand the drivers, the why, behind the coaching engagement. This situation immediately creates tension between the coach and those being coached.

A much more effective introduction can be guided by asking your stakeholders to complete the Agile Coach Entry-Prep Canvas in figure 9, using it as a way of planning their introductory meeting with those you'll be coaching.

Your coaching clients could be individuals, groups, teams, or the entire organization. What's important is that you clearly communicate your role and purpose and give those being coached an opportunity to ask clarifying questions.

I can't recommend this step strongly enough to you. It makes a huge difference to the successful entry of your coaching, whether you are being pushed into the organization or invited, chartered, and entered into the organization. (The latter approach is always more palatable.)

Coaching Ethics

When I first began to call myself an agile coach I was largely focused on the practice of coaching. While I consider myself a relatively ethical being, I really didn't spend a whole lot of time thinking about my ethics, operating standards, and client responsibilities.

Over time, I became more aware of the need for some ethical standards in the practice of agile coaching. The market has become inundated with coaches who aren't really competent or capable, and yet they can still call themselves an "agile coach" because there is so little clarity around what that is—and even less ethical clarity around how they need to operate.

Agile Coach Entry-Prep Canvas

The intent of the Canvas is to help the client identify, plan, and **communicate** the critical decision factors AND success factors (expectations) for bringing in a specific coach; **entering** them into the system.

Client:	Last updated:
Driving Forces? What are the drivers behind bringing in this coach. Why? What are you hoping to accomplish?	**Focus & Duration?** What will be the primary focus of the coach? Teams, Organization, what? Also, for how long? Journey map?
Key Selection Decision Criteria? As you searched for the coach, what were the 2-3 key competencies / skills you were looking for? What sets this coach apart?	**Expected Outcomes?** What are the expected outcomes, list the Top 3. What would a great success look like?
Internal vs. External; Why? You have choices about what sort of coach to bring aboard. If external, why over internal candidates?	**Push vs. Pull; Invitation; Welcome!** Be clear—is the coach a resource to be requested / pulled in OR are they being assigned to improve something?

This work is licensed under CC BY-NC 4.0

FIGURE 9. Agile Coach Entry-Prep Canvas

As you saw in the book's introduction, that's one of the big reasons I decided to write this book: to provide some firm guidance as to what excellence (or badassery) looks like.

To be clear, an Extraordinarily Badass Agile Coach needs to be aware of, in support of, and actively guided by an industry-standard and transparent set of operational ethics.

The Importance of Ethics

Basically, I believe we as agile coaches have a responsibility to our clients to provide a consistent level of excellence in our skills and capabilities, in our services, and in our intentions for how we will conduct ourselves. Ethics should be fundamental to the mindset of every coach as they interact daily with their clients. This serves a similar purpose to physicians having ethical standards: patients understand that there are skill differences between doctors, but can rely on a minimal set of operating standards for any doctor's competency and performance.

Formal codes of ethics have been too long missing from the agile coaching world, but that is beginning to change.

The Current State of Agile Coaching Ethics

I'm not going to reinvent the wheel here. Instead, I will explore a few of the relevant ethics models or initiatives that we can use to anchor this important topic.

ICF Ethics

The ICF has a long-held set of clearly articulated ethical standards, and every member is expected to sign off on their support of those standards. I consider it a wonderful baseline that any of us should be aware of and leverage.

The problem is that it doesn't directly relate to the depth and breadth of agile coaching, in that it only applies to the Coaching stance within the Wheel. In other words, it lacks breadth, clarity, and relevance for us.

Agile Coaching Growth Wheel

While I probably didn't emphasize it enough—or at all, so far in the book—the Wheel has some clear ethical guidance attached. The fact that ethics are an inherent component of the model is one of the reasons I like it so much.

The key ethical focus areas for the Wheel include:

- Professional conduct with clients
- Confidentiality
- Conflicts of interest
- Professional conduct toward the profession

Please review the Wheel's ethical framework and then deeply consider your personal and professional practice of agile coaching. At the very least, mentally sign off on your own active support of these ethical principles going forward.

Also note that the Wheel's ethical standard links to the ICF ethics as a baseline, so please review, reflect on, and sign off on those as well.

Agile Alliance

In January 2020, the Agile Alliance embarked on an initiative to define a Code of Ethics and Code of Conduct for the profession of agile coaching. Here's the statement of the driving force for the initiative, from the Agile Alliance website (as of October 2021):

> Something that has become a burning issue for us and one that we think belongs under the auspices of the Agile Alliance is the lack of consistency in the discipline of Agile coaching and the lack of any ethical framework or code of conduct for that profession.

As of this book's publication, this initiative is a work in progress with no clear completion targets. But I'd like to see the results of this effort become the de facto standard for our profession.

The volunteer team has made another unique contribution by creating a partner set of scenarios exploring the use of the code of ethics. Because ethics can be difficult to navigate at times thanks to real-world complexities, the scenarios are quite helpful in navigating the nuance of ethics in application.

There's a link to the Agile Alliance's Agile Coaching Ethics page at the end of the chapter.

My Own Ethics

Because there was such a gap in agile coaching ethics, a while ago I wrote my own set of ethics and published it on my Agile Moose website. I've also shared it with every client since then. Early in our coaching relationship, while I'm establishing our agreements and contract, I'll usually ask the client to review my ethics statements. I want them to fully understand how I plan on showing up, how I plan on operating, and how I will hold myself accountable to myself, the profession, and to them as my client.

While I'm not holding my set of ethics up as an exemplar, it does capture the essence of my ethics. I encourage you to read it as well. There's a link to it at the end of the chapter.

A Real-World Example

Quite a few years ago I was coaching a client's leadership team when the CEO and COO asked me to give feedback on their PMO and project manager team. The question was, Which ones will make it to agile and which ones won't? In other words, the leadership team was looking for performance feedback in order to understand who needed to be terminated and replaced.

To say that I was uncomfortable with the request was an understatement. While I've assessed many organizations on their agile readiness and how their competencies aligned with the requisite change in mindset, I've always avoided giving individual feedback based on my observations as an external coach. But I'd never clearly articulated this as part of my own coaching ethics.

This event was the genesis of my personal ethics stance and my motivation to clearly communicate it to each of my future clients.

Saying no to this client's request wasn't easy for me at the time, nor did the client receive it very well. They were looking for me to do their performance management job for them. But my stance was the right thing to do for me and, I firmly believe, for the client as well. That said, we did part ways soon after.

Holding the Profession Accountable

I want to wrap up this chapter with a call to action.

In many ways, I'm incredibly privileged as an agile coach. In fact, we are all privileged to be doing something so awesome with our clients. And with that privilege comes great responsibility. I believe a part of that responsibility includes holding ourselves, as Extraordinarily Badass Agile Coaches, to an ethical framework and a code of conduct for our wonderful profession.

I challenge everyone reading this book to sign off on some sort of ethical standard—pick one or develop your own—and then hold yourself to it. No matter what.

Further Reading

Here's an ICF Coaching Contract example. Remember, it's contractual in nature and only an example. But it does provide a template for an agreement: https://coachfederation.org/app/uploads/2018/01/SampleCoachingAgreement_2018.doc.

Eight Must-Haves for your coaching agreements: www.performancecoachuniversity.com/8-must-haves-in-a-coaching-agreement/.

Examples of Agile Coaching Codes of Ethics:

- Agile Coaching Growth Wheel, v2_1 ethics statement: http://whatisagilecoaching.org/code-of-ethics/.
- ICF Code of Ethics: https://coachingfederation.org/ethics/code-of-ethics.
- Agile Alliance, Code of Ethics working group/page: www.agilealliance.org/resources/initiatives/agile-coaching-ethics/.
- My Agile Moose ethics statement: www.agile-moose.com/moose-ethics.

An article focusing on the dynamics of entering coaches: https://rgalen.com/agile-training-news/2020/6/2/entering-a-coach-into-a-team-group-or-organization.

5

The Badass Agile Coaching Arc

You would think that something as organic as agile coaching would simply emerge from ongoing organizational interactions. And it does, but it's not totally emergent—nor should it be.

Contrary to popular practice, agile coaches should guide engagements with clear upfront agreements and a plan, apply some common patterns, and follow a consistent conversational arc with a beginning, middle, and end. The arc should also include thoughtful consideration of context, situation, and organization culture dynamics.

In other words, there should be a conscious rhyme and reason to your coaching conversations. And there's a lot to consider. That is, if you aspire be a Badass Agile Coach.

Introduction

This chapter covers three topics. First, I'll discuss a few basics around preparing for and executing your coaching sessions. Then I'll share a conversational arc metaphor that I've used quite effectively to guide my overall coaching conversations. Finally, we'll explore an idea from Len Lagestee: a coaching life cycle arc that can be applied to many group or team coaching contexts.

But first, let me explain what I mean by a Coaching Arc. It's composed of

- a **beginning**, or how you enter each conversation;
- a **middle**, how you guide the ebb and flow of the conversation toward pre-agreed goals or outcomes;
- and an **end**, where you leave the conversation and set the stage for the next conversation.

While we explore it in more detail later, I want to encourage you to begin thinking about your coaching as a series of conversations that follow this arc.

Before you dive too deeply into this chapter, please be sure you've explored chapter 4 on coaching agreements. It sets the stage for your Coaching Arcs and is a step that you will not want to skip.

Situational or Context-Based Coaching

You could think of the Coaching Arc as context-based coaching. As you approach each arc, I want you to think about your context or situation. One aspect of it, in an agile sense, is the experience or maturity of your client.

I'll be using the aikido Shu Ha Ri metaphor for determining maturity levels. In its simplest terms:

- **SHU** is a beginner or novice—someone with perhaps book-level experience, but little to no direct or practical experience. These folks need more prescriptive guidance to get them on the right

track. Using our coaching stances here, they need more focus on teaching, mentoring, and consulting.
- **HA** is someone with moderate experience. They've been practicing for a while, following beginner recipes fairly well, and are now in a position to benefit from a bit of experimentation and learning. From a coaching stance perspective, you want to become less prescriptive by leveraging the mentoring and modeling stances more often and the consulting/directing stance less often.
- **RI** is someone with expert or master-level experience. They often will have similar experience to yours, though perhaps less varied and deep. In this case, you are often serving as a sounding board and a reminder of the basics, perhaps motivating them to take more risks and explore new areas of learning as they widen their expertise. This is where you'll largely adopt professional coaching stance with a bit of mentoring and modeling.

There are other situational contexts that you'll want to consider beyond simply skill maturity or experience. For example:

- Empathy for their personal situation (loss of a loved one, financial challenges, recent relocation, etc.)
- Empathy for and understanding of their professional context (role, challenges, pressures, culture, etc.)
- Personal growth (how far they've come)
- Previous coaching plans, goals, and Coaching Arcs
- Their level of self-care
- Environmental factors (COVID-19 or working remotely)
- StrengthsFinder results or Leadership Circle Profile results

These are all examples of the contextual awareness factors that you might want to keep in mind as an agile coach. Remember, situational awareness is not something that you'll gather overnight. It takes time. It also takes curiosity and solid listening to glean details over time.

I want to take just a moment to explore another aspect of the Coaching Arc, which happens continuously within it. You as an agile coach have a responsibility to be nimble, to read the tea leaves, and to seamlessly adapt to your client in the arc. I'll use two phrases to try to capture what I mean and explore this more subtle aspect of your Coaching Arc flow.

Sense & Respond

Sensing and responding, the first phrase, starts with having your listening radar fully activated as a coach. In my ORSC coaching training, we talked about multiple communication channels: verbal and nonverbal, but also emotional.

This is not just about you sensing and responding to the client. It's about sensing and responding to yourself as well; for example, staying tuned into detecting whether you're triggering on anything the client is saying, or noticing if you're bringing your own biases into play while coaching. I sometimes refer to my Spider-Sense, as an homage to Spider-Man and his special skill for sensing danger.

The final part of sense and respond is trusting your intuition and instincts when you coach. Much more often than not, I've found them to be a true compass for me.

Dancing in the Moment

The second phrase to describe this subtle flow is the notion of *dancing in the moment* with your client. This isn't something you plan, necessarily; it's more fluid than that. The more experience you have coaching, the better you will become at dancing.

A huge part of dancing in the moment is leaving your plans behind you, along with your metaphors, tools, techniques, and everything else. It's not that you forget them, it's that you don't plan for them. Instead, you organically pull just the right approach out of your mind at just the right time—just as you would when you are dancing. There's also a bit of spontaneity to it that's hard to describe, but I've found that you'll know it and feel it when you're doing it.

Cynefin as a Sense & Respond Framework

Speaking of sensing and responding, here's another example: Dave Snowden's Cynefin Framework.[12] This model can be helpful in agile coaching, even though that's not its primary target. As illustrated in figure 10, it's essentially a four-quadrant model (plus disorder in the center), showing how our context drives our actions.

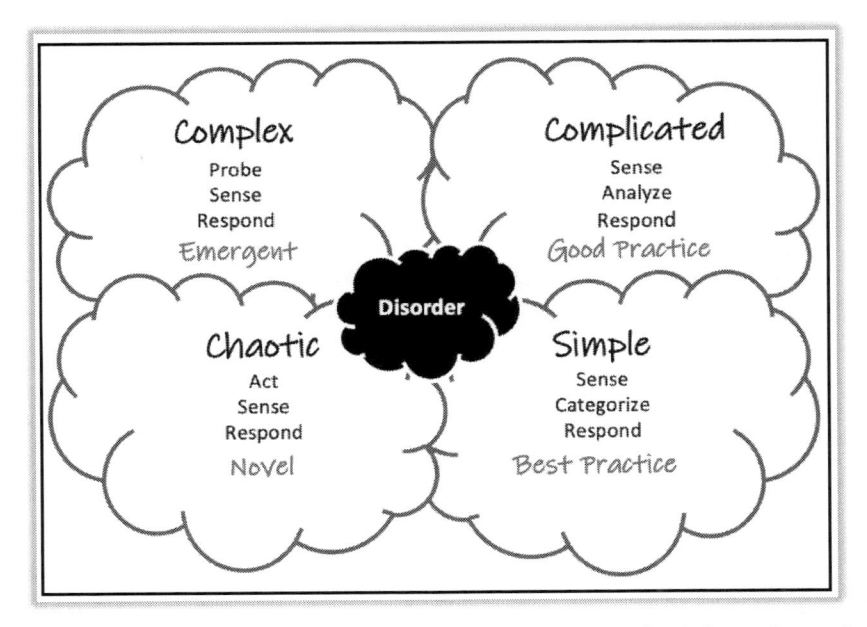

Complex
Probe
Sense
Respond
Emergent

Complicated
Sense
Analyze
Respond
Good Practice

Disorder

Chaotic
Act
Sense
Respond
Novel

Simple
Sense
Categorize
Respond
Best Practice

FIGURE 10. Dave Snowden's Cynefin Framework. *Source*: Derived from the various Cynefin Framework models, released under CC 3.0.

Cynefin is often used is as a situational model for organizational leadership, where you adjust your actions based on the context (organizational, process, product, technology) and the complexity associated with that context:

- If your context is **Simple**—then you would Sense, Categorize, and Respond to the situation. Consider this the land of *Best Practices*, where we largely know how to respond.

---

12. www.everydaykanban.com/2013/09/29/understanding-the-cynefin-framework/

- If your context is **Complicated**—then you would Sense, Analyze, and Respond to the situation. This is a land of *Good Practices*, but where you've perhaps not seen exactly this situation.
- If your context is **Complex**—then you would Probe, Sense, and Respond to the situation. Here, you're investigating options to see what might be appropriate and your understanding *emerges* over time.
- If your context is **Chaotic**—then you would Act, Sense, and Respond to the situation. In this case, you're running experiments and observing—acting in multiple directions, trying things out—and you discover a *novel* approach over time.

Can you see these same types of reactions applying to badass agile coaching? I can. When we enter a Coaching Arc, we normally sense with questions. Based on the answers or our dialogue, we quickly determine if there is some direction we should explore. Simple and Complicated spaces are more normalized and the client will be apt to sort things out on their own with only light-handed guidance.

But when we enter Complex and Chaotic situations, I believe the coach needs to become more engaged in helping the client. This is the area where a coaching stance may be insufficient. Sure, the client needs to be part of the discovery process, but we might need to be engaged more as well.

Keep in the back of your mind that the more complex the situation, the more frustrated our clients can become if we stay too long in a pure coaching stance. Cynefin gives us a framework for exploring various stances, in the service of our clients, as the complexity increases.

The Arc of a Coaching Conversation

Pre-Arc Planning

First, determine why you are planning on having a coaching conversation. What are the key factors? This will ensure you're focused. In other words, have a clear why for doing the coaching.

I like this framework

The Badass Agile Coaching Arc 75

1. Consider the why, context and empathy
2. Co-create shared agenda, plan, and goals
3. ARC: Opening Moves, Middle Game, and Endgame
4. Review agenda/goals
5. Commit to shared outcomes, next steps

The Arc of a Coaching Conversation

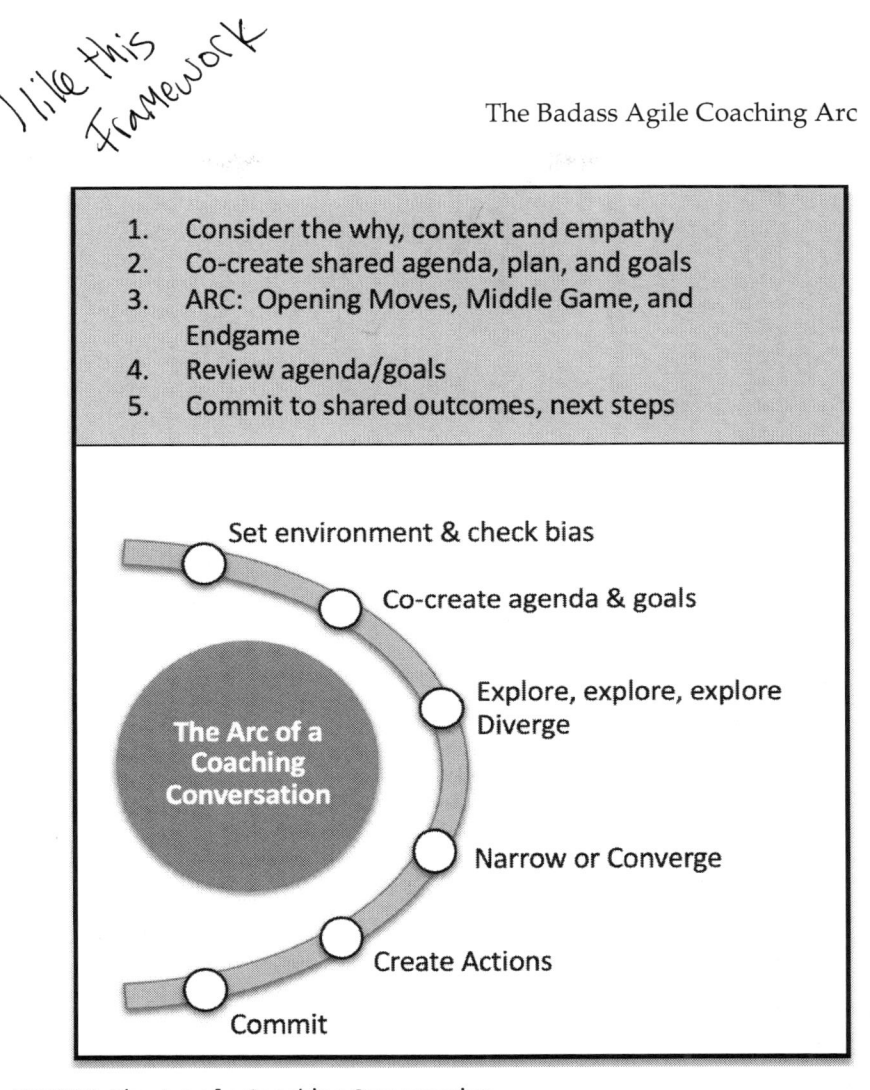

- Set environment & check bias
- Co-create agenda & goals
- Explore, explore, explore / Diverge
- Narrow or Converge
- Create Actions
- Commit

FIGURE 11. The Arc of a Coaching Conversation

The why includes priority and driving forces. For example, is this an urgently needed emergency conversation or the next in an ongoing series of conversations? Is this part of your coaching role and responsibilities or a challenging peer-to-peer chat?

Next, consider the context. This is this empathetic part of your preparation. Put yourself in the shoes of your client. Are they under stress or suffering because of some external event? What happened the last time you had a similar conversation? What was the emotional field and how did the conversation land? You'll want to at least spend a few minutes getting into the head of your client.

Finally, think about what shared outcome you are endeavoring to create with your coaching client. Again, narrow it down. This shouldn't be multifaceted or overly complex. Have a single outcome in mind. Remember, this is *your* goal. Once you get into the conversation, you'll want to *co-create* the goal with your client.

The Coaching Arc

I've been using a chess metaphor for a number of years in my coaching conversations. The arc, as illustrated in figure 11 and figure 12, is composed of:

- Opening Moves
- Middle Game
- Endgame

The Coaching Arc

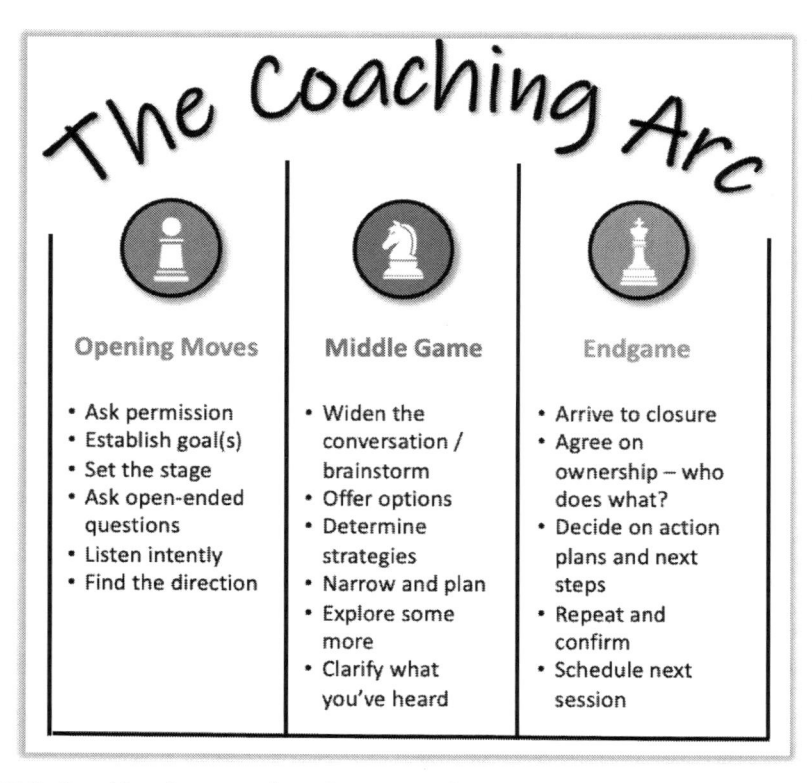

Opening Moves
- Ask permission
- Establish goal(s)
- Set the stage
- Ask open-ended questions
- Listen intently
- Find the direction

Middle Game
- Widen the conversation / brainstorm
- Offer options
- Determine strategies
- Narrow and plan
- Explore some more
- Clarify what you've heard

Endgame
- Arrive to closure
- Agree on ownership – who does what?
- Decide on action plans and next steps
- Repeat and confirm
- Schedule next session

FIGURE 12. Coaching Conversation Chess Metaphor

Each of the three primary conversational sections has its own focus and intent, but the arc flows smoothly from beginning to end.

Opening Moves

During the opening moves you establish rapport for the coaching conversation. This is a stage-setting moment. I always enter the conversation by asking permission to *have* the conversation. This goes beyond "Do you have the time for it?" and explores whether the client is in the right mindset for coaching. I've found that asking permission is a respectful first step.

Of course, you'll explore the plan and goals you envision and then co-create them with the client. I usually begin the opening moves by adopting the professional coaching stance, asking questions as part of our initial discovery. And because a large part of questioning is listening, my sensing radar is immediately active.

You should also be carefully sensing their mood and the emotional field. This is the place for situational awareness, so be prepared to pivot from the original plans if you need to. Think of this as amplifying your directional awareness.

If your coaching session is an hour, you should spend about 10 minutes in the opening moves.

Middle Game

The majority of coaching work is done in the middle game. Here, you create a space for the client to explore around their coaching goals. Sometimes I call this *divergent-then-convergent conversations*—you're allowing some randomness in the beginning, but midway through you'll want to help the client start focusing on their original goals.

A big part of the middle game is allowing for exploration while trying to keep it focused. It's a balancing act. I like to mention the outcome we've both established as a means of refocusing. The exploration allows for ventilation and can give you an incredible amount of information across all channels of communication (verbal and nonverbal).

As in your opening moves, you'll want to pay close attention to the emotional field as well.

Sometimes you'll realize in the middle game that you need to shift your coaching stance in order to meet the client's goals. Another way to think of it is veering off your plans and pivoting to a new course. This is usually seamless to your client, as it's something you sense and respond to as you are coaching. Building on the chess analogy, it's like the middle game in a chess match. You might enter it with a generic plan in mind, but as your opponent makes a move, you respond appropriately. Same for your coaching journey in the middle game—you're reacting to the moves of your client.

Another part of the middle game is developing a strategy by exploring options. This is, again, a creative process, and your coaching should focus on expanding your client's vision rather than problem-solving. As you approach the end of the middle game you'll want to switch to converging on an approach or an option with your client. As you do, asking clarifying questions will help.

If the coaching session is an hour, you'll typically spend about 40 minutes here.

Endgame

Endgame is your landing. This is where you wrap things up and review. You can start with the desired outcome or goal and review how that was met (or not met). Ask your client to reflect on and articulate their journey in the coaching session and see where they think it landed.

The endgame is also the place for accountability—meaning realigning with their goals and setting up any follow-up actions.

Finally, the endgame is rarely a complete ending. I think of it as a trampoline event for the next coaching conversation, so talking about what's next is a fair way to close things. And if you both agree, this is a perfect time to schedule the next coaching conversation.

If the coaching session is an hour, you'll typically spend about 10 minutes here.

Agile Coaching Client Canvas

While the client can surely figure out how to plan for and execute their coaching follow-up actions, I've found that these often fall to a lower priority until right before the next coaching session.

I've created the Agile Coaching Client Canvas (see figure 13) to help your clients reflect on, internalize, plan, and execute their resulting coaching actions. I've found it helps to keep their responsibilities in the coaching partnership top of mind. I'll often reference it as part of the endgame and remind them to visit (or revisit) the canvas as part of being accountable for their forward movement. The canvas just seems to help the client focus and stay centered. I'd encourage you to use it with your own clients, whether individuals or groups.

Post-Arc Conversation

Too many coaches skip the post-arc conversation. It has two parts. First, separate from coaching your client and switch to more of a relationship-building posture. You might want to ask how the coaching went from their perspective or catch up on their plans for the weekend. Or simply offer some small talk. The point is, decompressing from the coaching can be a healthy exercise for you, your client, and the system.

The second part of the post-arc conversation is for you as the coach. This is a time for reflection on what just happened. While the coaching session is fresh, you might want to jot a few things down in your journal. Consider how things went against what you had planned. Reflect on the arc and how well you navigated and pivoted within appropriate stances.

But also, consider how you might want to carry things forward into the next arc. In chapter 17 we'll explore aspects of starting your day. These considerations can then jump-start those plans and learnings on your part.

Agile Coaching Client Canvas

The intent of the Canvas is to meet yourself where you are, to pursue relentless, incremental (baby) steps, to model your future state, and to find the courage to challenge your system.

Client:	Last updated:
Goals *What are your goals for the coaching? Personal, team, organizational?*	**Outcomes** *How will you know when you've achieved your goals? What does success "look like" for each goal?*
Short-Term Actions *After coaching session reflection, what are your Top 3-5 short term actions you will take?*	**Longer-Term Plans** *As you continue to reflect on your coaching, what plans are unfolding in your mind for the long-term?*
Growth *As a result of the coaching, how have you grown? And what's next in your growth?*	**For Your Coach** *Coaching is a two-way street. What feedback do you need to give your coach to improve your results?*

This work is licensed under CC BY-NC 4.0

FIGURE 13. Agile Coaching Client Canvas, v1.0

Example Coaching Arc

At this point, it's probably useful to share an example of a conversational Coaching Arc. This example starts with a situation very similar to the scenarios in a coaching dojo presented in chapter 18. This is a leadership coaching conversation. A senior leader in the organization is looking for organizational structure advice for setting up their teams. This is probably the first coaching conversation of many, so there will be some stage-setting (see figure 14).

Commentary

The key focus for this arc was understanding the goal and establishing a plan. The most important point was the switch from coaching stance to consulting stance so you could advise your client on options and help them in decision-making. Partnering with them, but not taking sole responsibility, was an important part of your stance.

A Caution

I've found the Coaching Arc to be a useful model or metaphor for thinking about the flow of my conversations. But I've seen folks make a huge mistake with it (or any other conversational flow models): They think the coaching should end with one fell conversational swoop, or that there should be some huge outcome and epiphany each time. That simply doesn't happen that often.

More commonly, your coaching conversations and most meaningful outcomes will happen over a series of conversations or arcs. It takes time to accomplish something significant. So, it's probably better to think of the arc as overarching in time, perhaps with a major coaching goal, with a series of smaller arcs (conversations) happening within it. Arcs within an arc, if you will. But the key point is to not try to pack too much into a single conversation.

Opening Moves
- Set metaskills before the session
- Refer back to coaching agreement
- Ask powerful (or open-ended) discovery questions: Why are we here?
- Establish the goal for this coaching session
- Switch from Coaching stance to Consultative stance

Middle Game
- Explore:
  - The drivers for organizational change
  - The scope
  - Hoped for outcomes, dreaming/envisioning
- Look at options (expressed as options) for setting up the organization
  - Develop a minimum of three options-small, medium, all-in
- Ask the client for obvious pros and cons
- Perhaps perform a force field analysis to view options
- Start winnowing down options

Endgame
- At this point, what would be the best option to explore further?
- Is there a possible experiment to run? A way to engage the teams in the experiment?
- Switch back to Coaching stance
- What will the client do in parallel with the experiment to become more independent?
- Were the goals met? Determine if follow up required-how and when?

Note: *Force field analysis might be a good tool to use for winnowing things down and planning strategy for the experiment.* [13]

FIGURE 14. Example Coaching Arc

---

13. Force field analysis is a technique for analyzing the forces for and against a particular strategy or situation. Here's a reference: https://asq.org/quality-resources/force-field-analysis.

Storytelling and Exampling

Early in this chapter, I shared some common patterns to consider as part of your coaching conversations. The final one I'd like you to consider putting in your toolbox relates to telling stories and sharing examples (metaphors, models, etc.) as part of your coaching.

I've found that the more we can weave stories and examples into our coaching conversations, the better we communicate the nuance of our ideas. It's a much richer way to share. And because it adds visualization to the conversation, it expands the meaning of our words.

It's not just for the coach to communicate in this fashion. Please model and ask your clients to do the same thing in their conversations. Storytelling is something to work on over time with each client in order to expand the richness of your dialogues.

Coaching Life Cycle Arc

While we're exploring arcs in general, I want to share the notion of a coaching engagement life cycle that follows a broader sort of arc. To do this, I'll leverage Len Lagestee's thoughts and his sketch titled "An Exit Strategy for an Agile Coach" (figure 15) as a model. You can see the following phases in Len's strategy:

1. Arriving, or Meeting Them—with the coach outside the group and entering or arriving into the system.
2. Teaching, or Sharing with Them—as the coach begins to teach the group about lean and applicable agile frameworks.
3. Modeling, or Interacting with Them—where the coach interacts with individuals within the group and models behaviors, approaches, and tactics for them.
4. Coaching, or Observing Them—where the coach encourages the group toward improved collaboration and delivery.
5. Connecting, or Bonding Them—where the coach steps back and allows team performance to emerge.

6. Leaving, or Proud of Them—the ultimate goal of any coach; that is, essentially becoming unnecessary to your client's journey.

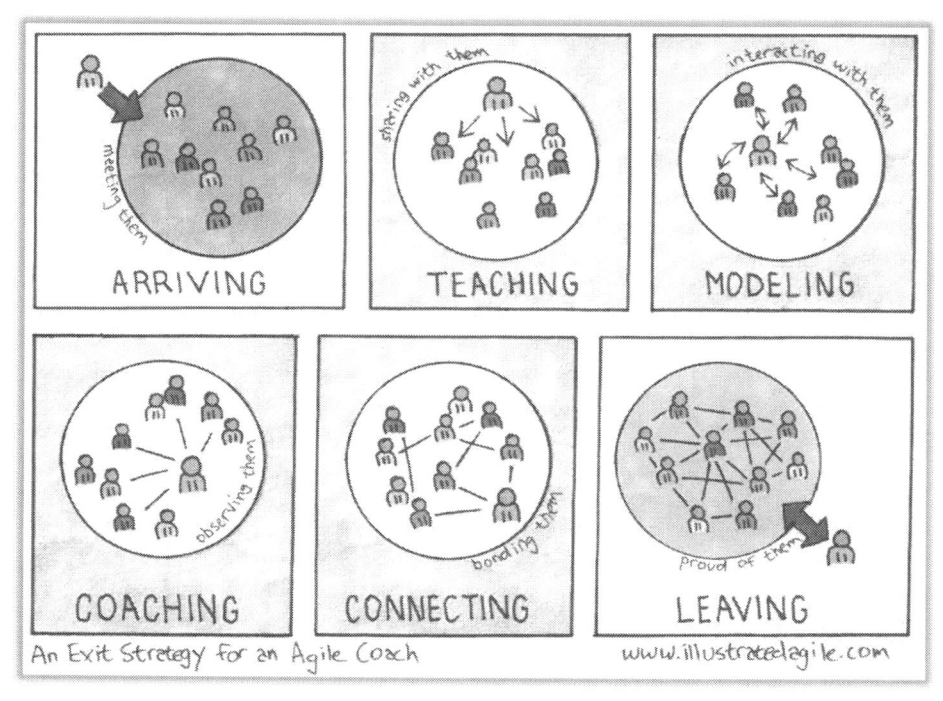

FIGURE 15. Coaching Life Cycle Arc (or exit strategy). *Source:* Len Lagestee. Used with permission.

As you can see, the coach enters the arc with a heavier hand of influence over and within the team. As time passes, the coach steps further and further back and creates space for the team to essentially coach themselves.

While I appreciate Len's model, I might add one more phase to the arc between Arriving and Teaching. I might call it Sensing or Assessing the coaching landscape and Preparing to Teach.

I believe the notion of an arc can apply to an individual coaching conversation, an ongoing series or set of conversations, an overall coaching engagement, or all of these. It's useful to think of coaching flows in this way so you are always connecting the dots toward whatever your client's goals are.

Further Reading

John Whitmore created the GROW model of coaching. It has four phases that align relatively nicely to our arc model:

- **Goal**—What do you want? (Opening Moves)
- **Reality**—Where are you now? (Middle Game)
- **Options**—What could you do? (Middle Game)
- **Will**—What will you do? (Endgame)

You can find out more about GROW here: www.performanceconsultants.com/grow-model. You might consider it a useful extension.

(could this be a retro)

6

The Badass Agile Coaching Operating System

I'VE ONLY JUST SCRATCHED THE SURFACE

> Beyond coaching stances, it's nice to have a mental model of the nuance that agile coaching requires. In many ways, professional coaching is an easier subset of skills, focused on a single technique. It's broad and deep, but it's *not* agile coaching.
>
> I suspect many people could spend years or decades refining agile coaching and still only scratch the surface of the craft. And that's ok. It's like a complex operating system. There are layers and relationships among the applications. There are well-trodden areas and less-traveled nooks and crannies.
>
> But it's nice to take a holistic view of the craft—in this case, as an operating system that helps us realize and refine the interconnections and situational nature of professional badass agile coaching in all its glory.

Introduction

In chapter 7 we'll begin exploring one of the anchoring models in the book, the Agile Coaching Growth Wheel. This model is fundamental to understanding the depth and breadth available across all of the agile coaching stances—at least when doing them well, as a badass.

But before we get there, I thought it would be nice to share another entry-level model. This one encapsulates an even broader ecosystem

this is a cool concept

The **Badass** Agile Coaching Operating System

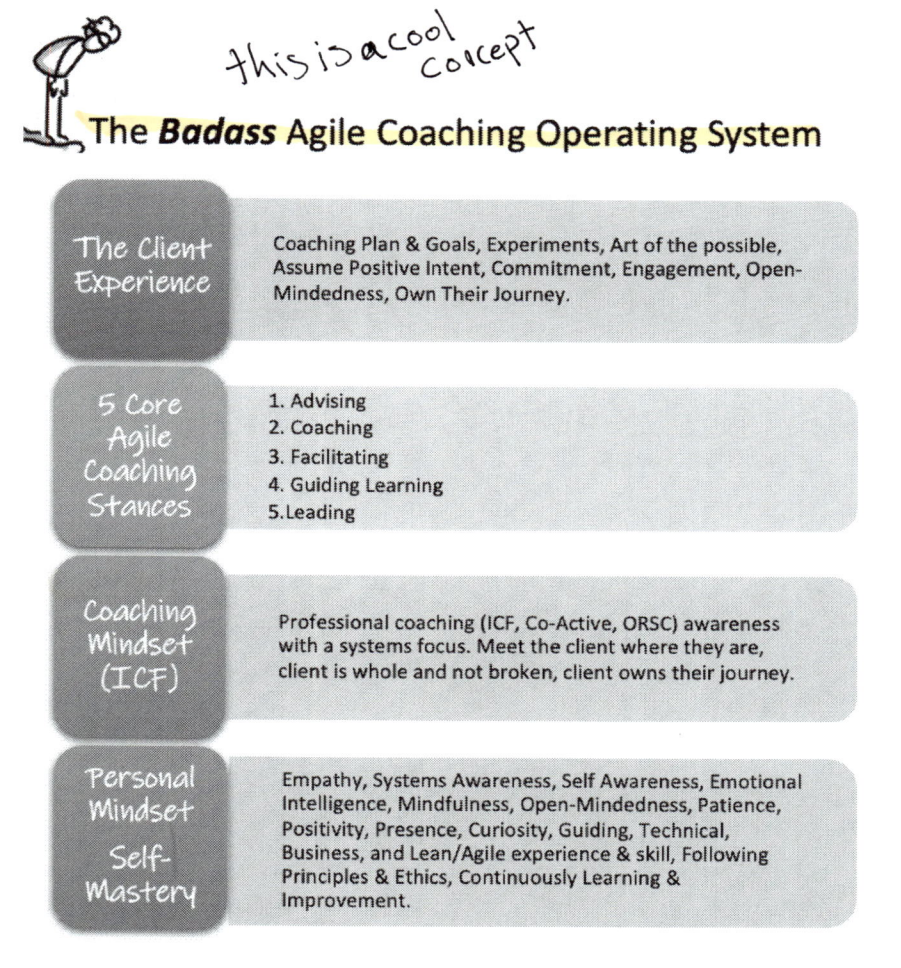

The Client Experience	Coaching Plan & Goals, Experiments, Art of the possible, Assume Positive Intent, Commitment, Engagement, Open-Mindedness, Own Their Journey.
5 Core Agile Coaching Stances	1. Advising 2. Coaching 3. Facilitating 4. Guiding Learning 5. Leading
Coaching Mindset (ICF)	Professional coaching (ICF, Co-Active, ORSC) awareness with a systems focus. Meet the client where they are, client is whole and not broken, client owns their journey.
Personal Mindset Self-Mastery	Empathy, Systems Awareness, Self Awareness, Emotional Intelligence, Mindfulness, Open-Mindedness, Patience, Positivity, Presence, Curiosity, Guiding, Technical, Business, and Lean/Agile experience & skill, Following Principles & Ethics, Continuously Learning & Improvement.

FIGURE 16. The Badass Agile Coaching Operating System

The Badass Agile Coaching Operating System   89

for your agile coaching and serves as a bridge from the generic coaching models in the previous chapter to the Wheel in the next. I'm going to call it the Badass Agile Coaching Operating System (figure 16).

Like any good operating system, the Badass Agile Coaching Operating System is multilayered and multifaceted. It's composed of four primary levels, building from the bottom:

1. **Personal Mindset.** Consider this the hardware level of the operating system. It amplifies the importance of the internal wiring (mindset) of the agile coach. Tactically, the coach's experience in the business, technical, scaling, and transformation/change domains resides here as a resource. This is the foundation for each coach, where they go when things prove challenging. We've touched on aspects of this in chapters 2 and 3, and will discuss it again in section IV.

2. **Coaching Mindset.** This is the device driver level of the operating system. It's tied to professional coaching skills and International Coaching Federation (ICF) principles, values, and competencies. These competencies and skill areas permeate the layers above and are fundamental to coaching, but are still somewhat subservient to the stances above this layer.

3. **Core Agile Coaching Stances.** These five stance areas represent the application level of the operating system. Whereas the two lower mindset layers are more foundational and fixed, here the agile coach switches between these five stances (and potentially more) in a fluid and nimble fashion as they serve their clients. This is where situational awareness (sense and respond) resides, which separates the badass from the merely good.

4. **Client Experience.** Finally, there is the windowing or UI layer of the operating system. This is the client layer, and is largely focused toward, on, and within the coaching client. Often in agile coaching we speak only of the coach—the coach's competency and skills, the coach's responsibility to coach. But the operating system and the success of the coaching are tightly coupled to the

client and to the client's engagement with their coaching plan, their goals, and their individual coach. This layer focuses solely on the client's experience from the perspective of the client. We've explored this layer in chapters 3 and 4, and will further explore it here.

Personal mindset was explored fairly completely in chapter 2, so we're not going to cover it here. We'll do the deepest dive on the coaching mindset level in this chapter. It's one of the most misunderstood and misapplied skills in agile coaching, and we need to explore how and where it fits and when (and when not) to use it. We'll also delve into the client experience layer in this chapter. (As I mentioned previously, the core agile coaching stances will be covered in chapter 7.)

Now, let's dive into the second layer, the coaching mindset.

The Coaching Mindset Explored

We'll start by exploring the ICF, the venerable organization that serves as the centerpiece of the professional coaching universe. The ICF's core certifications are:

- ACC – Associate Certified Coach
- PCC – Professional Certified Coach
- MCC – Master Certified Coach

Each of these certifications requires training, mentoring, and actual verified coaching hours with clients, and each is guided by a set of ethics and competencies established by the ICF. The organization places a strong emphasis on practicing the craft of coaching. One way this happens is an emphasis on having practitioners coach you while you practice your craft live and via recorded sessions.

The ICF Core Competencies fall into four areas, all of which are centered on the client:

1. Setting the Foundation
2. Co-Creating the Relationship
3. Communicating Effectively

4. Facilitating Learning and Results

For example, consider this Co-Creating the Relationship competency:

Coaching Presence

Definition: Ability to be fully conscious and create spontaneous relationship with the client, employing a style that is open, flexible, and confident.

This is representative of all of the competencies. In fact, you'll find that the word *client* shows up in all the ICF competencies except the first, Meeting Ethical Guidelines and Professional Standards, where it is implied.

Professional Coaching Programs

There are two ICF-approved coaching programs that agile coaches typically explore. One—Co-Active Coaching—is for individual coaching and is offered by the Co-Active Training Institute. The other is for more group- or system-based coaching and is called Organization and Relationship System Coaching (ORSC), from CRR Global.

Many agile coaches seem to find that ORSC is a good learning match because of its group and organizational coaching focus. But both programs strengthen skills and, most importantly, the client-oriented mindset that's so important in this layer.

The Essence of Professional Coaching

From an agile coaching perspective, within the operating system, the focus of professional coaching is entirely on the coaching stance. There are no other options. Given that, it's a fairly simple model.

However—and this is where the distinction between *professional coaching* and *agile coaching* gets confusing—agile coaching is much broader and more situationally aware. Although an agile coach may spend a significant amount of time in coaching stance with their client, they often switch stances while keeping the focus on the client in the back of their minds. This is implied in the coaching stances layer in the operating system. In the next chapter, you'll see that the nuance of the stances adds a significant challenge for coaches who are totally unaccustomed to the context switching from stance to stance.

Now I want to switch gears a bit and discuss questioning and listening, which are skills at the heart of professional coaching.

Powerful Questions

[handwritten: I rely on powerful/probing questions a lot]

If you do an internet search on *powerful coaching questions*, you'll see a long list of resources with question lists. Some lists will be focused on life or personal coaching, others will be focused on business or professional coaching, and still others will be focused on leadership coaching. You'll find most of them useful, but it can be overwhelming. However, I'd recommend doing this search just to get a sense for the different question lists and contexts.

What makes a coaching question powerful? First, it should be an open-ended question intended to do the following:

- Generate curiosity in the client
- Stimulate reflective conversation
- [Be] thought-provoking
- Surface underlying assumptions
- Invite creativity and new possibilities
- Generate energy and forward movement
- Channel attention and focus inquiry
- Touch a deeper meaning
- Evoke more questions[14]

Powerful questions are also **phrased more evenly, without any attached bias.** Remember, one of the keys to asking any question is whether there is genuine curiosity behind it. For additional context, Table 1 shows a subset of common powerful questions.

---

14. Amy C. Edmondson, *The Fearless Organization* (Hoboken, NJ: John Wiley & Sons, 2018), Kindle locations 3962–68; via Andy Cleff, "Stop Giving Answers … Ask Powerful Questions Instead": www.andycleff.com/2020/06/stop-giving-answers-ask-powerful-questions/.

TABLE 1. Examples of Powerful Questions

What else?	What have you tried so far?
What is important about that?	What's the worst part for you?
What would a simpler way look like?	What is your prediction?
What would an experiment look like?	If you got it, what would you have?
What's already working that you can build on?	In the beginning, how did you want it to be?
How does it look to you?	What other angles can you think of?
What is stopping you?	How do you really want it to be?
In the bigger scheme of things, how important is this?	What's the worst/best that could happen?
What is the lesson from that?	Which part is confusing, surprising, annoying, etc.?
When is it time for action?	
What part is not yet clear?	What is at risk?
Whose opinion matters on this topic?	What might "help" look like?

Source: Derived from the Powerful Question Cards by Debra Preuss, found on the Agile Coaching Institute website (*https://agilecoachinginstitute.com/agile-coaching-resources/* [at "Professional Coaching"]).

As an alternative approach, the Clean Language community uses a series of questions in the client's language, so as to not ask anything from the coach's perspective (thus, they are "clean" questions). The questions reframe the client's own words into a specific set of phrases. The intent is to allow the client's metaphors to emerge as part of their understanding of what's happening within and around themselves. We don't have the space to adequately explore Clean Language here, but I'd encourage you to explore it more if you find it interesting.[15]

Another method that I'm excited to share—one that I've come to use almost exclusively in my personal agile coaching journey—comes from Michael Bungay Stanier's book *The Coaching Habit*. When I happened upon it, I was struggling with finding the "right" coaching questions. I was so focused on picking the right questions from the

---

15. Judy Rees is one of the leading experts in Clean Language. Her overview blog post here is a good place to start: https://reesmccann.com/2017/08/01/clean-language-about/.

various lists that I lost the natural fluidity and conversational quality of my coaching. The simplicity of Michael's approach and his seven questions brought me back to a simple baseline in my use of questioning within my Coaching Arcs.

The Coaching Habit

Michael's wonderful book proposes seven questions to use in a coaching setting. I've found them invaluable as a setup in Coaching Arc conversations.

[handwritten note: Love this to open a retro.]

1. The **Kickstart Question**: What's on your mind?

    This is how we begin our conversations in a way that is focused and open. It can sometimes be too open-ended, so be prepared to narrow the response down with additional questions. Also, remember to connect this question to the client's coaching plan and their goals.

2. The **AWE Question**: And what else?

    Asking this question works as a self-management tool for the coach and as a boost for the other six questions. It's focused on curiosity and open for discovery. Remember to allow time (silence) for the question to do its work, which is a good practice for all of the questions.

3. The **Focus Question**: What's the real challenge here for you?

    This question begins to funnel the topic in a way that focuses the conversation. It works in conjunction with the next question. It's about narrowing, focusing, converging, and targeting. With this question, you might opt to go deeper using something like the 5 Whys for further discovery.

4. The **Foundation Question**: What do you want?

    This question gets to the heart things so our attention is on what matters. You can guide this question toward the art of the possible or dreaming, so the want is big, bold, and audacious.

It can also be reframed: What does the system want? What does the team want? What does the customer/stakeholder want? What does the organization/company want?

5. The **Lazy Question**: How can I help?

    By asking this question, we learn what the person wants our role to be (coach, teacher, mentor, facilitator, advisor, inspiration/encourager, or listener). It also gives us a chance to confirm that we're aligned with the expected role. Care should be taken not to overcommit in helping your client instead of them helping themselves.

6. The **Strategic Question**: If you are saying YES to this, what are you saying NO to?

    Saying yes more slowly means being willing to stay curious before committing. This can be another exploratory experience, so allow time for the question to work. If there's resistance to a choice, perhaps connect it back to the client's goals.

7. The **Learning Question**: What was most useful for you?

    The Learning Question pairs with the Kickstart Question to make what Stanier calls the "Coaching Bookends," ensuring conversations have high value. Keying on the book ends idea, think of leveraging the Kickstart and Learning Questions as endpoints for your Coaching Arc conversations.

That's it. A simple set of seven questions that nicely map to your Agile Coaching Arcs and client conversations. Do you have to use them all, or use them in a particular sequence? Of course not. But I would leverage the two bookend questions nearly all the time to frame your conversations.

Death by a Thousand Questions

There's one important point, or caution, that I want to mention before we move on to listening. You may remember from chapter 1 my story about a leader telling a coach that they were asking far too many questions and not helping them.

That's a true story. And at least in my experience, it happens far too frequently. Many coaches fall into a common anti-pattern that I call Death by a Thousand Questions—the slow, painful, sometimes catastrophic ruin of a coaching relationship.

Why does it happen?

- Because they're a professional coach who is uncomfortable with, or incapable of, switching stances.
- Because they've gotten too comfortable with one tool or stance. It's become a habit.
- Because they're not meeting the client where they are or sensing the need for another stance to serve the client better.
- Because they lack skill and experience and, perhaps, self-awareness.

These are common observations I've made. But one overriding thought is this: to truly be badass is to avoid Death by a Thousand Questions at all costs.

Now, let's move onto listening. *I need to work on this skill*

Powerful & Active Listening

I've not always been the best of listeners, and it's still one of the skills I work on continuously. Let me share a personal story to explain.

During the early days in my management journey, I had a lot of one-on-one meetings and did a lot of coaching. I discovered that I basically sucked at listening. I was one of those people who are always three steps ahead, planning my next five questions or challenges, impatiently waiting for the client to pause or take a breath so I could take my turn at grilling or fixing them and their views.

I'm not proud of it, but that's the way I was.

Then someone shared with me a metaphor that really helped. They likened my brain to a computer CPU and said that speaking or listening took up only about 40% of my brain's cycles, so I had idle time. I was choosing to use that idle time to look ahead and plan my reply rather than for active and deep listening.

This was an aha for me. So, I came up with a work-around to use those extra cycles. I started taking notes during every conversation, and I began to listen to all aspects of a dialogue—including inflection, tone, and body language. By deepening my listening and taking notes, I slowed my brain down so it didn't wander so much. This helped me to stay present and in the moment with each conversation. To this day, I practice this to varying degrees to maintain my focus.

Six Steps for Active Listening

[handwritten: good reminders]

The Center for Creative Leadership has a six-step model that I appreciate and leverage in my agile coaching.[16] If you are challenged at all as a listener, I would recommend taking the following steps to hone your listening skills:

Pay Attention. As I shared in my earlier story, paying attention and staying fully present is one of my personal challenges. It's also fundamental to your listening, so if you have challenges staying engaged, it's something you'll need to work on. And don't be shy about borrowing my work-around.

Withhold Judgment. It's important to stay open-minded when you're listening. Don't allow what you're hearing to cause you to judge or trigger on what's being said. The other insidious thing about judgment is that you often lose your connection to the conversation and miss important things.

Reflecting. Essentially, this is confirming what you're hearing by reflecting back to the client—paraphrasing, if you will. For example, you might say something like "So, I hear that Bob is an inexperienced Scrum Master that shows some promise. Is that right?" Remember, in

---

16. www.ccl.org/articles/leading-effectively-articles/coaching-others-use-active-listening-skills/.

reflection you want to reuse your client's exact words. Don't translate them into your own terms first.

Clarify. While reflecting does clarify, it does it more subtly. In this case, you clarify more directly. For example, "I heard that your teams don't do Scrum very well, and are challenged with self-organization. Did I get that right?" Powerful questions (or open-ended questions) often fit here as well. So, a part of clarification is probing and exploring for more details.

Summarize. This isn't necessarily for closing a conversation. You can summarize any time you think you're either ending a topic or approaching a transition to another topic. For example, "All right, do I have this right? Bob has the following strengths as a Scrum Master: facilitation, listening, open-mindedness, courage, and respect. Did I miss anything?" You can see that this adds clarity as well.

Share. Sharing is when you connect yourself to the conversation by sharing something from your own experience and perspective. I did that at the beginning of the chapter, and have used that story many times when coaching clients. You probably need to build the client relationship a bit before you start sharing often, but it's a powerful way to stay connected with your listening.

Beyond these steps, there are other considerations to keep in mind during your coaching conversations. Many of them are situational, so not all of them need to be combined at once, but they are useful considerations:

- Listen on all channels—the specific language chosen, body language, tone, and emotional field.
- Be comfortable with and embrace silence.
- Remember to appreciate and normalize the conversation; that is, share how normal your client's reactions and feelings are.
- Focus on relationship building and establishing a connection.
- Extend empathy and understanding.
- Keep a 70:30 ratio in mind—70% listening and 30% speaking.

Listening to What's Not Said

I want to conclude this section by discussing a special case in listening. While it might sound odd, listening to what's not said might be your most valuable listening skill.

I'll illustrate it with this story: You're coaching an agile leader on their role within the agile transformation that you're leading as a coach. During several coaching sessions, your client asks you no questions. None. Not one question about agile methods, strategies, or tactics; not a single question about the role or posture they need to take for the effort to be successful.

As a coach, you need to stay tuned in and aware of this gap, but you might also want to start lightly exploring the why behind this. Possibilities might include impostor syndrome, a lack of self-awareness, lack of safety, or general disinterest. But there could be many other reasons, so you'll want to uncover them with your client.

Can you see how powerful this might be?

The Client Experience Layer

At the end the chapter, we're finally getting to the highest level of the operating system. How can that be? The coaching level was my priority in this chapter, but don't think that because this section is last or short that it's unimportant. It's not.

Your client experience, as maintained throughout this book, is paramount to your agile coaching success. But, it's not simply about you. It's also about the client and how they're showing up for your coaching.

In chapter 4, we explored agile coaching agreements, and that's where the client experience begins and ends. But I want to amplify how important it is for you to hold the client responsible for their coaching. Sure, you might adopt the role of guide and partner, but the client is solely responsible for the results.

The client also owns the metaskills that they're showing up with. Imagine that; metaskills aren't just for you. They're for the client as well.

Early on in each coaching engagement, I'll share the notion of metaskills with my client and explore some that they can leverage when showing up for coaching. For example:

- Commitment
- Engagement
- Being and staying present
- Staying open-minded
- Considering the Art of the Possible
- Accountability and responsibility

[handwritten note: Could this fit into a retro intro?]

This is a set that I often share and emphasize to set my expectations regarding the client's responsibilities. So, remember to assume your clients are creative, resourceful, and whole (our Prime Directive), but also hold them responsible!

Further Reading

I would highly recommend that you read *The Coaching Habit* by Michael Bungay Stanier (Toronto, Canada: Box of Crayons Press, 2016) cover to cover. It's that simple, useful, and good!

Coaching Questions: A Coach's Guide to Powerful Asking Skills by Tony Stoltzfus (Virginia Beach, VA: Tony Stoltzfus, 2008) is a wonderful reference for helpful questions.

Reflections

I want to encourage you to stop and reflect at the end of each section of the book—going back and reviewing to answer these questions.

- What were your key learnings? What was your personal big idea or takeaway from each chapter?
- Did any aha moments emerge, either from the reading or from later reflection?
- What ideas have your tried? What were the results?
- What ideas do you plan on trying? Why? What outcomes do you expect?

Think about your agile coaching journey.

- What areas of growth do you have?
- What superpowers do you need to amplify or leverage more?

Take a look at the Wheel-based learning references in our Badass Agile Coaching Repo (registration link in the afterword) and pick two or three books or articles that you're willing to commit to exploring.

Explore some of the ideas and inspiration from this section with your coach. Use them as a sounding board for your growth, experimentation, and learning.

Visualization

I want you to close your eyes and get quiet. Center your attention on the notion of a Badass Agile Coach. That's you.

Envision what that looks and feels like. What are you learning and doing to become that coach? Consider how to better leverage your superpowers and strengths in becoming that coach. What specific tactics from this section are you already using? Which ones do you want to try as a result of reading about them?

Now open your eyes and jot down those ideas, aspirations, insights, plans, hopes, and dreams in your journal.

Haven't started journaling yet?

Well then, read this: www.agile-moose.com/blog/2019/6/23/journaling-how-to-get-started, and consider using our Agile Coach Journaling Canvas, which you can find in the repo.

II • Agile Coaching Models and Practice

The Agile Coaching Growth Wheel

An Agile Coaching Story, Part 1

An Agile Coaching Story, Part 2

Badass Extensions to the Agile Coaching Growth Wheel

The Badass Agile Coach's Guide to Coaching UP

7

The Agile Coaching Growth Wheel

It can be lonely out there as an agile coach. Am I acting professionally? Am I doing it right? How do I grow to better serve my clients? These are some of the questions the Agile Coaching Growth Wheel was designed to help Badass Agile Coaches reflect on.

The Wheel is also a view of the competencies of an agile coach, which are the foundation for the profession of agile coaching.

In this chapter, Mark Summers of Beliminal describes the Agile Coaching Growth Wheel and its application. Mark was a volunteer lead of the coaching retreats that created and defined the Wheel, so there is no better guide to explore its genesis, evolution, and vision. In chapters 8 and 9, Mark shows you the Wheel in action in your badass agile coaching.

Introduction

I was working in a relatively large organization when I was introduced to an agile coach from another part of the business. This interaction was a crystallization of what I had long feared: There is a problem with the profession of agile coaching. I sat down with the coach for 30 minutes, hoping to discuss how we could share and learn from each other to better serve the client. He spent the entire time talking about himself, trying to convince me how expert an agile coach he was. He left me with a stern warning to stay off his turf.

From my perspective, this is strange behavior for an agile coach, although not necessarily uncommon behavior inside organizations. The agile coaching community is wonderful, and the peers that I meet at conferences and retreats are warm and sharing, with a passion for learning. This coach was none of that. Yes, he was confident and energetic, but he had no depth of knowledge or experience.

The next thing I knew, the leadership team stopped me from working with some teams. I had planned to run some workshops to explore whether Kanban would be an option for them. "You don't need to spend all that time with Mark. My agile coach can implement Kanban in a team in 15 minutes," one of the leadership team members told his colleague. Yes, this coach was going around to every team in the place creating a cookie-cutter board and showing them how to move sticky notes. Let's be clear, this is not just the fault of the agile coach. It's also the system that is wrong; as a coaching profession, we are also failing him, so he ends up damaging the client and potentially himself.

My vision is that we can do better as a profession to help agile coaches grow, and we can do better to help organizations understand what to look for in an agile coach. To that end, a team of us got together at the Scrum Coaching Retreat in London in 2018 to look at how we help agile coaches reflect on where they are and how they might grow. What emerged from that collaboration was the first version of the Agile Coaching Growth Wheel.

The Agile Coaching Growth Wheel   109

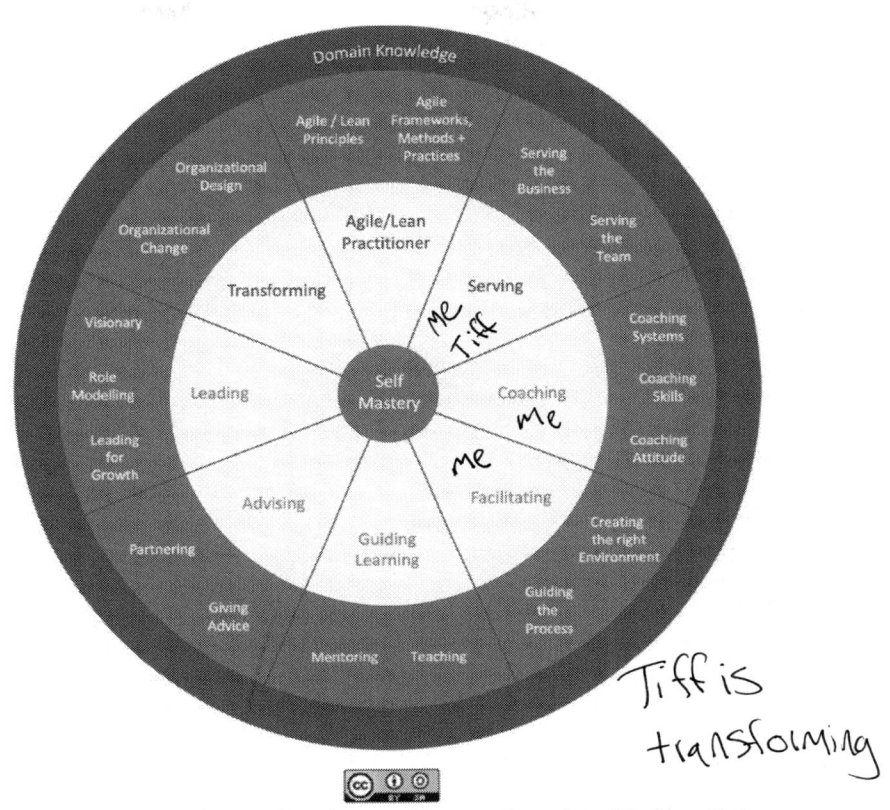

[Figure: Agile Coaching Growth Wheel diagram with handwritten annotations "Me Tiff", "Me", "Me", and "Tiff is transforming"]

Agile Coaching Growth Wheel by Joel Bancroft-Connors; John Barratt; Shannon Carter; Rickard Jones; Martin Lambert; Stacey Louie; Helen Meek; Tom Reynolds; Rohit Ratan; Andre Rubin; Kubair Shirazee; Mark Spitzer; Mark Summers; Josh Tasker; María Thompson is licensed under a Creative Commons Attribution-ShareAlike 4.0 International License.

FIGURE 17. Agile Coaching Growth Wheel. *Source: http://whatisagilecoaching.org/agile-coaching-growth-wheel/, CC-BY-SA 4.0 (https://creativecommons.org/licenses/by-sa/4.0/).*

The current version of the Wheel as of November 2021 is shown in figure 17. This is the result of a community-driven effort, and was published for all to leverage under a Creative Commons CC-BY-SA licensing agreement. I always refer to the Wheel as a draft, because it will continue to change as we learn more about the profession of agile coaching. Indeed, the version described in this book is an evolution based on the work of a Scrum Alliance volunteer team of agile coaches, for which I am acting as product owner. The competencies described here are now relatively stable, but the team will continue to update supporting guidance that will make it easier for coaches to reflect on these competencies. Iterative guidance will be released as it becomes available.

So, let's explore the Agile Coaching Growth Wheel.

Exploring the Wheel

The Agile Coaching Growth Wheel covers multiple professions, multiple leadership styles, and several domains of mastery. In terms of depth, the model tries to strike a balance, giving just enough guidance to drive reflection without being too prescriptive. It does this by focusing on your behaviors, the outcomes you achieve, your experience, and who you are as an agile coach. Where possible, it avoids prescribing specific methods and tools, for there are many and including some would exclude others. New tools and techniques continually emerge, so the Wheel would soon become obsolete if based on specific practices. Instead, the Wheel acts as a reflection tool to help agile coaches focus on what's important for them at the moment and invites the coach to go and discover more.

At the Center

Being a great agile coach starts with self-mastery: knowing yourself and your ability to choose how you show up in any given situation. This is placed in the center of the Wheel as it is a foundation on which the other competencies sit.

Competency Areas

Around Self-Mastery are eight competency areas. The five at the bottom represent the core skills or stances an agile coach uses, depending on the coaching context. Each stance relates to a profession and its standards, competencies, and associated body of knowledge.

1. **Advising.** The Advising stance draws from the profession of consulting. Recognition as a professional consultant is often

specific to the context. For example, bodies like the International Council of Management Consulting Institutes exist to raise standards in management consulting.
2. **Coaching.** Many agile coaches refer to the coaching stance as *professional coaching* to distinguish it from agile coaching. There are many schools of coaching and professional organizations; for example, the International Coaching Federation.
3. **Facilitating.** Facilitation is a profession in its own right, with certification bodies such as the International Association of Facilitators.
4. **Guiding Learning.** Guiding learning is about the professions of teaching and mentoring, complemented by years of research on how we support people's learning.
5. **Leading.** The profession of leadership is vast and includes a great number of theories and bodies of knowledge. This stance includes a subset of leadership styles and approaches that an agile coach is likely to need.

View the Wheel as a guide to a vast world of learning opportunities. Badass Agile Coaches have looked outward and drawn from these professions to enhance their skills and practice. In chapters 8 and 9, we will explore how an agile coach might switch between these coaching stances as their client context changes.

The remaining three competency areas represent an agile coach's mastery. As we operate in these areas of mastery, we may call on any of the core skills and switch between them as the context demands. Mastering which skill to use in the current context is what separates the merely good from the truly badass.

1. **Serving.** As an agile coach, it is not about you; it's about the growth and well-being of those you serve and the impact that they can make. This section is about how you serve the team and the business.

2. **Transforming.** Transforming is how you serve the organization as an agent for change, using all of the core skills to help you navigate change.
3. **Agile/Lean Practitioner.** The final core competency area is the Agile/Lean Practitioner area—obviously a critical domain for a Badass Agile Coach. Think of this as a reminder to stay rooted in the agile principles and practices so you can serve as a guide to agility.

Coaching Competencies

Further out in the Wheel there is a ring of competencies that coaches can reflect on in each core competency area. So, for example, the Agile/Lean Practitioner area contains two competencies:

- Agile/Lean Principles
- Agile Frameworks, Methods and Practices

The behaviors and knowledge illustrating different levels of practice within each competency area were abstracted into supporting guidance. The current draft of that guidance will be available in the Wheel-based learning references in our Badass Agile Coaching Repo (registration link in the afterword) and the master version will ultimately live on the Scrum Alliance site. We envision agile coaches using the Agile Coaching Growth Wheel Guidance to take deep dives into specific areas as part of their personal growth plans (discussed in the next section).

Domain Knowledge

The final area of the Wheel is the outer ring of Domain Knowledge: knowledge of the team's work, your business domain, and the organizational context. These supporting knowledge areas are represented as the "tire" on the Wheel—the domain context where your skills as an agile coach come into contact with those that you serve. Your knowledge in these areas may help you build rapport with your clients and serve them better, but as an agile coach one must guard against always being the expert in your client's domain, as this can get in the way of your ability to serve the client.

Guiding Your Personal Growth Plan

The primary purpose of the Wheel is to help agile coaches reflect on their current level of competence and identify areas for future growth. It is also best used with another coach who acts as your learning or accountability partner, mentor, and coach.

Within each of the eight core competency areas, the individual competencies provide opportunities for reflection. The Agile Coaching Growth Wheel Guidance identifies five levels for each of those competencies:

1. **Beginner**—knows the theory but has no real practical experience of its application.
2. **Advanced Beginner**—has applied the competency in at least one situation and may still require support in its application.
3. **Practitioner**—can apply the competency independently in most situations.
4. **Guide**—unconscious competence; has mastered the application and knows when to bend and when to break the rules. Acts as a guide to others.
5. **Catalyst**—can change to meet the current situation and innovate to create new techniques, but is always looking for new ways to grow and new skills to master.

Using the Wheel to Grow

There are many inventive ways you can use the Wheel to assess yourself or support someone else. If I am guiding someone else through the Wheel, I tend to start more broadly, walking through the eight competency areas to ensure understanding. You might ask the coach to rate themselves on a scale against each competency area, at a very high level, before diving into the detail. Then I may suggest that reflection on their current context, and ask, "Given where you are now, which competency area would you like to reflect on deeper?"

Once a competency area has been selected for reflection, it's time to look at the competencies within it. So, for the area of Agile/Lean Practitioner, you would read through the guidance for the competencies of Agile/Lean Principles and Agile Frameworks, Methods, and Practices. For each of these competencies, there is guidance for the five practice levels, Beginner through Catalyst. This guidance is not meant to be a checklist, but should be enough to give you a gut feel for where you are. Again, if I am coaching somebody through it, I may challenge their thinking, asking them to reflect on examples to aid the learning process. Once the client has established where they are, you can turn your focus to what that means for the future and identify actions for personal growth.

Here's how you might use the Wheel to self-assess.

Step 1: Identify an area of improvement. Look through each of the core competency areas (the eight sections in the middle). You can't improve everything at once, so select an initial focus area.

Step 2: Reflect on a core competency area. For each competency within the core competency area, review the guidance and assess your practice using the five levels. Some people will sell themselves short, others will overestimate their competence; so, it may be useful to think of some examples from your recent practice.

Step 3: Brainstorm options and generate actions. Use the insight generated in the reflection to brainstorm options for growth and then formulate a plan of action.

Helping Groups of Coaches Reflect with the Wheel

When working with a group of agile coaches, I like to create a version of the Wheel on the floor, using tape and cards as seen in figure 18.

FIGURE 18. Using the Agile Coaching Growth Wheel in a group coaching session

Once I have introduced the Wheel, I will usually invite participants to walk around the different segments of the Wheel in pairs. Having people physically occupy the different segments deepens the reflection as they step between the core competency areas.

Walking around the first time, they are exploring, making sure they understand each of the core competency areas and sharing stories of where they have used a competency. After a while, I bring everybody back together to see what questions they have. Then, I let the pairs dive into the guidance, each focusing on one core competency area, to identify some things they can try to improve and some actions they can take.

If I am working with a group of coaches, or maybe a Scrum Master chapter from the same organization, I take it a bit further. I ask everybody to stand in the core competency area that they most want to grow. Then I use a variation of an informal constellation, to reveal more information about the system. I start with an opening question: "Given where you are standing, how competent do you feel when working in the competency area?" The more competent they feel, the closer to the center of the Wheel they should stand; the less competent they feel, the further away they should move. Where everybody places themselves instantly reveals information to the system, without anyone speaking.

I then ask them to consider the polling question: "Why are you standing where you're standing and what's that like?" I invite some of the participants to share, starting with someone closer to the center, then someone about halfway out, and finally someone at the back.

Next, I ask them to move again in response to a question designed to unfold their thinking: "How active have you been in improving in this competency area?" More active people move toward the center of the Wheel. Once again, I ask a few to respond to the polling question, starting with someone in the center who has been active in this area. People share interesting stuff about what they have been doing, and others sometimes realize that they could do more.

Then, I ask people to move in response to a final question: "How actively are you going to be improving this competency?" Often, people want to improve so there is a very close group in the center. I ask the polling question for the final time and allow some people to share.

I often find that you get some really useful insights if a few people aren't standing close to the center at this point, so it's worth taking time to hear from those people. Someone might say, "I would love to improve, but given that I am busy with X, Y, and Z, it doesn't seem realistic." That's useful information. Or someone could say, "On reflection, I feel I have about the right competence in Serving the Team, given what my team needs from me right now, so maybe I would be better focusing on Serving the Business." Again, useful insight.

An informal constellation tool or practice, where people position themselves relative to each other based on a question, is a great way for a system to quickly reveal information. The form that I use for the Wheel is similar to a circular constellation, from Organization and

Relationship Systems Coaching, where people place themselves close to a central point in the room the more positive their response is to a question.

The rest of this chapter will explore each of the competency areas in a bit more depth.

Five Primary Coaching Stances

As I stated earlier in the chapter, there are five primary agile coaching stances in the Wheel: Advising, Coaching, Facilitating, Guiding Learning, and Leading.

Advising

As an advisor or consultant with an individual or team, or within the wider organization, you are responsible for setting the work up for success. The competencies within Advising are:

- **Partnering** with leaders, teams, and individuals, taking shared responsibility on the journey toward the goal. This covers creating agreements around how the relationship will work, establishing clear goals, and agreeing on a way of working that allows for inspection and adaptation. Important aspects of this competency include communication, transparency, and establishing trust within the relationship.
- **Giving Advice.** Consider this the consulting part of your coaching approach, where you're providing examples and ideas, and sharing your stories of success to help your client envision possible solutions. And yes, you might even occasionally tell them what to do.

Coaching

There are a number of definitions of coaching. The International Coaching Federation defines coaching as

> partnering with clients in a thought-provoking and creative process that inspires them to maximize their personal and

professional potential. The process of coaching often unlocks previously untapped sources of imagination, productivity and leadership.

I also like the definition by John Whitmore, which simply states:

> Coaching is unlocking a person's potential to maximize their own performance. It is helping them to learn rather than teaching them.[17]

When working with an individual, this is clear—we are helping them move forward in some way, helping them grow.

The competencies within Coaching are:

- **Coaching Attitude.** This is explored in depth in chapter 2.
- **Coaching Skills.** This is the very essence of this book.
- **Coaching Systems.** The skills and coaching approaches when working with more than one person; so, teams/groups and relationships between people.

Facilitating

[handwritten note: Can we truly be neutral when facilitating a retro for our teams]

Facilitation is a process of guiding a group or team through interactions that help them create meaningful outcomes. Facilitators are neutral to those outcomes; their focus is on creating the right environment for group participation and guiding the process.

Facilitation helps everyone in the group align in a collaborative way, interpret their context, and mutually identify the most valuable outcomes so they can be the best they can be.

Before facilitating any workshop it is important prepare, understanding the current situation of the team or group and the desired outcome. Once you understand that, designing the workshop is about taking them on a journey that allows divergent thinking around the topic and ultimately allows the group to converge toward a new state.

The competencies within Facilitating are:

---

17. Whitmore, J. (1992). *Coaching for Performance*. London: Nicholas Brealey.

- **Guiding the Process**. A large part of facilitation revolves around planning and supporting the journey toward a specific outcome. Helping the group to navigate conflict, using the positive tension created by new ideas to create better outcomes, but not allowing behaviors that let the conflict become toxic. Evoking creativity through the use of activities and games that get participants to think differently and examine the situation through different frames of reference.
- **Creating the Right Environment**. This starts with fostering a safe environment where everyone can share their concerns, fears, and challenges. Then, as a facilitating coach, you guide the group to a co-created ecosystem where they can explore possibilities and emerge toward an outcome.

Guiding Learning

Learning is at the heart of being agile. As an agile coach, you will need to facilitate the learning of people around you, helping them acquire new skills and knowledge. The competencies within Guiding Learning are:

- **Mentoring.** I think of this as a form of apprenticeship where an agile coach partners with others, models behaviors and skills, and helps them grow.
- **Teaching.** You could spend your entire life working on becoming a better teacher. So, as a coach, you need to become a better teacher over time, by working with individuals and groups.

Leading

For an agile coach, leading is about being the change you want to see to make the world a better place. As a leader, you are capable of partnering with others to inspire the realization of a shared vision. The competencies within Leading are:

- **Visionary.** At times you may need to be a visionary leader, co-creating a vision of the future that acts as a positive attractor for

change. Inspiring people, that change is possible, using positive language and focusing people on what could be possible.
- **Role Modeling.** As an agile coach you model the behaviors that you want to see in others: be the change. This competency is always on. You are always showing the way by what you do and what you say. Role modeling requires you to be vulnerable—to be yourself and be prepared to take a failure bow when you mess up.
- **Leading for Growth.** Being a leader in an agile context is about creating an environment where others can learn, grow, and ultimately thrive. As a leader for growth, you understand that the potential of people is limitless.

Areas of Mastery

The remaining competency areas can be considered areas of mastery. They are: Self-Mastery, Serving, Transforming, and Agile/Lean Practitioner.

Self-Mastery

This is integral to the entire Wheel, which is why it's in the center. Knowing yourself and gaining the experience to know when to switch stances is the key to being an effective agile coach. Being an agile coach is less about your knowledge than it is about your self-awareness and how you show up.

Helping the growth of others starts with knowing and growing yourself. A deep understanding of your drives, beliefs, values, and strengths can be valuable in managing your emotions when interacting with others.

As an agile coach, I try to spend a third of my time in this area of mastery, reflecting, writing, reading, attending events, or experimenting with new ideas. Investing in yourself is key to being a Badass Agile Coach, because serving yourself leads to being able to better serve your clients.

Serving

A servant leader focuses on people, helping them grow and looking after their well-being. While traditional leadership is more about the accumulation and exercise of power—the higher up you go in an organizational pyramid the more power you have—the servant leader shares power, puts the needs of others first, and helps people develop and perform as highly as possible. Being a servant leader is central to the very essence of an agile coach.

The competencies within Serving are:

- **Serving the Team.** This is about staying tuned into the formation and evolution of the team toward a mature instantiation of an agile mindset and behaviors. You are actively engaging the team in their ongoing learning and growth.
- **Serving the Business.** The competencies here are often an area of specialization for the coach. You may need experience and skill within the business and product domains to be effective here. Serving the business may involve facilitating business stakeholders to create a greater understanding of customers and users, developing practical product strategies, product planning, forecasting, product economics, or validating assumptions. You may spend time guiding teams to help them effectively manage the backlog, differentiate outcome and output, define value, order items, and refine the product backlog.

Transforming

Transforming is about guiding sustainable change that will allow the individual teams and the organization to be more effective and learn how to change for themselves.

Organizations are complex, and changing them is an even more complex proposition. An empirical and informed approach to the change process improves the chances of success of an agile transition. Successfully helping an organization with change needs a certain level of emotional intelligence (see Self-Mastery), understanding of organizational design, and the knowledge and skills to help people navigate change.

The competencies within Transforming are:

- **Organizational Change.** Introducing change into a system will be unique every time, and it's not like installing a piece of software. It's a matter of guiding an organization through a series of experiments to help them inspect and adapt toward a desired future state. We also want change to be sustainable, so it's about helping people change, not inflicting change on them—growing everyone's capability to affect the system around them long after the agile coach is gone.
- **Organizational Design.** An agile coach must be able to understand an organization's current state, opportunities, and challenges and how this impacts their ability to reach their desired goal or solve their problems. As an agile coach, you guide people in understanding which patterns are appropriate and help them to adapt those patterns to their context. Nothing seems to inspire more coaching conversations than how to scale agile in larger organizations. Conversely, as a Lean coach, you'll want to consider the opposing forces of simplification or descaling.

Agile/Lean Practitioner

For you to work as an agile coach, most clients would expect knowledge and experience here. Many agile coaches come from agile or lean backgrounds, but reflecting here helps us stay rooted. If you are coming to agile coaching from a non-agile background, then investment in personal growth is likely to start here. There is also a lot of synergy between an agile/lean mindset and a coaching mindset— an underlying belief in people, the idea that change is possible and people can be the best that they can be.

Agile/Lean Principles

This competency includes the agile values and principles, which guide our thinking and actions when approaching new situations. A deep understanding of agile allows an agile coach to apply frameworks and practices in the way they were intended. An agile mindset requires belief in yourself and others; people are the foundation of agile working. We trust, support, and nurture people to unleash their full human potential—being agile over doing agile.

Lean Manufacturing and Lean Product Development provide us with some foundational concepts that underpin the agile frameworks and methods.

- Focusing on the value that gives the most delight to our customers.
- Optimizing our organizations for flow with small batch sizes with the shortest possible lead time.
- Maximizing quality and minimizing waste.

At its heart, Lean is about total respect for the people involved and a continuous improvement mindset.

Domain Knowledge (The Tire)

Domain knowledge is represented around the outside of the Wheel. It is the expertise that may better help you serve the client and build trust with the team or organization. However, there is a risk: The more domain experience you have, the harder it will be to remain objective in your coaching. Therefore, it may be valid for an agile coach to allow a reduction of expertise in some areas (i.e., choosing not to stay up-to-date with the latest changes in technology) while seeking to increase knowledge in other areas.

Closing Thoughts

If you think about it deeply, the Agile Coaching Growth Wheel is actually several models in one:

- Coaching stance model
- Coaching mindset model
- Coaching competency model

- Coaching service model
- Coaching skills growth model

My point is, there's a lot of nuance in this simple diagram. We wanted it to be something that you could grow into (pun intended) and that would serve you well no matter how experienced you were as a coach.

Remember, it's all about growth—your growth as a Badass Agile Coach in service to your clients. And trust me, you're never done growing, so get on the Wheel and continue your journey.

Further Reading

It's not what you know, it's who you are. This blog explores being an agile coach: www.beliminal.com/being-an-agile-coach/.

The Agile Coaching Growth Wheel blog and guidance: www.beliminal.com/the-agile-coaching-growth-wheel/.

Facilitation skills for agile coaches: www.beliminal.com/facilitation-skills-for-agile-coaches-and-scrum-masters/.

Greenleaf, R. (2002). *Servant Leadership: A Journey into the Nature of Legitimate Power & Greatness*, 25th anniversary edition. Mahwah, NJ: Paulist Press.

Kaner, S. (2014). *Facilitator's Guide to Participatory Decision-Making*, 3rd edition. New York: Jossey-Bass.

Whitmore, J. (1992). *Coaching for Performance*. London: Nicholas Brealey.

8

An Agile Coaching Story, Part 1

In this chapter, Mark Summers of Beliminal explores how agile coaching conversations look when taking different stances. Through a fictionalized case based on Mark's coaching engagements, we will see how an agile coach moves between stances based on the context they face. Even within a single conversation, we will see how adaptable an agile coach needs to be.

Our Setting: Julie, an experienced agile coach, has just been engaged by Shepton Bank. We will join her as the engagement begins, highlighting specific conversations to demonstrate the Coaching Arc when using different coaching stances. The conversations are concise to demonstrate the arc; real-world conversations may take longer.

The Beginning – Julie's New Engagement

I am excited, as I always am at the start of a new engagement. Shepton Bank has just hired me to help them with their agile transformation. The Digital leadership team promised the board that they would implement agile in this financial year, but they have been struggling to get off the ground. The pressure is now on, as very little progress has been made since making this commitment. One of the leadership team members spent two months doing a gap analysis and designed an operating model based around the Scaled Agile Framework (SAFe), and they want help implementing it. This was the context I had ahead of my first Zoom call with Paul, the director of digital, and the heads of user experience and project management.

Planning

Our email exchanges tell me that they are in a rush, so it will be important to try and keep this initial conversation focused on some specific goals. Once we establish those, I will probe their thinking with some questions specifically around why they wanted to transform and their current challenges.

I suspect we will be talking about SAFe at some point in the conversation. When that happens, it will be important for me to challenge their thinking, as they are new to agile. I have also seen enough big upfront transformations attempted by other organizations to know they rarely achieve the desired benefits, so I need to be prepared to step into an Advising stance when discussing how to run the transformation.

The Conversation

Once we've completed the introductions, I ask my first question: "What would you like to focus on today?"

There is a brief silence. Ryan, the head of project management, is the first to break it.

"Well …" After checking to be sure no one else is going to jump in, he continues. "As you know, our head of change, Debbie, has recommended that we implement SAFe, and I for one feel a little lost. We hope you can help us."

My first opening move is to seek permission to ask questions and explain that I will be listening while we explore. "Let's explore this together," I start. "I would like to ask you a few questions. I will mostly be listening at this point. Is that ok?" Everyone agrees that it is.

"Tell me more about feeling lost."

"Debbie seems confident, but apart from her and Zara we have very little experience in agile," Ryan says.

"And SAFe seems very different from the agile I have experienced before," adds Zara, the head of user experience. "Although I guess we have a lot more people involved this time, so maybe it makes sense to be more structured."

I decide it's time to establish a goal for this conversation. "Where do we need to get to by the end of this call?"

"Well, it would be good to understand where we start with implementing SAFe, and how you will support us," Paul offers.

I wait for a few moments. I notice Zara slightly furrowing her eyebrows, but she doesn't say anything. "Anything else?"

After a fairly long pause, this time Ryan speaks. "We have had a lot of discussions in the leadership team about if SAFe is right for us, and I would love to know your opinion."

"Ok, so that's three things: where to start, how I support you, and is SAFe right for you." They are now nodding and making positive noises.

"We only have an hour for this conversation, so it's unlikely I will know enough about your context to advise you if SAFe is right for you, but we should be able to get to a point where you understand how we could start and how I engage." They give me knowing smiles and indicate they are happy with this.

At this point in the conversation, I want to help them connect with the why behind their agile transformation. "I would like to explore your context with you for a little while first. Is that ok?" Yes, they say. "Apart from meeting your commitment to the board, what are your motives for this agile transformation?"

"Well, whenever we work on anything that needs significant IT changes it takes forever," says Ryan "and we have a big new program of work coming up that will mean a lot of change across the full stack of our online banking platform. Given how we normally work, these changes will take 18 months at least. We need to be able to deliver faster."

Paul adds, "Complaints have gone up over the last year and most of them are due to quality issues, so better quality is a driver."

"Anything else?"

"We have been struggling to hire great user experience people," says Zara. "And, when we do get them, they don't stay very long. I want to make this department a great place to work so that we can attract and retain the best people."

"Anything else?" I ask again.

"I am sure there are more, but I think those are the main points," says Paul.

We will come back to the why as a whole team, but for this conversation, I take the cue to move forward and explore challenges.

"Ok, so what is stopping you from delivering fast, achieving high quality, and creating a great place to work?" I ask.

There is a long pause this time. Eventually, Ryan says, "Not enough hours in the day to fit everything in." Zara and Paul chuckle.

"What was it that made you laugh?"

"Relief, I guess just being able to talk about it," says Paul.

"Everybody is so busy. It's just the way it's always been around here."

"How does being busy stop you from being fast?"

"To get any significant changes out the door we rely on IT and their third-party suppliers, Commercial, Legal, Security, and Operations," Ryan says, counting out the department names on his fingers as he goes. "And everybody's busy, so managing and scheduling the work is a massive task. When it's just simple front-end changes we can turn them around really quickly, but this new program is going to require a lot of change within IT, and that's when things really slow down."

"So, is SAFe the answer?" presses Paul.

I smile. Paul is not going to let me off the hook for some advice around SAFe. I sense that their lack of knowledge about SAFe is making them nervous. I decide it's time to switch to an Advising stance and use their context to explain what it will be like to engage with me.

"I would always recommend to my clients not to start with a scaling framework. Learn with some initial pilots what being agile might look like at Shepton Bank. It may be that SAFe or parts of SAFe will be a good answer, but organizations are complex, so if we start with a solution, we won't know if we are addressing the real needs of the organization."

"So, that makes sense," Paul replies, "but it is more than a little scary. How do we get started?"

"This is where I can make a proposal. As it is the Digital leadership team who are engaging me, this is where the change must start. I propose that I facilitate a session to identify the first pilot. However, I haven't met all of the team yet and I think it would be good for me to speak to the others first."

"Why can't we just start a couple of Scrum teams?" says Ryan. "I am a bit worried about how much time this may take if the leadership team needs to be involved."

"Often, creating teams is the easy bit, but it is not always the place to start with an agile transformation. The other thing I notice about what you have told me is there is no agreement among the leadership team about how to adopt agile. If we can agree on the direction of travel, then we can sense the challenge that needs to be addressed first and design an experiment around that."

"Won't the leadership team need some training?" asks Zara.

"That is a possible outcome of this first workshop, although I will include an exploration of the what and the why of agile so that you can be clear as a team about your motives."

"There is a lot that is not clear for me in how we adopt agile," Paul says. "Don't we need a roll-out plan and to design a new operating model and processes?"

I am still advising them about how to approach the engagement, but I want them to have input into the conversation, so I am going to rephrase the question back to them.

"That is how many agile transformations start. What risks can you see with that approach?"

"I guess it is the same as adopting SAFe, we wouldn't know if a new operating model would work," says Zara.

"Exactly. And that brings me to how I will work with you. Once we have identified one or more experiments and set them in motion, we will agree on a review cadence. In this way, we will be able to make adjustments as we help guide the organization toward our goals."

"So, we are going to be agile about the change, continuously planning over following a plan," jokes Zara.

"Yes. And this is important, as this gives the leadership team a chance to learn what it means to be agile. I notice we are coming toward the end of this meeting, how are we doing against our goals?"

"I am happy to start like this, and I am actually relieved that we don't start with SAFe. It did seem daunting," says Paul.

"I just hope Debbie will be on board with this. Julie, I can work with you to get things scheduled," says Ryan.

"Thank you, Ryan. What else would you like to talk about today?"

The meeting finishes with a few logistics.

Reflection

Straight after the call, I open my notebook to do a post-coaching review while it is still fresh in my mind. After any client interaction I practice self-reflection to learn about both the engagement and myself. I have found this process critical to grow in the competency of Self-Mastery; the self-awareness it creates helps me to learn and evolve how I show up next time.

The important thing with a post-coaching review is not just to look at the *what*, what happened, but to also explore the *so what*, what it means, and the *now what*, what I need to do as a result, or what changes I need to make in our coaching agreements, plans, or strategy.

What. What Happened?

- At the start, I was very consciously taking a Coaching stance, and together we co-created some clear goals for the conversation.
- When pressed for an answer on SAFe, I switched to an Advising stance, and I stayed in that stance to describe how I would engage. So, I was both giving advice and starting to partner.
- I switched back to a Coaching stance by asking questions toward the end of the conversation, like "Can you see any risks with that approach?"
- I sensed relief that I wasn't going to come in and start changing everything straight away.
- The conversation around SAFe diverted the conversation away from exploring the challenges.

So What. What Did I Learn? What Does It Mean?

- As I switched to an Advising stance, I noticed that I was a little anxious; I think I recognized this as a critical point in the conversation. I also felt relief when I was able to ask a question again.
- From my perspective, it felt like I chose the right time to provide advice about not starting with SAFe. My motive in advising was to challenge their thinking.
- I was even more anxious when offering advice on how I would engage, and I picked up a degree of uncertainty here from Ryan because of the time investment and from Paul due to the lack of an upfront plan.

Now What. What Do I Need to Do as a Result?

- From a personal development perspective, I need to get better at telling the story of what coaching is, how I engage as a coach,

and why. A good first step for me would be to write that as a blog post, as I find writing helps me get my thinking straight in my head.
- Within the initial leadership workshops, we will need to allow time to explore how to become agile, as well as what it means to be agile.
- Schedule one-on-one time with each of the leadership team members to learn more about their challenges.

Advice from My Pair-Coach

I met with my pair-coach (mentor) prior to starting the engagement to work out my initial strategy. After the call, I met with Bob again to close the loop and hear his views. After recounting the conversations, we settled on the following:

- Bob emphasized how important the "beginning" was as a coach. It's about establishing many things—setting the stage for coaching, establishing your relationship, explaining what agile coaching actually is, meeting the client where they are, establishing coaching goals and plans, and so on. He reminded me not to rush to accomplish all of this at once, but to remember these things as I started the overall Coaching Arc with this client.
- He also reminded me of the importance of my metaskills, and of being intentional in how I enter each and every Coaching Arc. In other words, deciding on the best way to show up for the client (and me) to create the most effective conversations.
- Finally, he reminded me that he had my back and was there if I needed him, but that he had confidence in me, my skills, and my instincts.

The Interviews – Building Rapport

Over the next week, I have calls scheduled with all of the leadership team to build up a rapport with each of them and listen to their concerns. In addition to a follow-on to the initial Zoom call, I will meet with the function heads for Development (Neil), Testing (Nimesh), and Change Management (Debbie).

Planning

My main goal for the calls is to build rapport with each member of the Digital Leadership Team, since this is still part of my opening to the engagement. I decide to hold a metaskill of curiosity, through my listening and questions. This will show that I am interested in them, and it will help me surface information that is useful to the client.

My second goal for the calls is to surface and try to address any issues that might hold the team back in the workshops. So, the call will have two parts. Part one will focus on listening to build rapport and identify obstacles. If needed, I will be ready with part two, trying to bring attention to any obstacles and challenging thinking where needed.

The Conversation

I am feeling a little apprehensive before the call with Debbie, as I don't know how attached she will be to her recommendation of implementing SAFe. Before the call, I go for a run—that tends to put me in a positive mindset and free my mind so that I am a better listener. During my run, I reminded myself to be calm and take things slow; when I am anxious or excited, I tend to talk when silence might be better.

So, after the initial pleasantries, I smile, nod, and wait for Debbie to speak. I don't have to wait long. "I am so glad we are going to start this agile adoption; it is long overdue."

I decide to go with the positive vibes I am picking up around agile. "Paul mentioned you had previous agile experience. What can you tell me about that?"

"It was a few years ago when I was working in IT. We had a large program to re-platform our retail banking system, and I took on the role of a product owner. I just loved it. It was the first time in my tenure at the bank that I had been able to make decisions for myself and we got stuff done."

"That sounds like a great experience. What happened?" I focus on being curious.

"We delivered, and then slowly we went back to business as usual. A few of us tried to push to continue with agile, but the teams were disbanded and people went back to their managers, who were reluctant to release them again."

"What are your thoughts about adopting agile in Digital?"

"Well, I left IT for Digital because I thought there would be a greater opportunity to adopt agile, so I am very excited. I believe you know I had recommended that we adopt SAFe, as it worked very well on the retail banking program. Although I hear you are not a fan." says Debbie, with a hint of a smile.

At this point, I still want to focus on building rapport and exploring Debbie's motives. So, I acknowledge the topic of SAFe in a neutral way, but focus attention on what's going on in the leadership team. "It may well be that SAFe is right for you, but at the moment the leadership team all seem to want different things out of this agile transformation, and seem nervous about how to move forward."

"Well, I can see you know us quite well already. The main reason I suggested SAFe was so that we had something to hang our hat on. That lot would procrastinate forever. I thought SAFe would give us something that we could start to implement and that the structure of SAFe would give the team confidence to move forward. Although it seemed to confuse them even more. Which did prompt Zara to reach out to you, so maybe something good came out of it."

"Can you tell me more about what made your previous agile experience great?"

"I worked across two teams and they were both amazing. We didn't always see eye to eye, but we learned how to work together and we delivered. Every two weeks."

"What else?"

"Oh gosh, it was just so much nicer to collaborate with people rather than spending my time writing documents to hand over the wall."

After taking Debbie back to the experience, I decide it's time to address the elephant in the room, but in the context of her previous experience. "What role did SAFe play in your successful experience?"

"Well, we didn't adopt SAFe straight away, and we only picked bits of it as more teams came online. I think having a single view of demand helped align all of the product owners and also helped us prioritize work across the program."

"So, what do you want out of adopting agile in Digital?"

"Lots, but the main thing I think we would benefit from is that sense of purpose we had on the retail banking program. Currently, it feels like we just do stuff, without any understanding of the value or impact we are having."

"What else?"

"I would love to get that team culture back again. That's what I miss." I don't say anything, and Debbie changes tack. "So, how do you think we can get the agile transformation moving forward?"

Up until now I've been exploring in Coaching stance, but I recognize now that I am going to switch stances to advising the head of change about change. So, I will start with something I know she already agrees with, but then it's time for honesty about why I don't think they should start with SAFe. Then, I will invite reflection by ending with a question.

"First we need to get some alignment with the leadership team. Also, we need to recognize that this transformation is coming top-down. Rolling out SAFe risks imposing change on people. It's typically not change that people don't like; change is a constant and we humans are quite adaptable. What people resist is *being* changed. So, rather than the leadership team starting with a solution, I would suggest finding ways of inviting people into the change and working with them to co-create the solution. What does that bring up in you?"

Debbie looks thoughtful for a moment. "Well, we didn't start with SAFe in IT, and it now makes me think it would be the wrong thing to start with here. However, I also think Paul will struggle with us as a leadership team not having the answers. That's what he sees as our job."

"Thanks for sharing that," I reply. "How do you see it?"

"Well, you have probably guessed I like to get things moving. I like to lead by example and encourage people to come with me.

Although—what did you call it?—'inviting people into the change' sounds like a very different kind of leadership and I worry that we are not ready for it."

"Well, one of my mentors always said, 'Start before you are ready because if you wait until you are ready, you will never start,'" I joke.

By the end of the call, Debbie and I have built up a good rapport and explored further challenges and opportunities for adopting agile within Digital.

Reflection

What. What Happened?

- Throughout the conversation with Debbie, I was mainly holding a Coaching stance but did switch to an Advising stance to advise against starting with a scaled solution.
- I was able to keep the tone lighthearted and use my curiosity to bring out what was important to Debbie. In addition to using the metaskill of curiosity, I tried to be a bit playful as we went along.
- I stuck to my plan of focusing on building rapport before dealing with any challenging topics.

So What. What Did I Learn? What Does It Mean?

- I discovered Debbie was not attached to SAFe; she just wanted to see action or movement.
- I learned that there had been previous agile initiatives within the bank.
- The run helped me clear my head before the call, so I was calm at the start of the conversation.
- I share some traits with Debbie around driving forward to action, and this helped build rapport.
- The time I spent thinking about the calls ahead of time was really useful. I was able to hold back and not dive into challenging topics before we had established some rapport. It was just enough structure while still allowing me to dance in the moment.

- I feel confident about the upcoming workshops, now that I have met all of the team members individually.

Now What. What Do I Need to Do as a Result?

- I must be conscious when working with the leadership team that I don't get carried away by Debbie's enthusiasm, as we will need to move forward together.
- I will go for a run before the first session with the whole leadership team; I am finding that helps get my head in the right space before a session.
- I will continue to set aside a similar time for planning these types of conversations in the future.

Advice from My Pair-Coach

- Bob mentioned that Debbie and I are both pushing, "get things moving and done" types of personalities. He cautioned me to be aware of this in my coaching—teasing out when it was strategically right to push as opposed to being influenced by Debbie's energy.
- He also reminded me that rapport takes time and that I need to continually work on it while trusting my coaching Spider-Sense, switching stances, and pushing (Advising) when I feel it is in the best interest of the clients' goals.
- Finally, Bob mentioned that SAFe might be a bit of a red herring to this client—a silver-bullet solution that might be masking deeper challenges, obstacles, or goals. He recommended I keep thinking more deeply about SAFe in this way throughout my coaching journey with this client.

Workshop 1 – Opening Moves

Now that I've met all the leadership team members individually, we have scheduled a series of morning workshops over the next couple of weeks. Because of the pandemic, we are all working from home and will join the workshops virtually.

Planning

This is my first time working with everyone as a whole team. I am aware that they have not been functioning well as a team, so I need to make sure we have a solid foundation to work together for the series of workshops. I also want to give them a baseline understanding of agility. I establish some high-level goals for the first two workshops.

Workshop 1 – Opening Moves

- Create an environment for the team to work together effectively.
- Co-create the goals for the workshops.
- Create a baseline understanding of agility.

The initial training will be minimal; I will introduce concepts as they support the conversation, both during the workshops and into the engagement.

Workshop 2 – Explore Motives and Agree on a Direction of Travel

- Create alignment around the why of their agile transformation.
- Agree on the indicators for success.
- Create a common vision for their direction of travel.

After we safely navigate these two workshops, we can use the following workshops to start designing pilots and agree on how they as a leadership team will work to support the transformation.

Clearly some of my time will be spent in Guiding Learning stance throughout the workshops. But I do expect to dance between that stance and the Facilitating and Advising stances.

The Conversation

It's Monday morning, two weeks since my first conversation with Shepton Bank. I am delighted that everybody is almost on time for our first leadership workshop. Ryan, the head of project management, is the last to dial in, with apologies that his last meeting ran over.

I like to start meetings like this with a check-in. I find that every check-in creates connections between team members, so if you do it often it can have a huge positive impact on the team. Some of my favorite check-in questions are:

- What is your earliest childhood memory?
- What has inspired or motivated you in the last few weeks?
- Who would play you in a film about your life?
- What's the best advice you have ever been given?
- If you had to teach a class on one thing, what would it be?

Since this meeting will be so important to our overall results, I decide to focus the check-in on being present in the moment.

"Welcome," I greet everybody "It is important to start with a check-in. If we do this every time we meet, it can help us to grow as a team. I would like to start with a question. What's going on in your head right now that needs to be unloaded in order to be fully present today?" I wait.

"Morning, Julie." It is Zara. She is used to my check-in questions from working with me in a previous company. "I had a great weekend. It was lovely weather so I went cycling with my husband, Jack, and we had a lovely picnic overlooking a beautiful lake. I woke up excited but nervous this morning about these sessions. I am checked in and ready to start."

Nimesh, the head of testing, goes next. "I found out this morning that one of my senior testers is leaving. Pam has been with the company for over 20 years and her product knowledge is irreplaceable. So, I am sad about that, but as there is nothing I can do about it today, I am fully present."

"Well, I'm spinning plates as usual," says Ryan "We have various stakeholders jumping up and down wanting to know when their changes will be live. That's what my last call was about, but I think we are on top of things."

142   AGILE COACHING MODELS AND PRACTICE

Once everybody is checked in, I want to make sure we have the right goals for these workshops.

"Thank you for being present. Based on our conversations last week, we agreed on the following objectives for these sessions:

1. Create a common understanding of agile;
2. Gain alignment around why we want to be agile and identify a direction of travel; and,
3. Identify where to start and agree on leadership's role to support the change.

"Does anybody have any objections to this focus?"

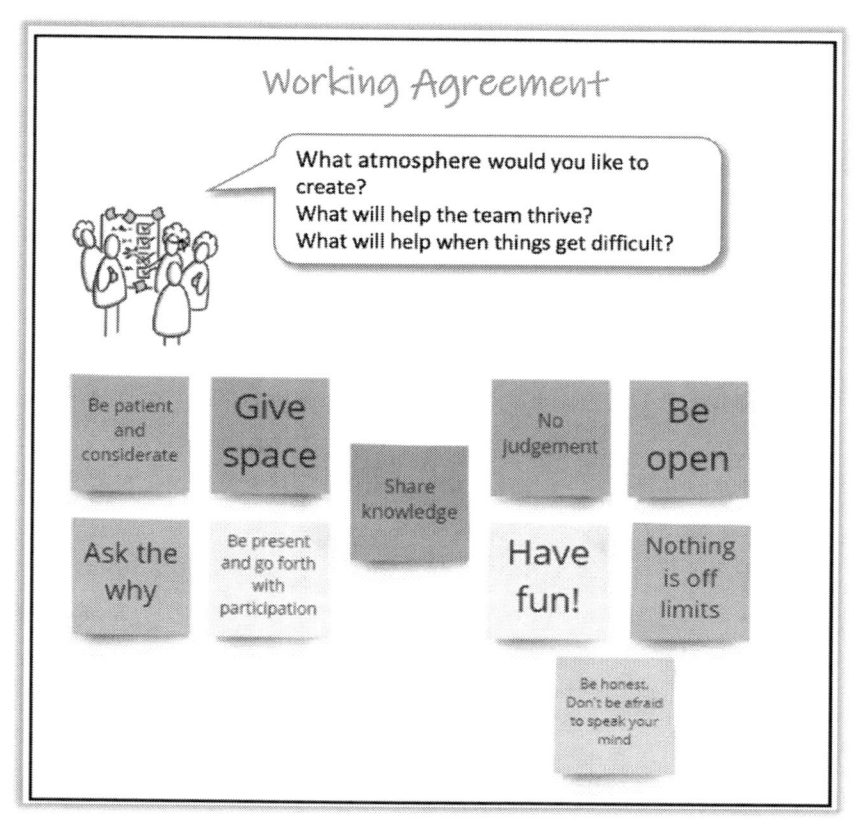

FIGURE 19. Team Working Agreement Ideas. *Source*: Mark Summers' facilitation and coaching group examples. Used with permission.

There are no objections, so I make it clear we can review these objectives at any time and adapt our approach. I continue.

"Before we dive in, we need to create our agreements for how we will work together." I share the virtual collaboration board we will be using for the workshops and point them to three questions:

1. What atmosphere would you like to create?
2. What will help the team thrive?
3. What will we do when things get difficult?

"I am going to put you into two breakout rooms. I want you to discuss these questions and propose agreements for the team. Capture them on sticky notes. You have 10 minutes. Is it clear what I am asking you to do?"

After nods of agreement, I open the breakout rooms. After 10 minutes, the two rooms have captured five items each (see figure 19). I ask a member from each of the breakout rooms to explain what is important about each item they chose.

Once the team understands the intent behind each item, I introduce the next step.

"We want to make these items useful for choosing how to behave toward each other. Now that we understand the intent behind each of the items, I would like to introduce you to *even over statements*. For example, if we are giving space, what are we prepared to give up a little of? It could be 'Giving space for everybody to be heard EVEN OVER getting things done.' Or maybe you mean 'Giving space to others to talk EVEN OVER making sure you are understood.' Notice how both sides of the statement are positive. That's important—it allows us to make tradeoffs."

I decide it's worth spending time doing this to make our working agreements less ambiguous and more useful when managing our interactions. So, I mix up the teams to allow more divergent thinking while making sure some people understand the original intent behind each idea. I ask one team to focus on the pink stickies and the other team to focus on the blue.

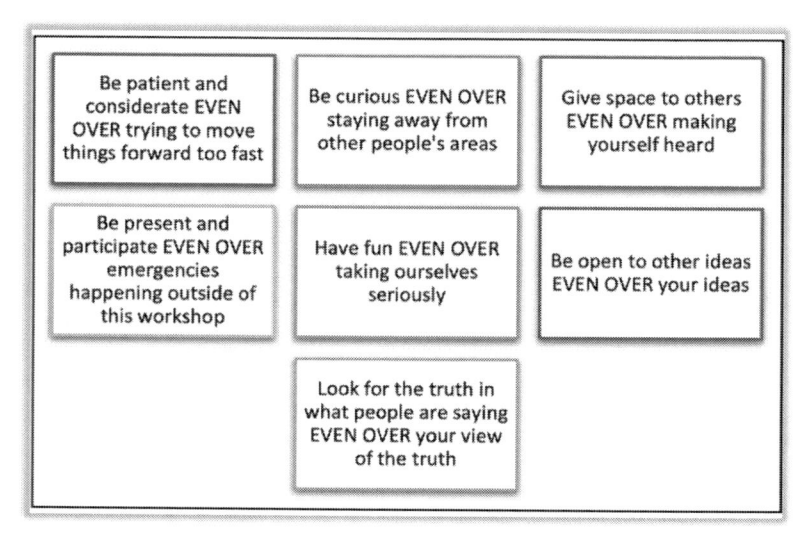

```
┌─────────────────────────────────────────────────────────────────┐
│  ┌──────────────────┐  ┌──────────────────┐  ┌──────────────────┐│
│  │ Be patient and   │  │ Be curious EVEN  │  │ Give space to    ││
│  │ considerate EVEN │  │ OVER staying away│  │ others EVEN OVER ││
│  │ OVER trying to   │  │ from other       │  │ making yourself  ││
│  │ move things      │  │ people's areas   │  │ heard            ││
│  │ forward too fast │  │                  │  │                  ││
│  └──────────────────┘  └──────────────────┘  └──────────────────┘│
│  ┌──────────────────┐  ┌──────────────────┐  ┌──────────────────┐│
│  │ Be present and   │  │                  │  │                  ││
│  │ participate EVEN │  │ Have fun EVEN    │  │ Be open to other ││
│  │ OVER emergencies │  │ OVER taking      │  │ ideas EVEN OVER  ││
│  │ happening outside│  │ ourselves        │  │ your ideas       ││
│  │ of this workshop │  │ seriously        │  │                  ││
│  └──────────────────┘  └──────────────────┘  └──────────────────┘│
│                        ┌──────────────────┐                      │
│                        │ Look for the     │                      │
│                        │ truth in what    │                      │
│                        │ people are saying│                      │
│                        │ EVEN OVER your   │                      │
│                        │ view of the truth│                      │
│                        └──────────────────┘                      │
└─────────────────────────────────────────────────────────────────┘
```

FIGURE 20. EVEN OVER Principal Agreements. *Source*: Mark Summers' facilitation and coaching group examples. Used with permission.

Once more I open up the breakout rooms. When they return, we talk through the statements, refine them together, and eliminate a couple that contradict or are covered by the others.

We are left with seven principles to guide the sessions (figure 20). To finish this session off, I ask "Who will hold the team accountable for each of these agreements?"

Straight away, Debbie says, "I am happy to hold us to giving space to others. I also want to own being patient and considerate, as I recognize that I tend to want to drive things forward, but I may need help."

"Who can help Debbie with that?" I ask.

"Well, I like to go a little slower so I will help Debbie," says Nimesh.

"I would also like to take responsibility for being curious. Given where we are as a department, we need to take a good hard look at ourselves, and I for one don't think we should hold anything as sacred."

"I will help you with that Nimesh," says Neil, the head of development. "How we are set up now is just not working and will only get worse when we start on this new program of work to improve the online banking experience. I am also keen on being open to other ideas."

This is a good time to recognize the positive steps they are taking around these agreements. "I would like to acknowledge the partnerships that you are making around these agreements and the sense of shared commitment. Who else will commit to holding one of these agreements for the team?"

"I would like to be patient and present," offers Ryan. "A lot is going on, but it will be all right. So shall I let others know if people seem distracted?"

"Well, I think that leaves fun," says Zara, "so I am happy to take on the role of chief joy officer."

"What emotions are you feeling right now?" I ask.

"Happiness," says Paul. "This is so different from our normal team interactions."

"What can you tell us more about that?"

"Well, it is more positive, and if we do what we have just agreed I can see how we can hopefully be more productive."

"I agree," says Zara. "I also feel relaxed."

"I feel a little anxious," says Ryan. "It feels like we have a lot to do, and we haven't even started yet." Everyone looks at Ryan. "I know, I know, I need to be a little patient." He smiles.

"Well, I am energized and ready to get cracking," says Neil.

With that, I once more acknowledge the sense of unity I am noticing and we move on. We spend the rest of the session focusing on the first objective—creating a common understanding of agile. We play some games to internalize the intent behind the Agile Manifesto for Software Development, which leads to some discussions of what it means to be agile as a business.

The day's session ends with the agreement that in the next session we will look at the why behind the agile transformation and try to identify some shared motives. I ask them to leave their thoughts about the session on a feedback board with quadrants labeled *lacked, liked, loathed,* and *longed for.*

Reflection

What. What Happened?

- The team came together well to create team agreements, and everyone seems positive about the results.
- Through the use of breakout rooms, I created space for them to explore in a safer environment. It also allowed for a divergence in ideas that ultimately converged to create eight agreements to guide us as a team.
- My primary stance here was one of facilitating to guide the process, however I used coaching questions to deepen people's thinking. Even in training, I stayed mostly in Facilitating stance, using games to guide the learning process. I also introduced techniques as I thought they might be helpful, such as the even over statements—very much learning through doing.
- I was careful as a leader to start to role model some of the behaviors that they expressed in their working agreement. Being patient meant being aware of my own tendency to move forward fast.
- One of the items on the feedback wall under *longed for* was "to know where we are going to start."

So What. What Did I Learn? What Does It Mean?

- Even though they have said they want to be patient, they are eager to get going.
- They enjoyed it when the sessions were mixed up, diverging their thinking in smaller groups.
- From the comments, they have not been a team in the past, so it was good to spend half of that first workshop on the team itself.
- "Even over" statements are normally used for making tradeoffs around strategy. Using them around the team's interactions was an experiment. It drove useful conversations, but we will need to see how useful they will be going forward.

Now What. What Do I Need to Do as a Result?

- It's time to cut them loose from agile theory and let them focus on themselves. I will then introduce other agile concepts as necessary.
- They seem to respond well to the team-building elements I am introducing, so as I facilitate them through the process it will be important to allow time for them to continue to grow as a team.
- There is tension between the work that needs to be done to become a team and the need to move forward with the agile transformation. If this becomes an issue, I will play this back to them.
- I want to learn how useful the even over statements are for making tradeoffs around interactions, so I will keep them in the team's focus each session and review with the team how useful they found them at the end of the workshops.

Advice from My Pair-Coach

- Bob mentioned that I might want to share with the clients when I'm switching stances (or hats). This level of transparency might limit any "stance confusion" on their part, as well as help them to understand the role and responsibility change for them (as clients) when I shift roles. I haven't done this before, but I like the idea. I think I'll try it as an experiment.
- He also gave me some very positive feedback that I had done a masterful job of setting the space in the beginning. But clients can sometimes become frustrated with this "fluffy, people-oriented" stuff, so he urged me to be aware of that in checking the clients' emotional field.
- He also thought this session was well planned and asked me if anything that happened today needed to be carried over into the next workshop. That made me think about potential adjustments, pivots, or experiments.

The story continues in the next chapter.

9

An Agile Coaching Story, Part 2

In this chapter, Mark Summers of Beliminal continues to explore how agile coaching conversations look when taking different stances.

One of the things Julie is learning is that planning for a coaching event and reflecting on what just happened are probably the most important activities for her to be a successful agile coach. This regular cycle of planning and reflection creates a pattern:

- Craft some directional ideas on client needs—goal-setting!
- Enter coaching with a sense-and-respond mindset, dancing with the client.
- Reflect on how well the goals were met and what you learned in the coaching.
- Pivot as required to meet your clients' goals and needs.

To paraphrase Forrest Gump, badass agile coaching is like a box of chocolates: You never know what you're gonna get.

Now let's move into the second phase of Julie's workshops with Shepton Bank: aligning on goals and direction.

Workshop 2 – Explore Motives and Agree on a Direction of Travel

Planning

For the second workshop, I have planned two major elements. Through the interviews I discovered many different answers to the question of why they want to be agile. I want the team to explore this, choose a few and agree on some measures of success. The second element I have planned is to explore the general direction of travel and create a potential vision for the future.

I plan the flow of activities to allow divergence and convergence around the two elements. There are a few elements I am not sure about, so I may need to allow for more divergent thinking around the measures of success. I may also need to use a game as we converge around the creation of a vision.

Agile Transformation Motives
- Improve accountability
- Remove roadblocks
- Create a sense of team
- Increase efficiency
- Increase effectiveness
- Make it a great place to work
- Deliver faster
- Improve transparency
- Improve communication
- Increase flexibility
- Create a sense of purpose
- Improve decision making
- Improve stakeholder engagement
- Improve quality

FIGURE 21. Group-Based Drivers or Motives for the Agile Transformation. *Source*: Mark Summers' facilitation and coaching group examples. Used with permission.

The Conversation

Wednesday morning, two days after the first workshop, everybody shows up early and enjoys a chat before we start. I start with a check-in question: "What is your first pleasant or fun memory as a child?" I have chosen this question so they will reveal something about themselves that is non-work related and to create an opportunity for them to see each other differently. Once everyone checks in, I begin with our first objective.

"On Monday we explored agile and we agreed that today we would start by exploring your motives for being agile. Through all of our conversations so far, I have been capturing the reasons you have expressed for being agile; you will see them on the virtual board (figure 21). So as a first activity, I am going to break you into two groups of three to discuss these reasons and identify any that are missing. I will see you in 10 minutes."

Ten minutes later, I welcome them back. "Did anything new emerge from your conversations?"

Paul starts. "We identified *improve customer satisfaction*. That was all we added in our group."

"And we added *reduce dependencies on IT*," says Neil.

"What else came out of your conversations?"

"Well, we didn't really understand the difference between *increase efficiency* and *increase effectiveness*, and we also felt they might be related to *deliver faster*," says Nimesh. "It would be good to explore this."

"Before we explore that, is there anything else that needs to be said about the potential motives you have been talking about?" There is a contented silence.

I switch to a Guiding Learning stance and use a game that allows them to explore the differences between optimizing for efficient task completion and optimizing for effective flow of value. This leads the team to decide to merge these ideas into "deliver value faster" (see figure 22).

> **Agile Transformation Motives**
>
> 1. Deliver value faster
> 2. Improve employee satisfaction
> 3. Improve customer satisfaction
>
> - Improve transparency
> - Increase flexibility
> - Remove roadblocks
> - Improve accountability
> - Make it a great place to work
> - Improve quality
> - Improve communication
> - Improve decision making

FIGURE 22. Group-Based Prioritization of Motivations. *Source*: Mark Summers facilitation and coaching group examples; used with permission.

After a short break, I introduce the next step. "Now we are going to line up our sticky notes from 'most important' to 'important but not as much as the others.' To do this, one of you will go first and place an item at some point on the scale. The next person will place the second sticky note above (more important) or below (less important) the first one. The third person can either choose a new item or move something that has already been placed. We will keep going until all the items have been placed and have stopped moving around. Make sense?"

They all have different thoughts around these motives, so I am trying to integrate these different frames of reference. We are entering the groan zone, and I am using a forced ranking to navigate it. I also ask them to do this silently and then gamify the activity so that they take turns. This speeds it up, and we only talk about the things where we have fundamentally different views.

By the end of this activity, an order has emerged and they have done this relatively silently. The only debate they needed was around quality and customer satisfaction. Ultimately the team decided that for customers to be satisfied, quality was important anyway, and focusing on customer satisfaction would be a little richer.

"Now I'm going to make a proposal based on that activity." I introduce consent-based decision-making—thumbs up if they agree with the proposal, thumbs out to the side if they have concerns, an open palm if they have the gift of an objection which we can use to improve our proposal. "How about we focus on the top three motives as our key drivers for this agile transformation." There are two concerns but no objections. We celebrate making a decision and then listen to the concerns.

We go on to talk about how we will know if we are having an impact on these three drivers, and agree on some metrics. An open discussion suffices for this part, as they already have some things in place for customer and employee satisfaction.

Customer Satisfaction

- They already have a regular survey of customer satisfaction.
- There are also industry tables that rate banks for customer satisfaction.
- They also want to see the number of complaints decreasing.

Employee Satisfaction

- They have an employee satisfaction form, which goes out annually, but they can use that more often.
- They also want to keep an eye on the impacts on retention and recruitment.

For the driver of *deliver value faster*, we agree to hold a workshop the following week to explore concepts that might help them measure success here. I'm thinking that I will introduce them to lead time (the time from a request being made to being delivered) and cycle time (the time from when we start working on something to when we finish).

This brings the first segment of the workshop to a close. "We have identified and agreed on the three key drivers for our agile transformation, how do you feel about that?" I ask.

"Well, if you told me beforehand that we were going to spend two hours talking about our motives I would have resisted," says Ryan, "but just looking at all the reasons we had come up with, I can see we were not aligned."

"I feel focused," says Nimesh.

"Given you now agree what's important, I want to give you time to dream about the future. Again, I am going to break you into two groups. I want you to imagine that in 12 months you have been asked by the bank's senior leadership team to present to them the success story that Digital has become. Consider what benefits you have achieved. What does it look and feel like to be in Digital? What are customers saying? What are employees saying? Create a poster that you will use to tell the story of your agile journey and highlight the successes. You have 20 minutes." I open the breakout rooms.

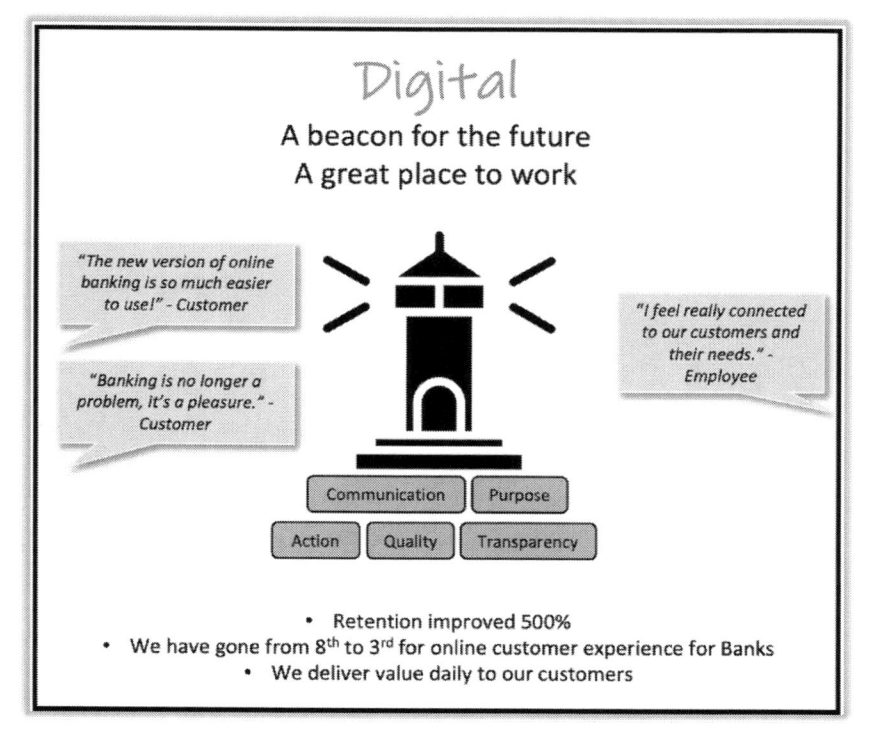

FIGURE 23. Imagining the Future of Digital, group one. *Source*: Mark Summers' facilitation and coaching group examples. Used with permission.

An Agile Coaching Story, Part 2   155

I end up giving them a little longer than 20 minutes, and when they get back, I ask them to present their posters as though they are presenting to the bank's senior leadership team.

Group one (see figure 23) includes Debbie, Paul, and Nimesh. Debbie starts. "We envisioned Digital as a shining beacon inside the bank that will be a guide for other areas as a great place to work. You can see the great quotes from customers and employees, and we have highlighted some of the benefits."

Nimesh continues. "And our shining beacon is built on solid foundations. We were talking about what was important to create this great place to work. Any questions?"

"I like how you have tied the benefits to the drivers we talked about. What do you mean by *action*?" asks Ryan.

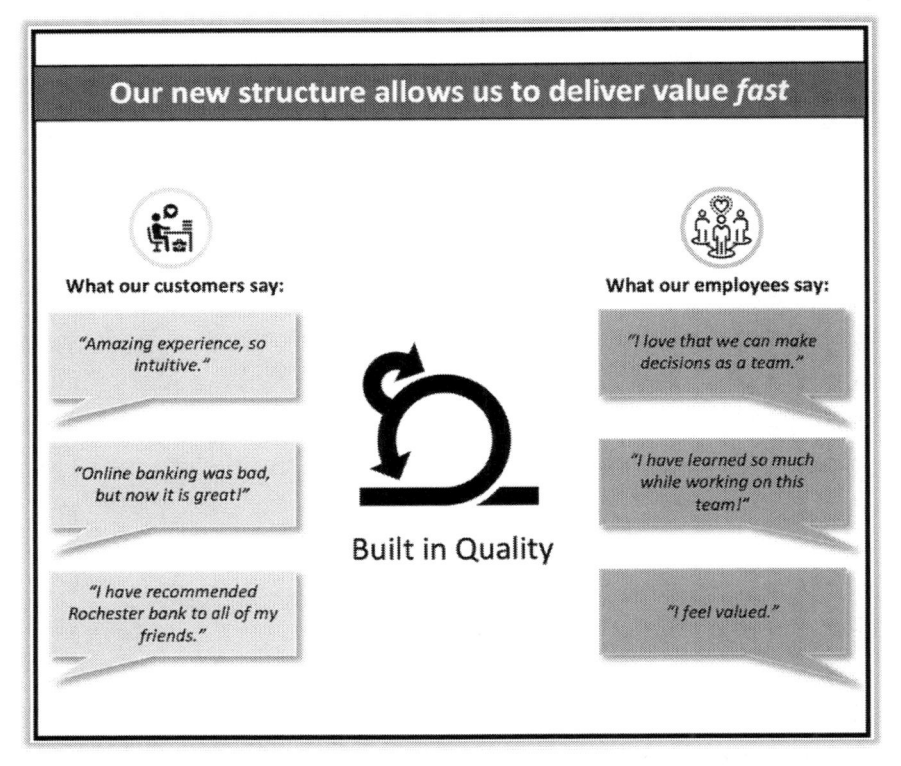

FIGURE 24. Imagining the Future of Digital, group two. *Source*: Mark Summers' facilitation and coaching group examples. Used with permission.

Paul replies "If something is getting in the way of becoming a great place to work, then we take action."

"Any other questions?" I ask. There are none. "Ok, let's hear from Zara, Neil, and Ryan."

"Well in the middle you can see a Digital team. They have all the skills they need to deliver value, including all the skills from our IT stack," says Neil, with a wide grin (see figure 24). "Defects now never escape the team; quality is king. As you can see this allows us to deliver fast and has a big impact on employees and customers."

Zara continues, "Now we have the best user experience for our customers, and we are attracting more thorough recommendations."

"And because there are fewer dependencies on other teams, I am much more relaxed," says Ryan. He chuckles.

At this point, I realize that the intent behind the posters is similar, as both have built on the key drivers we identified earlier and describe how the organization has changed as a result. I could leave it to open discussion to choose elements from each.

However, I decide to introduce a game to make sure everyone has a voice. Through the interactions during this game, the team will have an opportunity to improve their ideas further. "Ok, let's try and bring this together through an activity called *attract*. I want each of you to create an avatar on a sticky note next to your poster. Add an image and your name. Imagine you are standing next to the posters that you created. Now, I want you to go and stand by the poster you like best."

After a moment, Nimesh moves his avatar from team one to team two. "I just love the focus on quality, Neil sold it to me with his talk of no defects." Nimesh is the only one to make a move.

"You are two groups, and your goal is to attract others to join your group through negotiation. Find out what you would need to improve or change to get others to join. You are also free throughout this process to form new groups around new ideas that emerge. Each group can take turns to try and attract others. As team two is the largest group, you can go first."

An Agile Coaching Story, Part 2   157

> - Retention **improved 500%**
> - We have gone **from 8th to 3rd** for online banking customer experience
> - We **deliver value daily** to our customers

What our customers say:

"Amazing experience, so intuitive."

"Online banking was bad, but now it is great!"

"I have recommended Rochester bank to all of my friends."

What our employees say:

"I love that we can make decisions as a team."

"I have learned so much while working on this team!"

"I feel valued."

Communication | Purpose
Action | Quality | Transparency

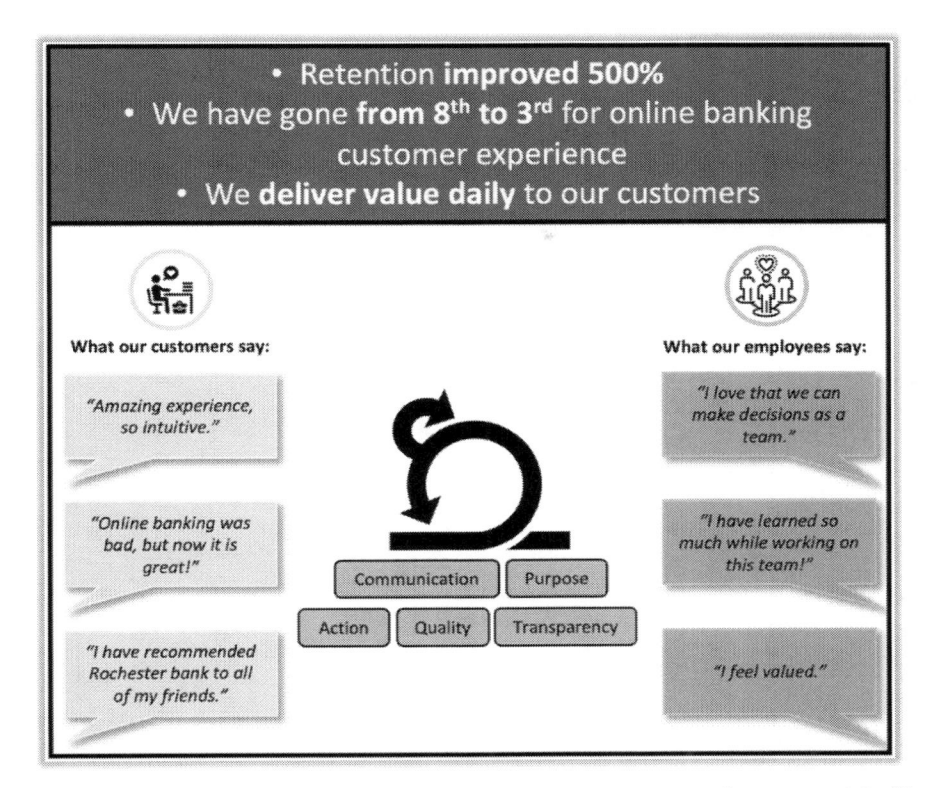

FIGURE 25. Imagining the Future of Digital, converged. *Source*: Mark Summers' facilitation and coaching group examples. Used with permission.

This activity can last for a long time but it can be worth the investment, because better ideas often emerge. On this occasion, the activity is relatively quick, as most of the work can be integrated onto a single poster (figure 25).

I comment on the fact that the team has removed the beacon.

"Yes," says Zara. "We didn't feel it fit with the story we would want to tell, and it works well with the foundations of communication, purpose, quality, action, and transparency underpinning our delivery."

Pleased with this outcome, I decide it's about time we look at where we are in the process. "So, today we have been focusing on our second objective, gaining alignment around why we want to be agile and identifying a direction of travel. How are we doing with that?"

"I think we are [...obscured...]," says Paul. "And I can see what we ar[...obscured...]less about how."

"I also like the w[...obscured...]t agile as we worked through our stuff," s[...obscured...]re impactful to how we are shaping thing[...obscured...]

"So tomorrow, wo[...] you prefer to spend more time exploring a direction of travel, or would you prefer to move on to our final objective, identifying where to start and agreeing on leadership's support role?"

"Move on" they all say, as I thought they would.

We spend the last 30 minutes reviewing how we are doing against our working agreement, and I ask them once more to leave feedback.

> [Sticky note: Why does this all kind of feel like a waste of time?]

Reflection

What. What Happened?

- The team was able to converge in both of the two main activities, and the feedback indicates surprise at how they have all come together.
- The element that felt slightly unfinished was how we would measure our key drivers, which emerged as we examined motives.
- This workshop was mostly done from a Facilitating stance, only stepping outside of that to explore team discoveries with a Coaching stance.
- I subtly introduced them to consent-based decision-making.

So What. What Did I Learn? What Does It Mean?

- In my eagerness to launch into a game to explore efficiency of task completion and effectiveness of flow of value, perhaps I rushed into it. I should have spent some time getting them to explore the differences. Starting with a Coaching stance would have probably created a better connection to the topic, and maybe the game wasn't needed.

- Things are going well in terms of progress and team unity. Maybe I could reflect this to them more often.
- In my session planning, I didn't give too much thought to how I would gamify the team's convergent activities. I decided on using the game *attract* in the moment, but it worked better than when we were converging around the motives, and the team was proud of the result.
- The team seems to like to learn by doing—we learned consent-based decision-making by doing it—but I need to make sure they understand the theory of different decision-making strategies so they will be able to apply them when I am not there.

Now What. What Do I Need to Do as a Result?

- If I am going to introduce a new concept, I need to make sure they are open to a bit of learning. Asking them would be a good idea. So rather than going straight from Facilitating to Guiding Learning stances, I will ask a few questions first from the Coaching stance.
- I think that at the opening for the final workshop this week, I should reflect with them on the progress they are making as a team. This can be done simply through the check-in question.
- I need to make sure I have a few different options in mind to gamify activities as the team converges its thinking.
- Next week I need to introduce the idea that there are lots of ways to make decisions, and get them to explore how they want to make decisions.

Advice from My Pair-Coach

- Bob agreed that I could have done more reflection toward the team, sharing with them their positive (agile-centric) discoveries, team formation progress, and willingness to play and experiment. He mentioned that I have a tendency to not share this with clients and that I should remind myself to do that in my planning efforts, or to perhaps "put on" a metaskill of reflection before coaching.

- In the same spirit, Bob mentioned that I seem to be getting better at sensing and responding to my clients (seamlessly switching stances). That was positive and encouraging feedback for me.
- The planning for this workshop seemed a bit lighter than the last one. He mentions this because it seemed to impact the flow a bit. Depending on the outcome and my comfort with the stances I'll be using (planned or ad hoc) I seem to be more comfortable in my coaching if I do a bit more planning. And the client outcomes seem stronger as well. But he's asking me to ponder this point, to see how it lands with me.

Workshop 3 – Identify Pilots

The groundwork is in place. I want them to end the week on a positive note, with their first steps agreed and ready to go. If they can achieve that, then the work can start next week on how they can unleash and support the change as leaders.

Planning

Given that we have a direction of travel, I want them to explore the first steps they can take toward that vision of the future.

I plan a check-in question to get them to explore what they are noticing about themselves as a team as they go through this process. I am keen to create awareness of how they are changing as a team.

The first facilitated section will be to identify their current tensions as they look toward that potential future state. I will allow them to brainstorm initially, but in order to converge I plan to break them into smaller groups to group, merge, eliminate, and identify the main tensions they want to address.

I will then introduce them to the idea of creating potential experiments to address the tensions they want to work with. Again, I will get them to work in groups to do this. If we end up with a lot of potential experiments, then we can assign value and cost to each using planning poker, so that we can get a feel for return on investment. My goal is to have them act on one to three at most, depending on how big the experiments are. This will all be very new for them as an approach, so as a leader I must make a conscious effort to encourage them.

The Conversation

"Today we will work toward creating some steps that you can put in motion toward giving that presentation to the senior leadership team. But before that, let's start with check-in. What's changed in the atmosphere of the team this week?"

"Well, we are being a lot more patient and considerate," says Nimesh, focusing straight back on the team's working agreement.

"What does that look like?"

"Well, the pace has been slower," continues Nimesh, "but as a result, we have done meaningful work that we are aligned around. Rather than arguing and not getting anywhere."

"Something else has changed," says Neil. "Usually, we only see each other at meetings. This week I have noticed us seeking each other out to talk about things."

"I feel an air of anticipation about what's going to happen next, which is great because before it felt more like denial, dread, when I thought of adopting agile," says Ryan.

The rest of the team members share their thoughts. Eventually, everybody is present and checked in and I begin.

"It feels like you are really enjoying the process so far and working well together." I observe. "Today I want to introduce you to the idea of tensions. I first came across them in the book *The Fifth Discipline* by Peter Senge.[18]

"Imagine a rubber band stretched between where we are now and our potential future state—it's in tension. Tensions are neither good nor bad, but they need to be released, either by making a change that

---

18. Here's a wonderful 5-minute video with Peter Senge explaining this tension: https://youtu.be/wz337pj-oLE.

moves us closer to our desired state or by changing our desired state. We will attempt to do the former initially, by identifying one or more tensions and designing an experiment we hope will move us forward.

"So, as you look forward to your potential future, what is coming up for you? You may think of these things as challenges, or maybe even opportunities, but I want you to silently capture on the board what is coming up for you."

After a few minutes, I stop them. The rate of new tensions had slowed down, and the big stuff should have come out by now (see figure 26). "I am going to put you into groups to explore the tensions. I want you to start to differentiate between tensions that are here now in the present and tensions which could happen but are future worries.

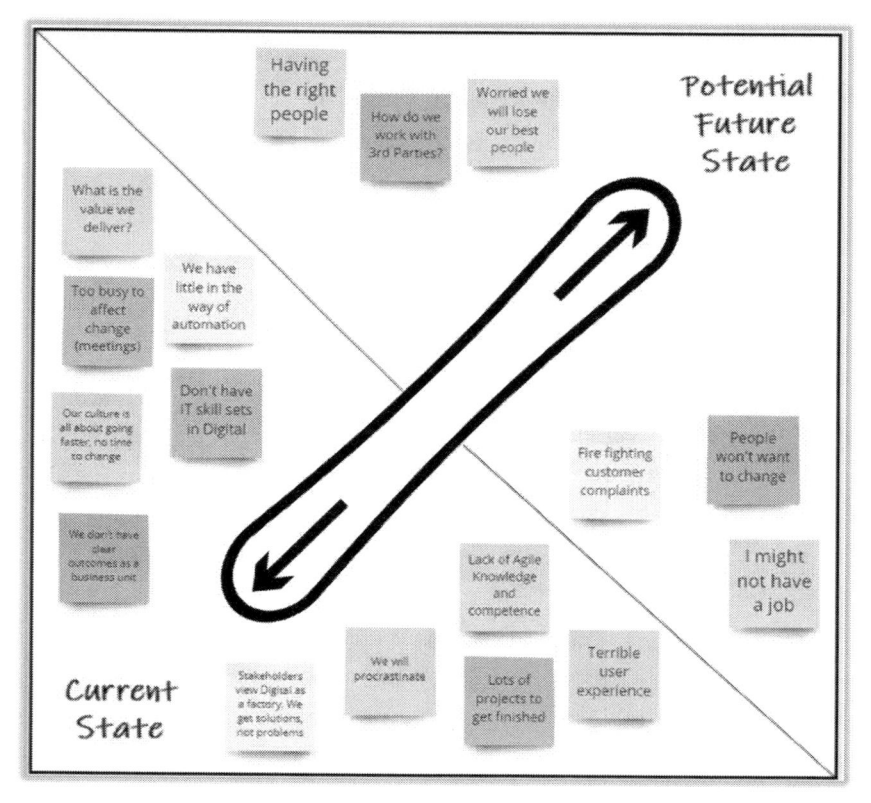

FIGURE 26. Current State to Future State, Tensions #1. *Source*: Mark Summers' facilitation and coaching group examples. Used with permission.

Set aside the future tensions. Also, see if you can overlap tensions that may be related, and give the group of tensions a name. Is this clear?"

I break them into groups, and after 10 minutes I rotate the groups, so that they share insight and understanding across the breakout sessions. When they finally come back together, there are fewer tensions, and some groups have started to emerge (see figure 27).

"What important information emerged from your conversations?"

"We talked a lot about how we are just a delivery function. We don't think like a product organization," says Debbie. "Mostly we just implement what business stakeholders have told us to do."

"Actually, that is probably a contributing factor to why our customer experience is so bad," says Zara, "as, effectively, our user

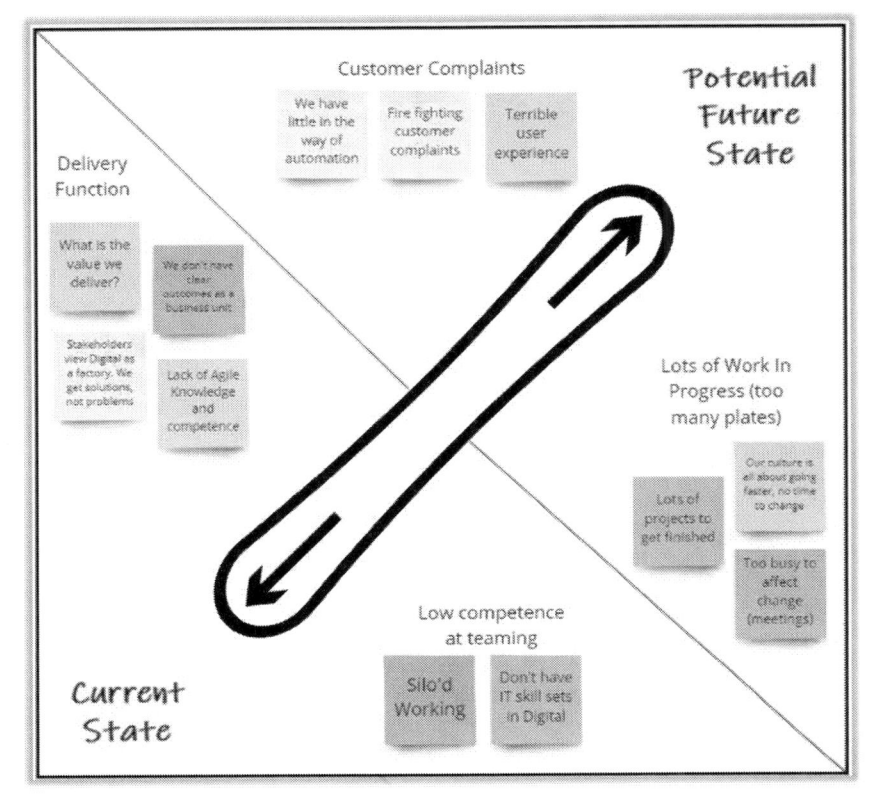

FIGURE 27. Current State to Future State, Tensions #2. *Source*: Mark Summers' facilitation and coaching group examples. Used with permission.

experience is the result of requests from different stakeholders with different needs. It's like a Lego house built from lots of different-sized bricks, all different colors, that we have been handed. We have never taken a step back and looked at our house holistically and asked, what do we need to build a nice house?"

"Nice metaphor, Zara," says Ryan. "And we don't have the time to do anything about it, because we have so many projects in progress."

"It looks like you are connecting some of these tensions. What about the low competence at teaming?"

Experiment Card

We have identified	We will experiment with
<Tension or Challenge>	<Practice or Change>

We expect	Context
<These visible benefits>	<Participants, Duration, Requirements >

FIGURE 28. Experiment Template. *Source*: Mark Summers' facilitation and coaching group examples; adapted from The Ready (*https://theready.com/cards*). Used with permission.

"That's an opportunity. It's something we haven't tried in Digital, and certainly not with IT either," says Neil. "It's something I would be keen to try soon, because we need to reduce the handovers and the dependencies if we want to be fast."

"We have mentioned the four groups. Is there anything else that is causing a greater tension at the moment?" The team members shake their heads; they are done. Now that we have explored some tensions, it's time to focus the team on creating some experiments.

"We are going to start to create some options describing changes we could make. To do that, we are going to design some experiments. Have a look on the virtual board at the format I would like us to use initially."

"These are experiment cards. On the board next to them you will see some guidance about what to think about when designing your experiment."

I have borrowed the format for the experiment cards from The Ready (see figure 28). They also have some predefined tension and practice cards. These make it safer to admit to tension being present, because lots of organizations have experienced something similar.

For this workshop, we have already identified some tensions, but I will have the practice cards available in case inspiration is required.

Over the next hour, the team co-creates two nicely envisioned and articulated experiments they could run.

Ryan takes us through the first experiment (figure 29). "We need a volunteer group to look at how we can reduce the number of projects to no more than 14. We don't know if that is the right number, but Nimesh feels that's how many we can actually test. We will run the experiment for at least six months; however, we expect that we will adjust the number of projects in progress as we learn. So, if everyone agrees then the next step is to do a call for volunteers. I would be happy to draft this."

"Thanks for that and to all who worked on that experiment," I say. "What else do we have?"

Experiment Card

We have identified
<Tension or Challenge>

We have a lot of projects in progress.

We will experiment with
<Practice or Change>

Reducing the number of projects currently being worked on from 20+ to no more than 14.

We expect
<These Visible Benefits>

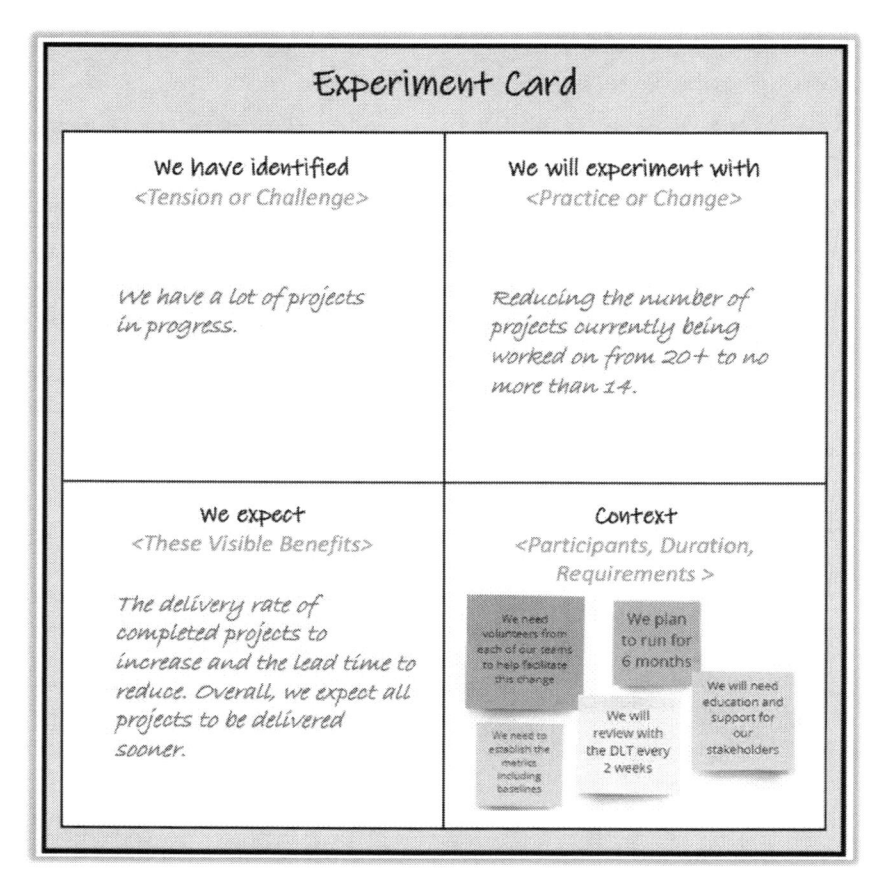

The delivery rate of completed projects to increase and the lead time to reduce. Overall, we expect all projects to be delivered sooner.

Context
<Participants, Duration, Requirements>

- We need volunteers from each of our teams to help facilitate this change
- We plan to run for 6 months
- We need to establish the metrics including baselines
- We will review with the DLT every 2 weeks
- We will need education and support for our stakeholders

FIGURE 29. Experiment 1. *Source:* Mark Summers' facilitation and coaching group examples. Used with permission.

"Well, we ended up combining the low competence in teaming and the fact that we are seen only as a delivery function," reports Paul (see figure 30).

"This is mainly because of the opportunity presented by the reworking of the online banking customer journey project, which is something we can own. So, it is a great sandpit to experiment with the notion of cross-functional teams and being more holistic and goal-oriented in our approach."

At the end of the session, I ask them to summarize once more what they are going to do and we capture actions, which we will review formally at the end of the following week.

An Agile Coaching Story, Part 2   167

Experiment Card

We have identified
<Tension or Challenge>

Low competency at teaming and we are seen as a delivery function.

We will experiment with
<Practice or Change>

For the simplification of the customer journey project, we will build a cross functional team of volunteers. We will be goal-driven and define value criteria to guide the work that we do.

We expect
<These Visible Benefits>

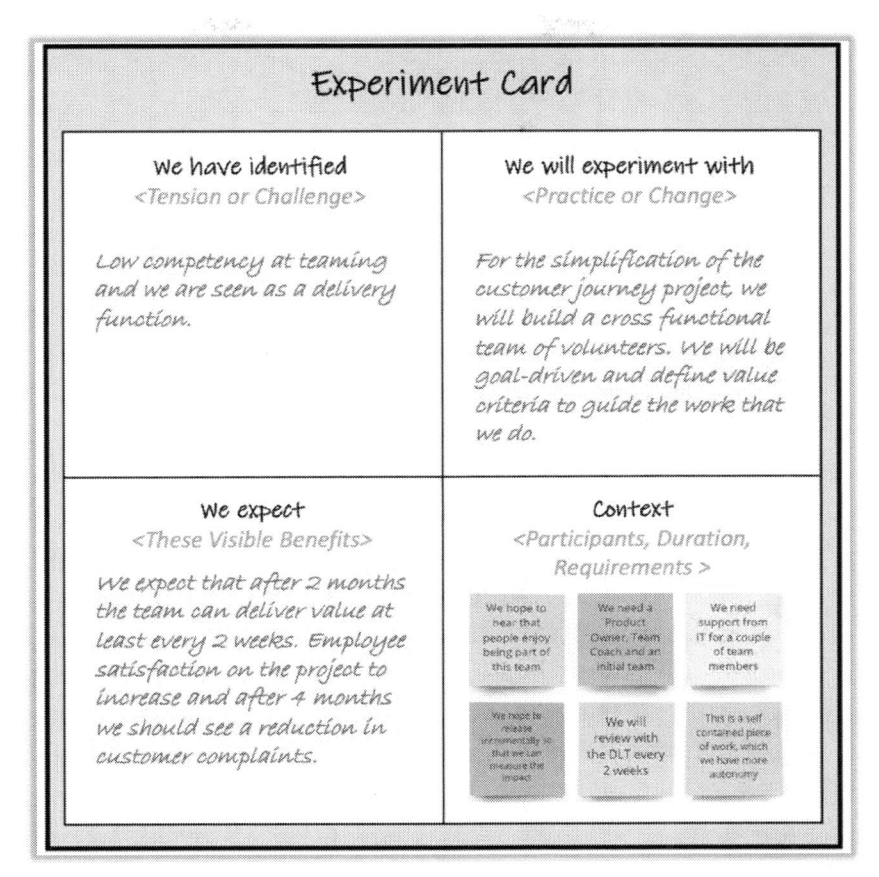

We expect that after 2 months the team can deliver value at least every 2 weeks. Employee satisfaction on the project to increase and after 4 months we should see a reduction in customer complaints.

Context
<Participants, Duration, Requirements >

- We hope to hear that people enjoy being part of this team.
- We need a Product Owner, Team Coach and an initial team.
- We need support from IT for a couple of team members.
- We hope to release incrementally so that we can measure the impact.
- We will review with the DLT every 2 weeks.
- This is a self contained piece of work, which we have more autonomy.

FIGURE 30. Experiment 2. *Source*: Mark Summers' facilitation and coaching group examples. Used with permission.

Reflection

What. What Happened?

- The check-in was positive, and they realized that they were forming as a team without me having to say it.
- As a leader, I was conscious of using positive language and tried to encourage them. This was important in the face of uncertainty about how this will work.
- I noticed that Paul had a strong reaction toward the end of the workshop when we started talking about involving volunteers in designing the details of the experiment.

- The two experiments they identified are not small things in terms of the impact on the organization, but the initial steps to start them seem clear.
- I rotated the team into different pairs. This helped them refine the experiments, including realizing that they could address two of their tensions with one experiment.
- Although I had planned on using the concept of ROI, or return on investment, to help them order their experiments, this did not seem necessary because they filtered the experiments naturally through the group conversations.

So, What. What Did I Learn? What Does It Mean?

- There is nervousness now around the role of leadership, as they start to realize that leading in an agile way is going to be different. Specifically, I sensed that Paul was uneasy at times during the workshop today. It happened when I mentioned the idea of volunteers who owned the experiment. I could have maybe tried to bring Ryan and Nimesh into the conversation here, before suggesting the idea myself.
- There is currently a lot of positive energy from the team about getting things moving. So, it would be good to harness that and help them to create and sustain their momentum.
- I may have gotten carried away with the positive energy toward the end of the conversation, mirroring back what I had heard in a group conversation, when perhaps I should have been fading out of the conversation a little more.
- Ryan and Debbie are both very action-oriented and have the potential to be driving forces and change artists. I might want to offer to coach and guide them more; offering more of a prescriptive and strategic Advising stance.

Now What. What Do I Need to Do as a Result?

- There are some concepts it would be worth exploring deeper with the team, like navigating organizational complexity and being an agile leader, as a starting point for how they are going to lead and support this transformation.

- At the end of the session, I offered Ryan and Debbie some one-on-one coaching time to support them with their actions. I will follow this up next week.
- I need to check in with Paul.
- I need to be careful not to get too carried away with the positive emotions of some of the group. I need to stay neutral. I write that on a sticky note and attach it to my monitor.

Advice from My Pair-Coach

- Bob's first bit of feedback is that I might be "too coach-y"—that is, leaning in too hard to my Coaching (professional) stance. He thinks I might be asking too many questions, staying too neutral, and not engaging situationally. He emphasized that this is not a binary point, but one I should consider by perhaps leaning into other stances more comfortably. As an aside, he's noticed over time that my least used stance is Advising and he wondered why.
- He really appreciates the facilitation tools I used, complimenting me on their selection and how they integrated well with the team. He also tells me that I danced fairly well with the tools.
- Bob also notes that this client (the team) seems to resonate with metaphors for communication. They seemed to visualize them and it helped with team alignment. He thinks I might want to consider this in future coaching situations—either encouraging them to create new metaphors or bringing my own into the coaching. And he reminded me that the use of metaphor was stance-agnostic, so truly general purpose.

An Ad Hoc Conversation with Paul

After the workshop, Paul requests a chat and invites me to a meeting with 15 minutes' notice. There has been no time for planning, and I had already got my head into designing next week's workshops. I just had time to step outside for a moment, to let go of what I had been doing and remind myself about the unease that I had sensed in Paul. I am keen to tune into this, and determined to do so if I get the opportunity.

The Conversation

"Hi, Julie. The first thing is that I wanted to thank you for the workshops you have run for us so far, I have never seen the team getting along so well and heading in the same direction."

"It was my pleasure, and I am looking forward to the next session. What else can I help you with?"

"Well, I realized that in the past I had been expecting the team to be professional and do their job, and as a result I hadn't even thought about working on them as a team. This also made me think that I'm not sure I have the skills required to make them into a team. I am also nervous about the kind of leader I can be in an agile organization. I wondered if I could talk this through with you."

I recognize that a Coaching stance could be valuable here, as Paul is the biggest expert on himself, however I sense he is also seeking some reassurance and guidance. But first, I check in with myself to see if my mindset is ready to dance between stances. I had been deep in designing the next workshop, but I had received enough notice before this conversation to put that aside. I feel I can focus my full attention on Paul.

Paul has surprised me with his self-awareness and vulnerability, and I want to call that out to him.

"First, I want to acknowledge your vulnerability and trust in me. I realize it's hard to admit your fears and I think that's a powerful step for you. I just want to say I appreciate your doing that. Now, what more are you feeling regarding the situation?" I ask this question to surface information, but I also want to understand if Paul is thinking rationally. If he is getting angry or panicky, then we are certainly not in a good place for a coaching conversation.

But Paul's tone is calm and measured. "I feel a little worried that my leadership style will get in the way of this agile transformation. I am used to feeling in control and providing answers to the questions."

This conversation could go anywhere, so I want Paul to focus on what is most important to him right now. "So, you have scheduled an hour with me, what would be a good outcome for you by the end of the session?"

Paul thinks for a few moments. "I guess it would be good to understand how I should be with the Digital leadership team in the next few weeks and what role I should play in the transformation."

"How would you describe yourself as a leader?"

"I have seen it as my job to get as much information as I can, so that I can make the best decisions possible. I saw myself as the glue that held this place together." Paul pauses for a moment. "My fear is that if I don't hold things together then everything will come crashing down."

"What's it like being the glue?"

"Sticky, really. It leads to some uncomfortable moments, as inevitably people see things differently than me at times. Luckily, I think I am well respected, having been in the bank for a long time." He pauses for a moment. "I am also spread very thin—too thin at times. It takes a lot of time to stay on top of everything, sometimes cracks appear and things seem to fall apart. Really the whole thing is very brittle. Ryan has been helping me keep it together, but that feels like we're putting tape over the cracks."

Paul really goes with the metaphor, with some real frustration evident in his voice at how things have been going. I decided to stay with Paul's current way of leading for a while and play with the glue.

"When does it work to be the glue?"

"It has worked for a long time. It has fitted the bank's way of operating. People get promoted here based on their ability to be in control. Before taking on the role of director of Digital, I was director of Infrastructure and I got the department humming. I guess the pace of change was slower there.

"In Digital it worked at first, as we set the department up. It gave us the needed structure. But lately the demands have ramped up and cracks are appearing everywhere."

I spend a little time getting Paul to articulate the differences between Infrastructure and Digital, but now I want to move his lens to be more forward-looking. However, I am aware that Paul does not have a frame of reference for the likely change ahead, so I decide to offer some input and try and frame the change in a positive way.

"In the workshops, we have created a vision of the future with autonomous teams responsible for their outcomes, able to make decisions themselves. I believe you sense this is going to require a change in the way leadership behaves." Paul nods and gives a wry smile at this. "I have noticed that you have been holding back at times during our workshops."

"I think it's helped to have you as a facilitator. Normally I would have just been making decisions trying move things forward. Out of the spotlight, it's been interesting to observe the others a bit more."

"See, you can do it. The team has been great this last week, and the whole group has contributed. As you are experiencing, teams don't need their leaders to make all of the decisions; they need support and encouragement."

Paul laughs at that. "Encouragement, like you are giving me now."

"It is hard to motivate people, and it's mostly about the environment that you will create for your teams, allowing them to make decisions, making sure work is meaningful and helping them grow. But nothing gives people a warmer feeling than when somebody they respect uses positive language and seeks out opportunities to encourage them."

Paul looks up, obviously thinking. After about 30 seconds, he says, "We need to support people in their growth, so that it doesn't need the leadership team and a bunch of managers holding things together."

"Do you want to think about that more now, or shall we focus on how you should be over the next couple of weeks?" I ask this to allow Paul to steer the direction of the conversation.

"I would rather think about that over a longer period, so let's focus on the next couple of weeks as we move into the transformation." Paul is ready to move forward.

"What does the leadership team not have that it needs from you in the next two weeks?"

"In terms of the agile transformation, very little. Ryan and Debbie in particular have jumped forward and are capable of igniting the pilots. They may, however, struggle elsewhere, at least while they get things moving, so I can help with some of the business-as-usual work."

"Where else could you provide value?"

Again, Paul thinks for several seconds. "I guess, make a point of being supportive, giving praise to things that are taking us toward our vision and almost visibly asking others to make decisions."

"How difficult on a scale of 1 to 10 will that be for you? 1 being almost impossible, 10 being easy."

"Well as you observed, I have been intentionally holding back in the workshops so far, but it's not easy, so I would say a 4."

"What would you need to make it a 6?"

"I guess I could be transparent to the rest of the team and ask them to call me out if I start becoming overly driven or start making all the decisions."

"That's great. What else could help?"

"Well, I think the fact that we have the workshops next week gives us all a chance to reflect on how we lead. It would be good to talk about next week's workshops," Paul says finally.

I step out of my Coaching stance once again and we talk about how best to shape the workshops next week so that we can get everybody to reflect on themselves as leaders. At the end of the call, I ask Paul to reflect on what he is taking away from the session. He makes a commitment to share with the team some changes he wants to make as a leader and to ask for their help.

We also agree that I will carry on working with Paul, and that we will schedule one-on-one coaching sessions every two weeks.

Reflection

What. What Happened?

- The highest-level sponsor requested help early on in the engagement.
- I was not entirely expecting this session, although I was pleased it happened, as I had noticed that Paul was concerned at the end of the last workshop.
- The glue metaphor really helped unlock the frustration Paul was feeling about the way he led.
- I predominantly used a Coaching stance in this conversation, but from my Leadership stance I encouraged Paul, and from an Advising stance I partnered with Paul to co-create the workshops.
- After gaining permission to enter a coaching conversation, we followed a typical Coaching Arc, closely following the GROW model.[19]
    - We established a **G**oal to focus on Paul as a leader in the next few weeks.
    - We explored the current **R**eality.
    - We brainstormed **O**ptions.
    - Finally, we **W**rapped up with some actions, which were repeated, and final reflections.
- I gave plenty of time and space for Paul's thinking.

So, What. What Did I Learn? What Does It Mean?

- Paul is very open to coaching and was prepared to be vulnerable, at least one-on-one with me, which I had not seen before in a group.

---

19. GROW is a popular coaching model. We're not going to explore it much beyond this brief highlight; to be honest, we feel we have enough models in the book, and the Arc from chapter 5 is a direct replacement for GROW. But if you want to research it further, you can start here: www.performanceconsultants.com/grow-model.

- The organizational culture supports a certain type of leadership; therefore, it is likely to require strong leadership to protect any pilots from the controlling culture.
- The conversation reminded me of how powerful metaphors can be in my coaching. They particularly resonated with Paul and they might with others on the team. I might want to use them more often.
- There are probably other things that Paul can be doing as a leader.
- The organizational culture came up; how leaders behave is likely tied to the organizational context.

Now What. What Do I Need to Do as a Result?

- The conversation with the whole Digital leadership team can follow a similar arc. Through the added team interactions, it's likely even more can come from the team in terms of what is needed from leadership.
- Before we explore the team as leaders, we should explore the organizational context.
- I need to book my next session with Paul.

Advice from My Pair-Coach

- Bob again provided feedback that I might be staying in Coaching stance too long. And he mentioned it might have been more of a problem here because Paul mainly needed some positive affirmation, appreciation, and guidance. This could have been achieved with more time spent in an Advising stance or even role modeling for him.
- This dialogue is also a good example of "death by a thousand questions," or overloading.
- I might want to invite Bob in to pair-coach with me some more and allow him to show/mentor/model how he might approach this same conversation, but with more nuanced stance shifting.

Wrap Up

Clearly, this isn't the end of the story, but a beginning. However, for the purposes of the book, we will leave Julie to her reflections and reflect ourselves on how a Badass Agile Coach like Julie operates.

During the arc of an agile coaching conversation, an agile coach may have to switch between multiple stances. Sometimes you are a facilitator guiding the process, sometimes you will be a coach challenging and supporting thinking, other times you may need to guide learning by teaching concepts or even give advice. However, as a leader you are always modeling behaviors, supporting and nurturing others and encouraging people as they move forward.

Two things are important here:

- having the competence to operate in different stances in all different contexts, and
- having the intuition and experience to sense the most appropriate stance at any given time.

There is no formula. These skills come through reflective practice. Notice how Julie reflects after each interaction. These reflections mostly improved her thinking about the engagement, but occasionally there were little gems that she could use to improve her self-mastery as an agile coach.

The other interesting thing to observe is how the agile coaching conversation arcs don't happen in isolation: The end of one arc is the beginning of one or more additional arcs. You may have also picked up through the workshops that we have several conversation arcs going on at different levels within the engagement at the same time:

- There is an overall arc spanning the two weeks of workshops. In the story we see that the first half of the first workshop is dedicated to opening that arc, with the working agreements and goal-setting for the series of workshops.
- There is an arc each day, starting with a check-in and usually ending with some reflection.

- Each facilitated game or activity will have an opening, middle, and end.

The key thing to remember is the pattern from the very beginning of this chapter: craft, enter, reflect, pivot. That, and the fact that badass agile coaching is an emerging activity—like that box of chocolates.

10

Badass Metaskills for the Agile Coaching Growth Wheel

> The statistician George Box said, "All models are approximations. Essentially, all models are wrong, but some are useful. However, the approximate nature of the model must always be borne in mind."
>
> We need to lean into the usefulness of our models without getting stuck in them. And we should not be afraid to extend our models based on our experience, learning, and experiments.
>
> At the same time, we must always be wary of creating something or interpreting something in a way that moves a model from useful to dangerous, restrictive, or useless.

Introduction

While I think the Agile Coaching Growth Wheel is currently the best model for representing the breadth of the craft of agile coaching and growing our competency within that craft, I do think leveraging a few specific metaskills can significantly enhance your use of the model. In this chapter, we're going to explore four metaskills (stances, mindsets or subtle capabilities) that are implicit within the Wheel that I want to ensure you don't miss as you become more badass as an agile coach. They are:

1. Leadership
2. Change Artistry
3. Inspiration
4. Role Modeling

I can hear what you're thinking: "Bob, the Agile Coaching Growth Wheel is complex, broad, and deep enough without you adding even more for me to consider as an agile coach." I realize that. But as I wrote the book and explored the model, I thought there were important points that might not be as clear, and I would be doing you a disservice if I didn't emphasize them.

So, think of this chapter as shining a light on a few more subtle aspects of the Wheel. First, focus on developing your skills across the Wheel, and when you feel your work is done in strengthening those competencies use these metaskills to continue and enhance your journey.

Metaskill 1 – Leadership

I've often oscillated on whether to describe leadership as a quality or a stance for agile coaching. The new version of the Wheel, v1_2, clearly establishes it as a competency. Leadership has always been a part of my coaching persona and skill set, but that's largely because I moved from leadership roles to my independent agile coaching practice. I also do a lot of my coaching at the leadership level.

But if you buy into my perspective that Badass Agile Coaches must have a leadership competency, then what exactly does that mean? What does it look like?

Principles of Agile Leadership

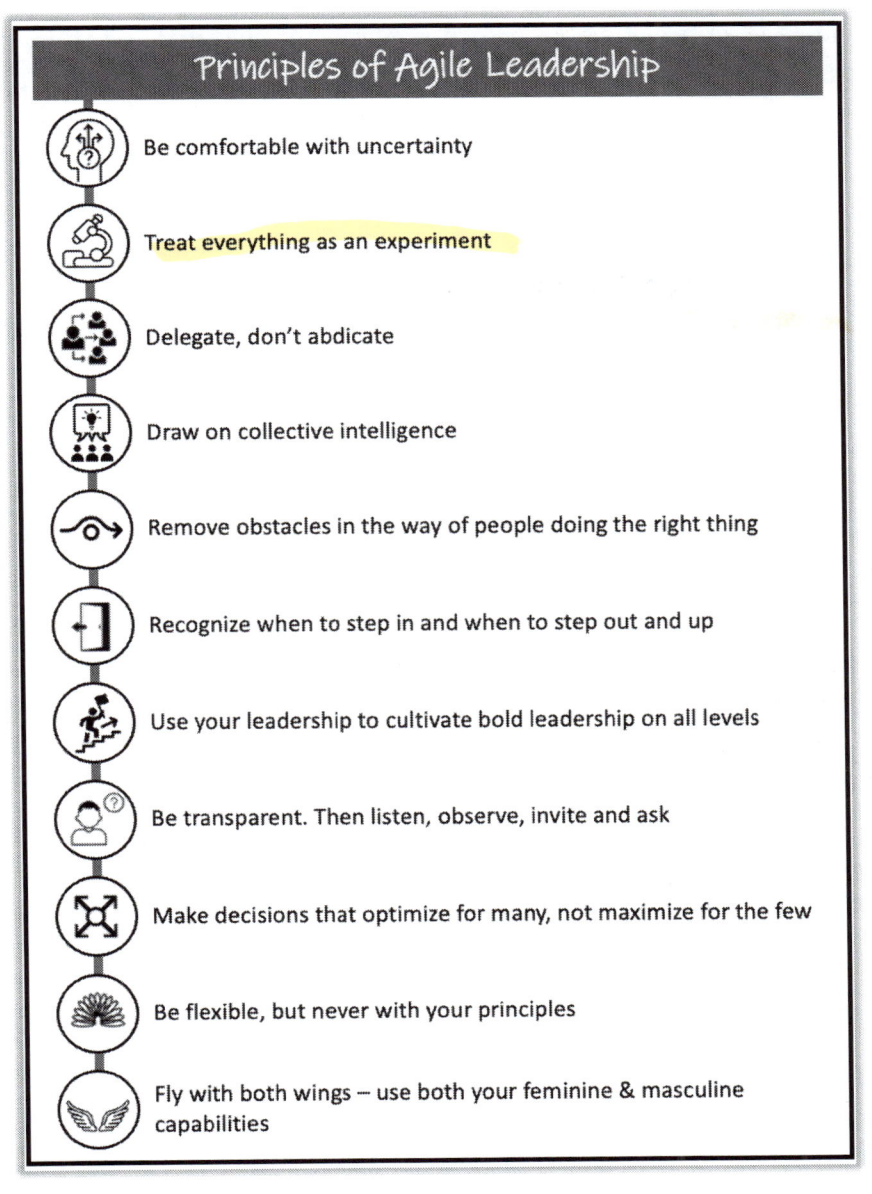

- Be comfortable with uncertainty
- Treat everything as an experiment
- Delegate, don't abdicate
- Draw on collective intelligence
- Remove obstacles in the way of people doing the right thing
- Recognize when to step in and when to step out and up
- Use your leadership to cultivate bold leadership on all levels
- Be transparent. Then listen, observe, invite and ask
- Make decisions that optimize for many, not maximize for the few
- Be flexible, but never with your principles
- Fly with both wings – use both your feminine & masculine capabilities

FIGURE 31. Principles of Agile Leadership. *Source*: From Anjali Leon. Derived from her Leadership workshop materials and used with permission.

There are myriad views of what makes for solid agile leadership. We could write an entire book about that. But I've decided the best way to explain what good agile leadership looks like is to share a set of principles from a friend and colleague, Anjali Leon. Figure 31 shows Anjali's 11 agile leadership principles. I recommend that you print this and keep it handy to remind yourself of how to center and focus as a leader within your coaching. I have a copy printed in my journal that I reflect on almost daily. It helps me to focus on my own continuous development and improvement activities in this competency.

Here are my reactions to some of these principles. See what they mean to you.

Be comfortable with uncertainty. As a leader and agile coach, there's pressure on me for outcomes and results. And, due to my management and project management history, my default stance to achieve results is to plan. And when I say *plan*, I do mean *PLAN*. I tend to try to dictate the path to a desired outcome. This principle reminds me that there is ambiguity and uncertainty in broad swaths of my journey, and of my clients' journeys. I need to become more comfortable with uncertainty, to expect it, to welcome it, to embrace it. And to get excited about what might *emerge* from it. Because my comfort zone is planning, I need to add this to my thinking daily.

Recognize when to step in and when to step out and up. How appropriate this is for agile coaches and coaching. When I think of this principle, I immediately think of "dancing in the moment" as an agile coach and leader. It's something that I often keep track of in my daily journaling—when I step in and when I stay out. And importantly, why am I stepping in? What are the triggers for it? Another important aspect of this principle is the modeling, or showing that you're doing. People will pay attention to how and when you show up, so modeling that you can leave space for them (step out and up) is valuable while you actively role model.

Fly with both wings—use both your feminine and masculine capacities. To be honest, I've struggled understanding this one and applying it. I asked Anjali what she meant by it and her answer was somewhat vague (at least to me). But as I've thought about it more, I've applied it to my support, learning, and growth in diversity and inclusion. For example, as a coach, I've studied the nature of microaggressions and I've become much more tuned into them in my group or system coaching sessions. I've also tried to be less binary in my thinking, working hard to be able to connect with empathy to everyone.

I hope you appreciate my transparency in showing you my own application of Anjali's principles. I hope the example inspires you, as a Badass Agile Coach (and Leader) to leverage them in your own journey and growth.

Metaskill 2 – Change Artistry

At its core, agile coaching is about guiding individuals and organizations through change. Don't misunderstand me: You're not changing the organization with your coaching, because people can't be changed. Instead, they need to decide to change for themselves. But with your badass agile coaching skills you can inspire people to change, show them the way by modeling the changes, and give them change models and metaphors to help them envision and navigate their own paths.

That last point is crucial.

There are two powerful models that I often use in my agile coaching to help my clients navigate change. The first is the Satir Change Model, shown in figure 32, and the second is Kotter's 8 Steps of Change. References for further exploration of both models are provided at the end of the chapter.

The Satir model is, in my view, more of a change mindset tool, and the Kotter model is more of a strategic planning tool for navigating a change initiative. While both are incredibly useful and should be in your coaching toolkits, I'm going to focus on Satir in this section. I'll leave the research into Kotter's work as an exercise for you.

Virginia Satir was a social worker and family therapist when she created her change model. Many in the pre- and post-agile communities have leveraged it as a model reflecting the phases that literally all changes go through. I've found that having the model and being able to explain it helps me to help clients think about, align with, and navigate their change experiences—individually, as groups, and as an organization.

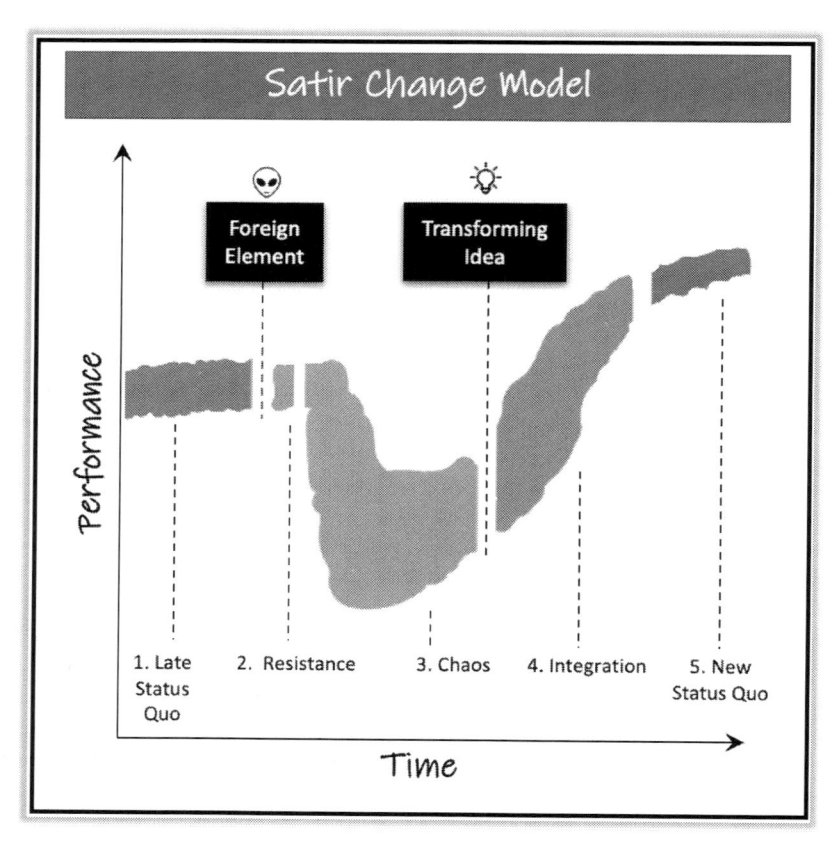

FIGURE 32. Virginia Satir's Change Model

Satir's change model establishes the following phases for any change:

1. **Late Status Quo**. This is the pre-change state. Don't consider it good or bad. Simply consider it as a stable or existing state that represents the status quo. It was delivering value and results in

some fashion, but someone has decided to optimize for continuous improvement in some way.
2. **Introduction of a Foreign Element.** This is the change. In agile contexts, it could be something related to agile adoption: a new team spinning up, adopting a new framework, installing a new toolset, or adjusting a set of approaches or tactics. But it could also be a promotion, business merger, reorganization, or work force reduction. Virtually *any* change (or group of changes) sets you down the path.
3. **Resistance.** Right after the foreign element is introduced, there is an immediate response to resist it. You could consider this pushback, raw denial, or hoping to go back to the Late Status Quo. Resistance can be short term or can continue until the change has been more fully integrated. It's important not to personalize this toward individuals, but rather view it as a normal part of the path through change. Resistance isn't good or bad; it's normal.
4. **Chaos.** Ah, chaos! This is the primary navigation curve for the change. It's where everyone is trying to make sense of things. To use Cynefin, as explored in chapter 5, everyone is in an Act–Sense–Respond loop. People aren't sure what to do, and need to experiment personally and organizationally to act within the change in order to navigate through the chaos. From an agile coaching perspective, the more you encourage experimentation and reflection within the chaos, the sooner the move to integration occurs.
5. **Discovery of a Transforming Idea.** Something needs to turn the ship around and show a way out of the chaos. This is the discovery of a transformative idea from the change. For example, a team might discover the why behind the change and see the value and sense of it—what the change might make newly possible. It's this idea, and its inherent excitement, that can generate the momentum to change direction.

6. **Integration**. This is the aha moment within the chaos. It's not an immediate exit, but it captures a recognition of what the change encompasses and a focus on integrating the change. While chaos is nondeterministic as to how long you'll stay there (because it's—well, chaos), part of integration is seeing the light at the end of the tunnel and increased value or impact from the changes.
7. **New Status Quo**. This is the ultimate realization of results from the change or changes. It's a period of newfound stability. But it's also, if you interpret the curve properly, a period of increased performance based on the change. We're not changing to reduce our effectiveness, but to enhance it. So, the system should see positive outcomes surrounding the change (or *foreign element*).
8. **Breathe**. I'm adding this phase to the model for agile contexts. One of the factors that create change fatigue is not pausing to allow a change to stabilize, settle, and grow in its impact before injecting another foreign element into the system. I liken it to allowing the system (individual, group/team, or organization) a little time to breathe and revel in the positive impact of one change before introducing another.

As you can see, the Satir Change Model provides a frame for discussing the path through change. One of the best books on Satir is Gerald Weinberg's *Becoming a Change Artist,* volume 7 in the Quality Software Series. He uses the model in the book and expands on its implications in system change. The model gives us terminology and context for our client coaching conversations. It also provides the client a model to help them understand their own journey through each change.

One of the primary reasons I use the Satir model is to sensitize clients to the impacts of change fatigue. One of the largest impediments to nearly every agile adoption/transformation I encounter as a coach is folks taking on too much change at one time. And the most common reason for change fatigue is introducing more and more changes before previous changes have been navigated into a new status quo.

Continuously dropping more and more change into the chaos extends the chaos—sometimes indefinitely.

As a coach, try to increase your client's awareness not only of the model, but of the danger of continuous change without allowing time to breathe.

Finally, being a Badass Agile Coach does not mean being a change artist by yourself. I've found that nearly all People or HR functions in companies have organizational development and change management capabilities. It makes sense to partner with them in those capacities.

Metaskill 3 – *Inspiration*

I facilitated an agile coaching clinic the week of the Agile Online Summit in October 2020. Twelve coaches joined me to provide coaching to about 50 attendees each day. Facilitating this free service for so many agile practitioners was a wonderful experience. The coaches were great and the feedback from attendees can be captured in one word—awesome!

For those who didn't want individualized coaching, we also offered an Ask Me Anything group-based coaching session each day. This went very well too. But I was struck by the variety of coaching replies to one of the questions. One day, one of the attendees asked "How do I develop myself as an agile coach and find a job?" Three different agile coaches responded:

Coach 1 responded from the perspective *of developing as a well-rounded coach*. They mentioned the Agile Coaching Competency Framework and the importance of learning and growing across all aspects of your craft. Being a well-rounded coach, they said, would make you stick out from the crowd and become more employable (a skills- and competencies-based approach).

Coach 2 focused on *career planning* first; that is, defining a journey map of your past, present, and potential futures. Included with that would be establishing your personal why, setting goals, and identifying what gives you joy. Then, depending on what you discover, targeting roles in that area (an essence/joy-based approach—do what you love).

Coach 3 focused on *being pragmatic*. For example, not taking on things that don't fall into your role. Setting realistic expectations and taking small steps. Minimizing your risks. Not trying to change the world, but staying within the lines. (In other words, do your job, get paid, be happy with small wins, stay safe, and don't rock the boat.)

I don't want to nitpick each response, as they're all valid and helpful, but I was struck by the pragmatism of the last one. It made me think about the role we might have as agile coaches to find a balance between pragmatic and inspirational stances.

You see, the pragmatic response, while valid, wasn't very inspiring. This was a very experienced coach and trainer who is a Scrum Alliance CST and CEC, a subject matter expert in the agile space, and a change agent, role model, and inspiration to many in our community. But they took a very cautious stance in their advice. My personal takeaway from the response was that it's fine to be mediocre—to keep trying to help an organization make an effective shift to agility, even if it takes decades, as long as you get enough small wins to keep your job. That may seem harsh, but that's the impression it left.

I think agile coaches have a responsibility to be inspiring. Beyond the coaching competencies and our own skills, I believe folks look to us as role models—exemplars of *YES!*

- Yes! And …
- Yes, you can do it!
- Yes, you can leap tall buildings; let me show you what leaping a tall building looks like!
- Yes, let me help you establish big goals!
- Yes, let me help co-create a large, all-inclusive vision for what's possible!

We exemplify yes by setting a tone, attitude, and stance and leading by example while strongly holding to the art of the possible. In every coaching opportunity, we should be putting on metaskills like:

- Evangelist
- Energizer
- Enthusiast
- Influencer
- Dreamer
- Change Artist
- Encourager
- Sports Coach
- Positivist

I guess what I'm saying is that, whether we like it or agree with it or not, we are influencers. And, since we all choose how we show up, let's intentionally show up with and as inspiration!

Metaskill 4 – Role Modeling

The final metaskill I propose is what I'll call *role modeling*, or the "walking our talk" competency. This is where we're coaching by showing the way, leading by example, and modeling behaviors. In other words, we're coaching not just with what we say or through a coaching conversation, but in what we do. This includes our actions, our language, our vulnerability, and our genuineness—everything that we bring to the table as a coach.

I've discovered that role modeling might be the most powerful stance for a coach. I know it's counterintuitive, but I believe it. Modeling isn't telling or coaching at all. Rather, it's showing everyone what it looks like to be an agilist. To walk in the mindset. To exhibit core behaviors when the going is easy and, more importantly, when the going is tough.

And there's a bit of a twist to this stance: You're always modeling, whether or not you like it or believe it. Because of the nature and privilege associated with your role, people are paying attention to everything you say and do. You are a walking, talking example every minute of every hour of every day.

The real question is—what are you modeling? Are you an exemplar or an anti-pattern? I am a bit of both in that I'm not perfect or an automaton. I am human. But I aspire to be an exemplar as often as I can because I'm aware of the power that my modeling brings to my badass agile coaching.

Wrapping Up with an Experiment

If you've read the chapters in sequence, then you know that chapters 8 and 9 contained a detailed client Coaching Arc that included a diverse mix of situational Coaching Arcs. Mark Summers did a great job of telling the story of the Wheel and then showing how to use it in your coaching conversations. So, here's my suggestion for a learning experiment for you.

First, take a detailed look at each coaching conversation. Read it a couple of times and get to the essence of it. Then, keeping the Wheel and stances in the back of your mind along with the client's context, consider changes you might make if you were doing the coaching:

- Would you change the conversation? Make it longer, shorter, or more focused?
- Would you use different metaphors or create new metaphors?
- Would you use different stances? Adopt the same stances at different times? Why?
- Would you use different tools or approaches?

Really dissect the coaching conversations and make them your own as a learning exercise. Don't be afraid to ignore what we did and do it your way. Then, reflect on the differences in approach and try to discover your *why* for making the adjustments.

Next, consider the additional metaskills from this chapter: leadership, change artistry, inspiration, and role modeling. Try to weave these metaskills into the coaching conversations from chapters 8 and 9. Include the workshops as well as the group and individual conversations. And remember the planning and post-coaching reflections. For example, review both chapters and see if you see opportunities to adopt the inspiration metaskill. I saw a few, but never directly mentioned them. I wonder what you might see. Or consider the role modeling metaskill. I can see several situations in the case study where a "show them" approach might be more effective than "tell them" or "ask them" approaches.

Once you identify opportunities, try reframing the conversation using the new metaskill. Really lean into it and see how it might affect the conversational flow, insights, and outcomes.

If you're feeling adventurous, you might want to try this as a stretch goal: Try doing everything I've suggested in this experiment with a Coaching Arc of your own. You can either use one you've already completed (a past arc) or try it as a planning exercise for a future arc. How cool would that be?

Have fun with the experiment and the learning!

Further Reading

I particularly like Steve Smith's take on the Satir Change Model, as his was the first reference I found in the late 1990s or pre-agile contexts: https://stevenmsmith.com/ar-satir-change-model/.

I mentioned John Kotter and his change model in this chapter. While he's written several books on the topic, I'd start with *Leading Change* (Boston: Harvard Business Review Press, 2012). Here's a link to his website for an overview of the model: www.kotterinc.com/8-steps-process-for-leading-change/.

While I didn't mention it at all in the chapter, Jason Little's book *Lean Change Management: Innovative Practices for Managing Organizational Change* (Happy Melly Express, 2014) is nearly a must-have resource for the Badass Agile Coach.

11

The Badass Agile Coach's Guide to Coaching UP

Leadership has never been for the faint of heart. It's a tough role to fill if you're doing it well. And in agile leadership it's even more challenging to get the balance right.

But I've found that success in an agile transformation, of any sort, requires the leaders to transform, change, and grow. And agile coaches can be an igniter for the leaders and leadership team to cross their own chasms and make this transition.

That is, those coaches who are extraordinarily badass in their courage, coaching skills, experience, and approaches can ignite this growth. Coaches who are leaders themselves—and not faint of heart.

Introduction

I spend a lot of time coaching other coaches, and coaching up is far and away the most challenging area for most of them. There seem to be two schools of thought: Either treat leaders as you would treat a team and coach them toward agile basics, or ask leaders a myriad of questions and hope they discover what effective agile leadership looks like on their own.

In either case, you're not going to be effective. These clients are leaders, and leaders are *different*. Their entire context is much different from the team's context, and you need to modify how you engage them as a coach.

From a Wheel perspective, you'll want to lean away from the stances of

- Coaching,
- Facilitating, and
- Guiding Learning

when coaching leaders. You don't want to stop using these stances entirely, but you need to be selective in their use. And you need to lean into the stances of

- Advising,
- Transforming, and
- Leading.

Why? Because at least in the majority of my experience, this is where these leaders need you to meet them in your coaching. These stances will resonate more with them and will co-create a better coaching alliance between you as a coach and your leader client.

But *how* you meet them isn't simple or easy; that's what I want to explore more in this chapter.

The Role of Your Experience

I've held several senior leadership roles, and nothing bugs me more than an agile coach who approaches me to "coach me." Often, they seem to be condescending, lacking empathy, and lacking any serious leadership experience. Yet, here they are telling me how my behavior isn't agile enough and that I'm not walking my talk. Or how to lead my organization more effectively. It rattles my bones, and I suspect it rattles most leaders' bones as well.

It's important in coaching leaders to show that you have some leadership skills and experience. It doesn't have to be in the same business domain as those you're coaching, but before you coach leaders you have to have walked in their shoes for a bit. If you've done this in some way, you can better understand them and their context, can have empathy for them, and can see where they're coming from. The following story further explores this idea.

A Leadership Coach Coaching Conversation

I was having dinner with Anthony Mersino, an agile coaching colleague from Chicago, and this very topic came up. He was challenging my assumption around having leadership chops in order to coach leaders and became frustrated with me around the idea. He said: "Bob, you mean to tell me that I can't coach leaders unless I've been a leader? I think that's nonsense. I'm coaching leaders right now. And I have been for quite a while."

I asked, "How's that going for you?"

"It's frustrating," he said. "They don't seem to take to my coaching and they don't seem to want to change. There's not a lot of open-mindedness to new ideas. And I'm always hearing 'But Anthony, that won't work in the real world.'"

"A part of that might be how you're showing up to them," I replied. "Are you showing up with empathy? And do you really know what's it's like to walk in their shoes? If you haven't been in a leadership role, then I suspect not. And, even if you have done this, coaching leaders in transformational change is still a challenge."

"What do I do?" asked Anthony. "Are you telling me I either have to stop or spend five-plus years in a leadership role before I can resume my coaching?"

"Of course not. What I might suggest is that you follow or interview or shadow leaders you are coaching for a few weeks. Don't coach them. Instead, listen and observe their world. Improve your understanding of their challenges, their goals, their insecurities, their fears, their day-to-day interactions and then factor this into your coaching— your coaching plans, stances, sessions and how you show up as a coach. Then, see if that makes a difference in the coaching effectiveness with your clients."

Anthony said he thought it was an interesting idea, and he might consider it. Then we amicably parted from our dinner.

A month or so later, I found out that, to his credit, Anthony had tried it. And I believe it made a significant difference in how he coached leaders (up) and the impact it had. He even wrote a blog post about the experience. (You can find a link to it at the end of the chapter.)

My point in sharing this story is that somehow, some way, if you're going to coach leaders, you have to gain empathy for them. And the only way to truly do that is to walk in their shoes. So, start walking.

Relationship Building

It's important to quickly build rapport with the leaders you'll be coaching, particularly in the Advising or Transforming stances. In these stances, you'll be providing advice that impacts them, their organizations, and their careers. In order to do that, you need to quickly build a trust relationship with them.

Of course, your experience, résumé, and reputation might do that for you initially. But those are simply your skills. You'll want to establish a *connection* with each of your leadership clients, not only in your abilities but in your judgment, motivations, character, and ethics. In many cases, they're placing their career and livelihoods in your hands, and you better well have the chops to deliver on your promises.

This is why I usually work so hard to establish a partnership with leaders that I'm coaching. I don't want them to view me as a contractual entity or a "resource" to leverage. Instead, in our very first conversation before I ever begin coaching, I emphasize the roles they and I will have as partners in the pursuit of their goals. That I will have "skin in the game" with them in our efforts, but that they ultimately have to shift their thinking toward a more agile leadership mindset.

Most appreciate this initial candor and shared partnership, but some do not. In those cases, we agree that now may not be the best time for them to be coached in this direction and we part ways.

Push or Pull

One early context point you should consider is whether you've been assigned to coach someone (pushed, prescribed, told to, or assigned) or whether they have asked to be coached (pulled you in, requested, asked for coaching). The initial momentum of your coaching engagement, push versus pull, makes all the difference in how things begin. And to the degree that you have control over it, you'll want to lean into pull-based engagements over push-based ones. It just makes things far smoother when the client has opted in to receiving your coaching.

That said, if I do encounter a push, I often try to turn it into a pull. By that, I mean I'll ask or determine if the client has been pushed into being coached by me. If they have, I'll try to allow them to opt out. I'll tell them that I'll do everything in my power to stop coaching them without ramification. I'll even use the push versus pull language to emphasize that I want to coach folks who want to be coached versus those who are told to be coached.

Simply having this conversation often flips them into a pull-based client. That is, simply giving them the choice can change everything and open the door for relationship building.

Leadership Styles

There are quite a few leadership style models that you can reference in your agile leadership coaching. Some of them offer the ability to independently assess a leader via a survey or tool; with others, you can simply ask the leader to self-assess based on a cursory review of the model. I want to share four models that I've personally used and have found quite helpful as I coach up in organizations.

I've used and am certified to deliver two models: the Leadership Agility 360, and the Leadership Circle Profile. Both are 360-degree survey-based models. The first, Bill Joiner's Leadership Agility work, is briefly discussed in chapter 17. I can't tell you how useful the Expert-Achiever-Catalyst model and language has been for me in identifying a leader's preferences and providing language to inspire them to reflect and grow across that spectrum.

The second, the Leadership Circle Profile, is another leader assessment tool that identifies an individual leader's alignment across creative competencies and reactive tendencies.[20] The creative competencies align more with our agile leadership principles and mindsets and are more forward-looking, growth-focused, and strategic in nature. The reactive tendencies align more with traditional leadership approaches, and are more tactical and now-focused.

The thing I find most useful in the Leadership Circle is how it highlights discrete behaviors within each of its major competency or tendency areas. For example:

- The Creative Competency of *Self-Awareness* breaks down into selfless leader, balance, composure, and personal learner behaviors.
- The Reactive Competency of *Complying* breaks down into conservative, pleasing, belonging, and passive behaviors.

The powerful insights the Leadership Circle provides for an individual leader are nearly priceless when trying to help them evolve and

---

20. https://leadershipcircle.com/en/products/leadership-circle-profile/.

grow into an agile leadership mindset. I go over the results with the client and have them reflect and gather insights and look for growth opportunities that the circle presents to them. I guess what I'm saying is that the survey does much of the heavy lifting of discovery for me and the client.

A third model that I've found helpful is from Gustavo Razzetti of Fearless Culture, creator of the Culture Design Canvas. Gustavo has created a four-quadrant Leadership Style Canvas[21] with the following quadrants:

> **Fearless**—Fearless leadership is comparable to transformational and visionary leadership. This style is built on a strong sense of purpose, inspiration, and disruptive vision.
>
> **Challenger**—Challenger leadership is comparable to pacesetting and transactional leadership. This style is built on high bars, accountability, and rewards. People often perceive challenger leaders as business-like, heroic, leading the charge, and relentless.
>
> **Coaching**—Coaching leadership is built on trust, respect, and strong relationships. It's comparable to participative, servant, or affiliative styles. These leaders drive team building, employee involvement, and participation. People often perceive them as gardeners, mentors, or parental figures.
>
> **Fearful**— Fearful leadership is comparable to coercive or commanding leadership. This style is built on positional power, hierarchy, and control. People often perceive fearful leaders as impersonal, autocratic, hierarchical, know-it-alls.

An important point about all of these models is to not interpret them as a binary representation of your client, and don't let your clients interpret them that way, either. Most leaders exhibit all of these styles in their ongoing leadership, depending on the situational context. However, we all have a dominant or go-to style, as well as a style

---

21. www.fearlessculture.design/blog-posts/the-four-different-leadership-styles-and-how-to-find-yours.

we revert to when we're under pressure. Understanding these individual style nuances can be helpful in your coaching conversations and for your client's understanding of themselves.

In addition, all of the models provide useful language for our coaching conversations. For example, if I were coaching a leader, I might say something like:

> Bob, that was a very "fearful leadership" style or stance you took with the Beta Scrum team today. Why was that? I'm not saying it was good or bad, but I'm curious as to your drivers and thinking behind it.

And then I would listen intently for what Bob had to say and explore it with him. I might then ask another question:

> Bob, I can see why you used that stance. What do you think another stance might be for that same situation and what would have been the difference in delivery and possible outcomes? For example, what if you leaned more into Coaching in that situation?

Can you see how helpful it might be to have this language at your disposal?

Finally, a fourth model I use is from the Co-Active Training Institute: their Co-Active Leadership Model.[22] It's composed of five situational leadership positions:

1. Leading from **Within**, or being a **Purpose-Driven** Leader.
2. Leading from the **Front**, or being a **Visionary** Leader.
3. Leading from the **Field** (left), or being an **Intuitive** Leader.
4. Leading from **Beside** (right), or being a **Collaborative or Co-Leader**.
5. Leading from **Behind**, or being a **Servant Leader**.

I appreciate the positional language in this model and how it speaks to a leader becoming very much like an agile coach. There are positions

---

22. https://learn.coactive.com/your-leadership-approach.

(or stances) that leaders need to dance across depending on a wide variety of leadership situations.

Unfortunately, I don't have the space to do a deeper dive into any of these models in this book. But I mention them because they can help you better connect with and coach your leader clients. If you're interested in any of them, I strongly encourage you to do more research.

Tactics and Tools for Coaching Leaders

Probably the most important tactics that you'll want to continuously grow and refine as a leadership coach are two habits that I feel most of us struggle with mightily. They are developing the skill and courage to speak truth to power and honing your active listening skills.

Many agile coaches talk about courage, psychological safety, trust, and a myriad of agile cultural principles and their importance while they're coaching. But when push comes to shove and the pressure is on for them to speak truth to power as part of their coaching, they either avoid it entirely or they obfuscate their message.

A wide variety of factors influence this—often the same ones that prevent teams and leaders from speaking up. But I'd argue that we must hold ourselves as Extraordinarily Badass Agile Coaches to a higher operating standard.

So, if I were to emphasize one and only one tool to sharpen in your tool belt, it would be your ability to speak truth to power under all circumstances and then to actively listen (sensing) to the reactions and responses to that truth.

A Crucial Story

I've been teaching a Scrum Alliance Certified Agile Leadership class since 2017. One of the highest priority modules in the class is focused on communication and feedback, leveraging the books *Radical Candor* and *Crucial Conversations*. Usually, the attendees want a recipe or checklist or tool to use for these tough conversations, and both books provide that.

But I always emphasize the following to attendees: It's not your conversation *skill* that will make or break the effectiveness of your crucial conversations. Skills are fine, they're great, but what trips most of us up is whether we have the *will* to have the conversation.

I can teach you skill, and you can practice and become more skilled. But you have to be able to dig deep for the will. And that I can't teach you.

Other Tools

While speaking truth to power and actively listening may be your most important skills to effectively coach leaders, they're not the only ones you need. In my coaching journey, I've often reflected on the critical skills, tactics, or approaches that I leverage in gaining positive outcomes. I've found the following to be valuable in coaching leaders or groups of leaders:

- **Providing options, stories, and examples**. The more experience you have, the more you have an inventory of experiences, both good and bad, to share with your clients as options. I recommend that you create an inventory of these things in your journals and writings so that you can bring them out when needed. This includes your ad hoc storytelling capabilities. I've learned that role modeling and storytelling are some of my most powerful tactics when adopting the Advising, Transforming, and Leading stances.
- **Pro/Con; Tradeoffs**. It's not good enough to say "try agile" or "agile will deliver different results." You must be able to illustrate your balanced views of every tactic, approach, and framework. I often share success and failure percentages I've seen. For example, I might talk about cross-functional teams versus not having cross-functional teams in agile contexts: that I've seen both work, but that cross-functional teams provide better organizational flow and delivery. That I've almost never seen a team be successful when they contain only a part of the organization's technology stack; or that 90% of the time they struggle to deliver value.

- **Keep It Simple, Stay on Principles.** One of my superpowers as a coach is an ability to not be enamored with or accepting of complexity as a fact of life. It's not. Instead, I think human beings—we—typically make things much more complex than they need to be. So, I relentlessly push back on complex designs, organizations, and solutions when I'm adopting the Advising, Leading, and Transforming stances. You might ask, who has to simplify things. Well, the client of course—perhaps with my help in Facilitating stance.
- **Systems Thinking.** One of the great blessings ORSC has given me in my coaching is increasing my awareness of the system in my coaching. For far too long, I only coached individuals and groups, but there is always a system around these folks, influencing their behavior. Being aware of the system, listening to and for it and actively bringing it forward in my coaching, has increased my own and my clients' awareness. Nowhere is this more important than when adopting a Transforming stance and guiding systems through change.
- **Patience and Self-Awareness.** I often talk to coaches who are triggered by or biased about the leader they're coaching, particularly when they're adopting more of a transformation, leadership, or advisory stance and the leaders really … aren't … listening or following their advice. I've encountered this myself, so I'm empathetic. But we need to heighten our awareness of our triggers when coaching leaders and stay vigilant and alert to them. In addition, stay open to every client growing and learning at their own pace. Patience is one of the most important metaskills for a coach when coaching up.

Coaching UP Scenarios

When I was coming with ideas for specific leadership coaching scenarios to share at this point in the chapter, it occurred to me that there are no recipes or checklists in your coaching. Particularly not in your leadership coaching. This discipline is incredibly nuanced and situational. I hope you'll see that in the following suggestions, as I share multiple approaches per scenario. These four scenarios just touch the tip of the iceberg of possible coaching strategies and approaches in each situation.

As we go through each of the scenarios, I want you to get into the habit of considering at least three possible drivers for their actions and behaviors so you don't trigger and assume there is one sole cause. You may recognize this as applying Weinberg's Rule of 3 (see the references at the end of the chapter).

Swooping Leaders

> Team managers are "swooping in" to their respective teams each time they (the team) encounter a critical problem. They keep taking away problem-solving and accountability, and you can see the morale, ownership, and empowerment waning across all of the teams. One particular manager, very senior, experienced, and respected, simply isn't responding to your coaching.

What Are Some Possible Drivers for This Behavior?

1. How the leaders are being measured.
2. Not understanding the detrimental impact to the team.
3. Traditional micromanagement (Joiner–Expert) behavior.
4. Top-down pressure to "get things done."
5. Simply not fully understanding their role as an agile leader.

What Are Possible Agile Coaching Responses?

Depending on the drivers, you could do any of the following:

- Get a group of managers together and do some Guiding Learning activities or group-based coaching to help them gain self-awareness of the behavior, understand the impact, and explore mitigations.
- Meet with individual leaders and have a coaching conversation focused on them, their role, their impact, and possible changes. This would largely be from an Advising stance. Depending on the relationship, you could ask them to serve as a role model for other leaders.

- Invite the leader of this group of managers for a coaching conversation. In this case, you're exploring the leader's role in their managers' behavior, the leader's awareness and intentions, and the possibility of the leader coaching their managers—again, from an Advising stance. You might even ask them for direct help in coaching the struggling (or resistant) manager.
- For the manager that you've been coaching with little/no effect, you might want to change to more of a Leadership stance, engaging in a crucial conversation with them.

And of course, you could do a combination of the above, or come up with your own options.

CPO Sizing

You observed the chief product owner (CPO) influencing estimates in more than one backlog refinement session. The good news is that she is very interested and engaged in these team meetings. The bad news is that she is influencing the estimates, and more importantly, the conversations. You've brought this to her attention several times, but the behavior if anything has gotten worse and is strongly impacting the confidence and morale of more than one team.

What Are Some Possible Drivers for This Behavior?

1. How the CPO, and the organization for that matter, is being measured.
2. Not understanding the detrimental impact to the team.
3. Traditional micromanagement (Joiner–Expert) behavior.
4. Top-down pressure to "get things done."
5. Simply not fully understanding their role as a product owner and the distance they must place between themselves and the sizing of the work.
6. Simple curiosity about better understanding the level of effort associated with their business needs.

What Are Possible Agile Coaching Responses?

I'd recommend sitting down with the CPO with Curiosity and API (assuming positive intent) metaskills and a Coaching stance to better understand the drivers for this behavior. Note that I said *drivers*. It may well be that there are multiple in play and you'll need to peel the onion to get to root causes to enhance the focus of your coaching. Depending on the drivers, you could do any of the following:

- If you find that this situation is driven by a lack of understanding of their role and/or the impact it's having on the team's morale and results, then you might adopt more of a teaching and/or mentoring stance in subsequent coaching sessions, helping guide them to a better understanding. A key here is determining whether they're curious and coachable.
- If I found that this is the result of organizational or personal pressure and micromanagement, then I might focus on a Coaching stance to better understand the dynamics with them and then switch to a partnership advisory stance to figure out what steps they and we can take to redirect and refocus the pressure. This might also mean coaching a broader group of leaders, changing the focus from the CPO to their peer group and beyond.
- There's another more subtle approach possible here. Let's say I've been coaching the CTO in this organization and they've been under the same pressure dynamics as the CPO. However, they've been changing how they interpret and act on the pressure and are making great progress in evolving toward more positive reactions. Perhaps I can "partner" these two peers, the CTO and CPO, by inspiring some collaborative mentoring and coaching among themselves. This can be incredibly powerful if done with finesse and respect.

And of course, you could do a combination of the above or come up with your own options.

Scenario – Pause

Are you getting a sense of the coaching mindset, thinking, and flow in these coaching up scenarios?

They can be incredibly nuanced and situational. There never seems to be a single strategy that is effective in all situations. This is where I've found that Cynefin (explored in chapter 5) or sense-and-respond thinking can be really helpful in my coaching. Keep in mind that sensing is not a one-time thing. Instead, you're continuously sensing how your coaching is landing, the outcomes, and the directional adjustments (stance changes, metaskills, and tactics) you need to make along the way.

If you're coaching an individual it's often simpler, because you are sensing and responding to one person. It can get quite a bit more challenging to coach a group or team, because in addition to coaching the group (the system) you might be coaching individuals within that system as well.

Now let's move onto a couple more scenarios to keep your coaching up mind working.

80:20 Rule

> You had hoped that your active coaching of organizational managers and senior managers would start seeping back down into the culture. That is, as the leaders began to better understand agile principles, their behavior would change and they'd begin to coach their teams toward solid agile principles. In other words, they'd start to "walk their talk."
>
> However, only about 10%–15% of the managers are actually helping the transformation. The others seem to be resisting the move to a more agile leadership mindset, and perhaps 20% are even undermining it. You are personally aware of three managers in the latter category.

What Are Some Possible Drivers for This Behavior?

1. Traditional, problem-solving management (Joiner–Expert) behavior.
2. Top-down pressure to "get things done" and hold managers "personally accountable" for the results.
3. Simply not fully understanding their role as a manager and the new role they need to play in empowering and building their teams.
4. Feelings of having power removed from them, fear of losing control, and feeling personally at risk.
5. Losing a sense of belonging, of seeing how they "fit" in the organization.

What Are Possible Agile Coaching Responses?

Depending on the drivers, you could do any of the following:

- I might consider starting at the top in this scenario and sitting down with the senior leader or executive that these folks report to. I'd begin by exploring how they are communicating the new direction and mentoring the individual managers. My initial metaskill would be Curiosity, but I'd also play into Courage and Lion's Roar so that I'm clear with what I'm seeing and the impact to the leader's overall strategy. From a stance perspective, I'd enter in Coaching stance, but probably quickly switch to either Leadership or Advising stance.
- Another strategy would be to spend some coaching time with the leaders who are navigating the shift well and to encourage them to model and mentor to their peers. This could take the form of some individual coaching, probably from Leadership-Partnership stance, or group-based coaching leveraging a Guiding Learning stance to surface alignment challenges and to look for opportunities to realign.
- In this situation, I sometimes use a manager-to-leadership role mapping exercise where we uncover the activities and focus points for a manager in the organizational context, and the responsibilities and activities for a leader in the organizational

context. Then, I facilitate a merging activity where the leaders co-create a new role understanding for the aggregate set of activities and responsibilities they need to adopt in their current organizational context.

And of course, you could do a combination of the above or come up with your own options.

Faster! Faster!

Your key leadership sponsor pulls you aside and tells you that they are a little unsettled with your coaching style, and more importantly, with the lack of results. She explains that of the 20+ teams in her organization, only three have consistent and increasing velocity. These same three teams seem to be working the hardest as well. She's challenging you that you only have two or three more sprints to get the remaining 15+ teams "up to speed" with the other teams, or else the senior leadership team will have to find another coach who can drive the results they are after.

What Are Some Possible Drivers for This Behavior?

1. Not fully understanding the how agile teams deliver their continuous improvement.
2. How the leader is being measured.
3. Not understanding the detrimental impact to the team and organization this behavior will have.
4. Traditional micromanagement (Joiner–Expert) behavior.
5. Top-down pressure to "get things done."

What Are Possible Agile Coaching Responses?

To be honest, this sort of conversation and reaction triggers me. I begin to assume bad intentions by the leader, which strongly colors my interactions with them. So, the first thing I would do before applying any coaching strategy would be to cool down, center myself, and allow some time to pass. I'd be looking to pivot my metaskills toward API (assuming positive intent), Empathy, Curiosity (seeking to understand the root causes behind the challenge), and Courage (to have the audacity to speak truth to the leader).

You can also look at previous scenarios for responses that might make sense in this context. There are a few to consider.

I also want to bring up an alternative conversation that I haven't mentioned yet. This in response to the remark that "they'll have to find another coach who can drive the results they are after." You might want to have a hard conversation that starts from an Advising stance and describes how damaging this approach will be—that is, if they're trying to truly create a high-performance agile organization. You might also need to say that if they continue thinking of this as an effective strategy, that yes, you might not be the coach for them.

And of course, you could do a combination of the above or come up with your own options.

Scenario – Pause

Among agile coaches, middle management is often called *the frozen middle* in agile contexts (among many other less useful euphemisms). Of course, we're stereotyping, but I thought I'd share this for context. There is a link at the end of the chapter to an article by Jeremy Braden that explores the term and the impact in much more detail.

The point, though, is a valid one. In all of my experience coaching agile transformations, the layers of management between the teams and executive or senior leadership—the frozen middle, if you will—are the folks who typically have the most challenges with personal and organizational change. I also consider them the critical success factor in any transformation because of the influence and power they have over their teams.

To that end, if you're coaching up as an Extraordinarily Badass Agile Coach, you'll need situational awareness, chops, and practice coaching the middle leaders. In my opinion, they are the key to your success in agile coaching at any level.

Dojo Practicing

I can think of no better way to end this chapter than to invite you to read chapter 18 to discover the power of practice.

Nowhere is it more important to practice your coaching chops than with your leadership coaching. Simply put, you can't have one tool, tactic, or stance here. You have to be nimble when dancing with your leader clients, and the stakes are too high for you to practice directly on them.

Variety is the spice of leadership coaching here. Given any scenario you encounter, you can:

- Run the dojo in a sunny-day fashion, having the person playing the leader assume a very cooperative and open-minded posture;
- Run the dojo in a rainy-day fashion, having the personal playing the leader assume a very closed and defensive posture;
- Run the dojo primarily from an advisory (or transformational or coaching or leadership) stance, with little or no switching of stances;
- Rerun the dojo with someone else playing the coaching role, to uncover variations of style, strategy, and approach.

Can you see how advantageous this would be for you to do *before* you engage in challenging leadership coaching sessions and stances?

It's also a great way to strengthen your weaker stances and to gain skill and comfort with them.

Further Reading

This is Anthony Mersino's post around building coaching empathy for and with leaders: https://vitalitychicago.com/blog/empathy-for-technology-managers-in-agile/.

This blog post explores different tools for gaining perspective in your coaching and facilitation. One of the tools is Weinberg's Rule of 3: www.agile-moose.com/blog/2021/7/19/gaining-perspective.

Jeremy Braden's article about "Thawing the Frozen Middle" on the Agile Alliance site: www.agilealliance.org/resources/experience-reports/thawing-the-frozen-middle-to-create-a-self-organizing-transformation/.

Joseph Grenny, Kerry Patterson, Ron McMillan, Al Switzler, and Emily Gregory, *Crucial Conversations: Tools for Talking When the Stakes are High*, 3rd Edition (McGraw-Hill Education, 2021).

Kim Scott, *Radical Candor: Be a Kick-Ass Boss Without Losing Your Humanity* (St. Marten's Press, 2019).

Reflections

I want to encourage you to stop and reflect at the end of each section of the book—going back and reviewing to answer these questions.

Spend some time digesting all aspects of the Agile Coaching Growth Wheel, paying particular attention to the competencies.

Mark spent a great deal of time exploring specific coaching conversations with you in this section. As you reflect on them:

- What were you thinking and discovering with each scenario?
- So, what was important in your observations and learning?
- And most importantly, now what are you going to do with that learning?

Take a look at the Wheel-based learning references in our Badass Agile Coaching Repo (registration link in the afterword) and pick two or three books or articles that you're willing to commit to exploring.

Explore some of the ideas and inspiration from this section with your coach. Use them as a sounding board for your growth, experimentation, and learning.

Visualization

I want you to close your eyes and get quiet. Center your attention on the notion of a Badass Agile Coach. That's you. Envision what that looks and feels like.

Think about your typical coaching conversations, stances, and approaches. Now reflect deeply on this section. What adjustments might you want to make in your overall coaching style and approach?

And, just for fun, run through a few of your own real-world coaching conversations in your mind using these newfound ideas and tactics.

Now open your eyes and jot down those ideas, aspirations, insights, plans, hopes, and dreams in your journal.

Haven't started journaling yet?

Well then, read this: www.agile-moose.com/blog/2019/6/23/journaling-how-to-get-started, and consider using our Agile Coach Journaling Canvas, which you can find in the repo.

III • Nuanced Agile Coaching

Badass Agile Coaching in the Language of the Client

Badass Pair-Coaching

Badass Role-Based Coaching

Badass Context-Based Coaching

Situational Awareness in a Badass Agile Coach

12

Badass Agile Coaching in the Language of the Client

Words matter. How we deliver them matters. Variations in our words over time matter. Consistency in wording, in intent, in body language, and even what words you choose not to say, matters.

This is a conundrum of agile coaching. I often say that coaches should speak about 30% of the time and their clients should speak the other 70% of the time. Partly, this is a means of giving the client sufficient space to communicate and consider. Partly it's in service to the client. But being frugal with our words only increases their preciousness, their value, and the impact that every word can have.

Consider your words carefully, craft them flawlessly, and deliver them clearly. And yes, I'm personally still working on this.

Introduction

Over the course of my career, as an engineer, a manager, a senior leader, and yes, as an agile coach, I've noticed that my language matters. I'll give you an example: the word *resistance* has always had a negative connotation for me:

- This Scrum team member is not on board with agile. They're *resisting* being agile within the team and it's causing the team to fail.
- This leader is *resisting* becoming agile or adopting the agile mindset. Sure, they're saying the right words, but their behaviors and actions are undermining the entire transformation.
- This organization is really not ready for agile. They're *resisting* it at every turn. They're not doing the things they need to do or changing their mindsets.

The word *resistance* in these instances, and in my mindset, has taken on a very negative, blocking, closed-minded, not-on-board connotation. And when I say that word, my tone and body language support that negative outlook. How I say *resistance*, what I think and perceive when I say it, and how the word is perceived by the receivers matters. And I have a very high degree of control over all of that.

The first point of this chapter is to sensitize you to the fact that your language matters. The second is that it's important for all of us to reframe our language, intent, and mindset to be in service to our clients. In other words, we need to stay in their language as much as possible.

In the Beginning, There Was Empathy

The first step in connecting with your clients in their language is to be empathetic. In this case, empathy means feeling into someone else's feelings—experiencing those feelings as if you were the other person—and then achieving better understanding. There's an emotional component to empathy that gives you an affinity for your client's feelings.

Empathy is not sympathy, which is understanding someone else's suffering. Another way to think about empathy that often helps me is the metaphor of walking in someone else's shoes. How can I be empathetic and feel into your feelings if I have no clue about your situation? I can't.

Figure 33 shows a spectrum of empathy. The origin of this figure is the Nielsen Norman Group, which is a UX coaching firm, so the empathy spectrum in this case is for the client/user. But I think it applies equally to empathy in all contexts.

The importance of empathy is one of the differences between agile coaches and professional coaches. Professional coaches lightly touch empathy and relationship, but they typically stay away from truly understanding their clients. It helps them to remain slightly distant from the client.

I believe agile coaching requires more intimacy and empathy with your clients. You're still holding the client as whole, capable, and competent, but you're increasing your awareness of and empathy for them and what it's like in their universe—both personally and professionally.

Spectrum of Empathy

EFFORT ↑

- Pity — I'm sorry for you.
- Sympathy — I feel for you.
- Empathy — I feel with you.
- Compassion — I am moved by you.

UNDERSTANDING & ENGAGEMENT →

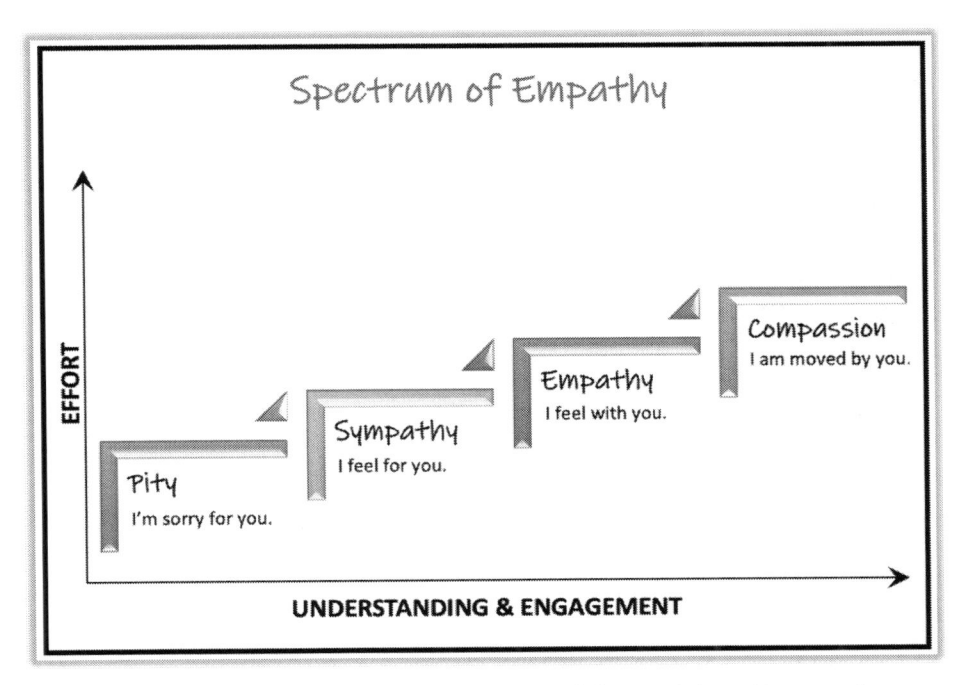

FIGURE 33. Spectrum of Empathy. *Source*: Adapted from Nielsen Norman Group, www.nngroup.com/articles/sympathy-vs-empathy-ux/.

The Client as a Persona

You may have come in contact with personas in your software UI or UX work. When doing UI development, it helps to have a picture or description of your client. Consider it a résumé and job description with personal details and a description of what the client does—the jobs they perform—in their role.

Understanding this background information can also be very helpful when you're designing your coaching alliance and plans and trying to decide which stances will be of most help to your clients and in which situations.

The best personas allow you to acquire a mental image of your client so that you can better envision them, better understand them, and better empathize with them.

Language Matters!

Our language as agile coaches matters as well. In some aspects, our coaching language can be the difference in our successes or failures as change agents.

I versus We language. As we move into agile contexts, we need to move from *I* or *me*-centric language to *you* and *we* language. The more often we can talk about the team, the group, the organization, and not ourselves, the better. From an agile coaching perspective, though, be careful that you don't overuse *we* when it's inappropriate; that is, when you're not part of the group.

Agile and Lean language. I once was teaching an agile leadership class for a C-level leadership team. At the end of the class, they were planning next steps on their agile transformation and making changes based on some things they learned in the class. One of their ideas was to stop using the term *agile*. It had become a buzzword and didn't help them when explaining things to their board, stakeholders, or customers. I thought this was an epiphany on their part.

Business language. Related to the above, it's important to continuously translate your agile language to language the business, clients, and leadership can understand. I'm not sure that always implies converting to ROI, outcomes, and OKRs, but it helps for us to make what we're proposing understandable by the entire organization.

Transformation language. What are some common buzzwords around an agile transformation? Well, for starters, *transformation*. Also, *business agility, digital transformation, DevOps,* and *agile scaling / SAFe*. Generally, I'd recommend you stay away from jargon and buzzwords as much as possible. When you do have to use them, provide equivalents or translations right away, to ensure clarity.

TABLE 2. Language Guidance for the Agile Coach

Focus less on this language	Focus more on this language
Velocity, throughput, flow	Predictability
Success and failure	Results
Agile/agile; "That's not A/agile"	Transparency
Self-directed	Autonomy and engagement
Servant leadership	Partnership and collaboration
Trust, but verify	Experimentation, learning, adjustment/pivoting
Testing phases and gates	
Developer vs. tester vs. business analyst	Trust
	Quality
SAFe, DAD, Less, etc.	Team members and team health
Scrum, XP, Kanban, etc.	Continuous improvement
DevOps	Customer value
Business agility, organizational agility	Leadership/organizational alignment
Organizational structures	

Table 2 shows some language and discussion guidance for you as a Badass Agile Coach. You want to be leaning to the language in the righthand column as often as you can.

Absolutely Don't Do This

To wrap this section up, I thought I'd share my top "don't say or do this" items for agile coaches. Hopefully none of you have experienced any of these, but I thought I'd at least mention them.

First up is a tendency to *weaponize* the term *agile* by saying things like:

- "That's not Big 'A' Agile; you're not agile!"
- "I'm the coach and an agile expert, so do it this way, it's agile."
- "Agile leaders don't behave/act that way, it undermines our agility."

Avoid these or any variations on this theme. In my experience, it's easy for agilists to fall into the trap of being the arbiter of what good and bad agile practices and mindsets look like. Stay away from that. It's truly up to your clients to discover what agile means for them.

Another habit I've seen, and unfortunately sometimes participated in myself, is *stereotyping* people and situations:

- According to common roles like tester, project manager, manager, leadership; for example, "All of the managers are undermining my coaching efforts by micromanaging."
- According to other attributes; for example, "All of the baby boomers are too 'experienced' to be able to understand and effectively operate with an agile mindset."
- Or "If only the managers would do their job, it would make my job so much easier."

It's hard to connect with a client if you're stereotyping them into a group. Rather, you want to meet them as individuals and connect with them as the unique and capable human beings that they are.

I often find that stereotyping behavior is coupled with blaming behavior. In the above, for example, I was blaming management and managers for their behavior.

Finally, and probably the most important for you to stay tuned into, is how you get triggered and what happens as a result. For example:

- On failure, "That team always fails. They've failed the last four sprints in a row."
- On resistance, "They'll never get to an agile mindset."
- On specific approaches, "Every team must use Fibonacci-based story points in their estimates in order to be successful."

- On frameworks, "Scrum is the best way to do IT support work. It works everywhere else, so you need to make it work here."

I equate triggering to a bias, and we all have experience which leads to biases. But triggering is often an absolute and judging stance, which is never good for a coach.

I often think in terms of *purist* versus *pragmatist* language, within agile organizations and as a coach. A purist is someone who has triggered on a method or approach or a tool to the point where it is the only way to do something. If they stepped back and thought about it, they would realize how ironic this stance is, given the core agile principles and mindset. But I digress.

A pragmatist, on the other hand, is much more flexible and less stuck (triggered) on their approaches. They're better able to step back, give some generic guidance, and then see what approaches emerge from their clients.

Language as a Maturity Measure

My friend Josh Anderson and I recorded a joint podcast with Jeff Bubolz and Jeff Maleski of the AgileWire podcast.[23] One of the tangents we went on was understanding the agile maturity (readiness, culture) of an organization by the presence of certain words in the overall culture, including everyone from teams to senior leaders.

We agreed that certain words or phrases indicate a less mature or agile-ready culture, and other words indicate more maturity. The overall usage and trending of all of the words together is the most interesting, and most indicative of overall maturity.

(Please don't get hung up by or trigger on the word *maturity*; you could just as easily say *readiness* or *receptiveness* or *fertileness*.)

We agreed that the following words and phrases are indicative of greater organizational maturity:

---

23. www.theagilewire.com/recordings.

- We, our, us.
- What did you discover? What did you learn?
- How will you avoid failing that way again?
- How can I help?
- Do you need help?
- I'm struggling and need your help.
- What can I do to help us achieve our goals?
- Always referring to the team or the group.
- Let's explore this together, or, Let's experiment together.
- Help me to understand your perspective.
- If we were to do that again, how would you approach it?

This is not an exhaustive list, of course, but it captures the ideas. In contrast, the following words and phrases are indicative of less organizational maturity:

- Me, my, I.
- Fixed scope and fixed dates.
- Get it done, now!
- I need you to do this for me.
- Who's to blame for it being late?
- Who's to blame (for anything)?
- Don't bring me problems, bring me solutions.
- I just need it to be done.
- You don't understand.
- Listen to me.

Again, this is not an exhaustive list, but you get the idea. The thought we had was to measure both sides of the conversations within a culture and then come up with some sort of agile maturity (behavior, walking your talk) metric or indicator based on the reality exposed by those conversations.

I shared this here because I believe this is a nice way to measure your agile coaching effectiveness as an individual or in your coaching team. So, as you are coaching your bad ass off, are you noticing a shift in the organizational language from the less to the more mature? You should be, or you should be reflecting on your overall coaching strategies and effectiveness.

Language Alignment

Another important point to explore is the notion of language alignment. For example, if one coach is using specific language in their coaching and another is using something different, it can create client and organizational confusion. I shared an example of this happening to me on my blog.[24] This can also happen organizationally, when leadership is unaligned as a team.

In both instances, confusion results, and the messaging gets muddled and hard to follow. Why? Because there is no consistency.

Now, I'm not saying that every agile coach in an organization or on a coaching team has to be a clone of every other coach and use identical language. That would be silly. But you should never assume that you're aligned. That's just plain arrogance. Instead, you should take the time to ensure that you're aligned. Make sure you are aligned on:

- The overall client strategy
- Specific principles
- Roles, such as who's taking the lead
- Compromises being made, meeting the client where they are
- Practices, tactics, mindset, lines in the sand, etc.

Here's an example: You should never have two coaches going into a client and disagreeing on Scrum sprint planning practices (whether to task or not). Or disagreeing on the level of estimation (points) that will be recommended. Or on the need for defining a sprint goal.

Alignment matters! And most of us believe that we're more aligned than we are. So, agile coaches, check your alignment and get aligned, before you confuse the heck out of your clients.

---

24. https://rgalen.com/agile-training-news/2020/8/28/a-coaching-alignment-story.

Coaching Leaders to Watch Their Language

One of the most powerful coaching conversations you can have with your leadership clients—and remember, everyone is a leader in agile contexts—relates to their language. I've used and shared the following guidelines with leaders who are trying to better navigate their language shift in agile contexts.

- Stop using the term *resources* to apply to people. You should charge and collect a "fine" every time someone does it. Then treat folks to lunch with the proceeds.
- Stop referring to groups by their functional name (QA or Developers or Architects or Management).
- Stop treating individuals as being fungible in any way. Consider and discuss everyone as an individual.
- Stop using "magic numbers" to calculate team member availability; for example, planning everyone at 70% of their availability. Instead, ask individuals for their capacity.
- Stop considering one or two voices representative of the opinions of an entire group. This is one reason I like Planning Poker dynamics; it encourages everyone to voice their opinion.
- Stop allowing one group, such as developers in the team, to be considered done with their work independent of the entire team. Doneness should be cross-team and cross-functional in nature. It's a team output.
- When you're approaching a near shore or outsourcing partner, don't think in terms of resources and staff augmentation. Think in terms of partnership and put the same care into that relationship that you do into hiring your own team members.

The real point is that teams are composed of individuals. Let's consider that in all of our interactions and not lose sight of the individual. I expect agile teams to behave respectfully in that way, and everyone outside of the team should too.

Further Reading

I'd recommend two books by L. David Marquet on this subject: *Turn the Ship Around* (New York: Penguin, 2015) and *Leadership Is Language* (New York: Penguin, 2020). I recommend reading them in that order. While they aren't classic "agile coaching" books, they do delve into two areas that will help your coaching: *Turn the Ship Around* illustrates what effective leadership looks like, especially under some very challenging circumstances, and the other book is squarely aimed at the theme of this chapter—language.

13

Badass Pair-Coaching

There are things in life that are best done alone, and there are things that are best done with someone else, such as a trusted colleague or partner. What those things are varies greatly from person to person, and self-awareness is required to figure out what's best for you.

If you are open to it, agile pair-coaching can be one of the most intense and accelerated ways to increase the depth and breadth of your agile coaching skills palette. And it happens to be fun—that is, if you find the right partner and check your ego at the door to your learning dance.

With the right coaching partners, you'll be on your way to becoming an Extraordinarily Badass Agile Coach, so don't go it alone!

Introduction

Not long ago a colleague and I had the opportunity to work together on an agile transformation engagement. As most of these engagements do, it had an initial training component and then a team-by-team coaching component. The idea was not just to get 10 or more teams up and running but to achieve some cross-team consistency in tactics and practices.

We quoted the client so that my colleague and I would be co-coaching periodically, with planned trips where we visited the client together. We had three reasons for not "living with the client." First, it wasn't our primary coaching model. We preferred a part-time model, engaging at the iteration endpoints. Then, we agreed that embedding often slows the client learning down, as they can become too dependent on the coaches. And finally, we each wanted our clients to receive the best (most experienced) coaches possible, and this model allowed for that.

Essentially the model gave the client space for execution, experimentation, and learning, which enhanced the impact of our visits. There are usually many questions and coaching opportunities in a model like this, but they are based on client ownership and real-time experience.

We noticed that it wasn't easy to sell pair-coaching to the client. The primary resistance factor seemed to be cost, including coaching and travel costs. But there were more subtle factors as well. For example, there was an undertone of "why can't just one coach do all of this?" — perhaps implying that our individual coaches weren't skilled enough to handle all of the client's needs. It reminded me of the resistance I heard in the early days of pair-programming. Many couldn't get over the simple economics and look to the intangible (but real) benefits to quality, risk mitigation, and execution.

The reality is that even the best coaches have blind spots and can miss important real-time aspects during their coaching. Having two sets of eyes working together can cover those blind spots, making each coach that much more effective for their client.

Those benefits need to be emphasized in pair-coaching to overcome or reframe the resistance. Of course, the context matters: Pair-coaching makes more sense when you're coaching organizationally across many teams or coaching up and down the organization.

It's Not Just the Teams

The other thing my colleague and I discovered is that we weren't always coaching at the same level. Although we paired on the engagement, we often split up for individual coaching. Let me give you a "day in the life" example:

- First thing in the morning, we pulled three teams together to discuss backlog refinement practices. We'd both noticed that these teams and their product owners were struggling with this, so we ran an ad hoc class focused on story refinement.
- Next, we split up and attended individual team backlog refinement sessions. This allowed us more breadth of coverage and let us coach by example or mentoring.
- Right after, we compared notes. Were there any common patterns? Were the individual product owners skilled enough? It turned out that a few of the product owners were really struggling. So, my colleague continued working with the teams while I pulled away to focus individually on product owners.
- At lunch, we compared notes—not just about the teams but also around what we were seeing at the organizational level. Each day we discovered aspects of the culture—both the teams and leadership. As our awareness changed, our strategies changed as well.
- In the afternoon, I spent time working with individual managers regarding their roles, talking about how their behavior and approaches needed to shift a bit in an agile environment. Part of this was coaching, but another part was establishing a sense of being a trusted partner.

- My colleague continued to focus on the teams. On this particular day, the focus was on architecture and how it fit into backlogs and team execution, so he spent a great deal of time with team leads and architects.
- We wrapped up our day with a retrospective, discussing what we'd observed and experienced throughout the day. We then discussed strategy adjustments we could/would make for the next day's coaching activities.

As you can see, our coaching stance and our focus (the lens) changed in real time throughout the day. That would have been hard almost to the point of impossibility with a single coach. And I can't emphasize enough how powerful it was to have a sounding board in real time, right there in the trenches with me.

Changing Your Lens

Changing focus can be a powerful tool in agile coaching. Pair-coaching facilitates your ability to focus across various aspects of an agile transformation. In the pair-coaching engagement just described, we could ensure we were attentive to all three levels of the effort:

1. Team-based coaching
   a. Direct teams
   b. Indirect teams (developers, business analysts, testers)
   c. Roles (Scrum Masters and product owners)
2. Skills and tactics
   a. Management-based coaching
   b. Directly involved managers (those managing agile team members)
   c. Surrogates (project managers, release managers)
   d. Activities (metrics, tooling, organizational structure, team management)
3. Leadership-based coaching
   a. Direct leaders (technology, development, quality, product)
   b. Indirect leaders (cross-functional leaders)

c. Stakeholders (direct stakeholders in the agile effort, could be with clients of our client)

And we pivoted across all of these in real time as conditions changed on the ground. It was incredibly powerful and proved highly impactful for the client.

Adaptive Coaching Strategy

Each day, as we prepared for our coaching, we would come up with an overall strategy for the day. This strategy was based on

- our original coaching contract (schedule and strategy),
- our learnings from the previous day,
- adjustments in the client team coaching opportunities, and
- adjustments based on our skills and client context.

Our focus became *opportunity – coaching – outcome* as we progressed through the engagement.

One Voice

It's important to have **one voice** in your pair-coaching—in other words, to be and remain aligned. By and large, all the coaches should be referencing the same techniques and approaches, and making similar recommendations for the organizational context. There should be an overarching consistency to the coaching stances, experience, and skills.

I'm not looking for the pairs to become automatons or clones of one another. That certainly wouldn't be helpful. But you can't have one coach providing some tactical advice one day, and then another coach providing diametrically opposite advice the next. There must be some sort of philosophical alignment between the coaches.

And the very act of pairing helps to identify misalignment and encourages alignment across your coaching team, which is crucial to ensure that your clients don't get confusing or conflicting advice.

Types of Pairing

There are several different types of pairing to consider. I've found myself adopting each of these across a wide variety of contexts in my pairing.

Strategic pairing. In this model, the pair-coaches are spending little time together in coaching sessions. Instead, they meet dynamically throughout each day to discuss the overall plan and strategy of the coaching; to use one other as sounding boards for discovery, ideas, and next steps; and to generally realign the overall strategy toward the clients' goals.

Tactical pairing. This is pair-coaching used for day-to-day activities. For example, in my earlier story, my colleague and I paired on backlog refinement coaching with specific teams. We felt that having both of us there, one as primary coach and the other as facilitator, would be the most helpful for the client. We didn't do this often, but it was a situational tactic that proved quite effective.

Mentor pairing. Here, there is a primary coach and a mentee coach. The mentee does little to no coaching, but learns from the coaching and debriefs later. Mentor pairing is a great way to develop coaching skills through direct observation, by sensing adjustments and using debriefing coaching sessions for learning opportunities.

Interview pairing. This is a twist on mentor pairing, leveraging pair-coaching—either in a real coaching session or in a dojo—to determine the skills, alignment, and compatibility of a coach. Interview pairing can be used to interview a candidate (internal or external) before they join your coaching team.

Agile Pair-Coaching Canvas

One of my discoveries while pair-coaching was the need for dialogue and clarity in the pair. One of the best ways to encourage this is using a canvas tool to focus the discussion before beginning your coaching. That's why I developed the Agile Pair-Coaching Canvas in figure 34.

Badass Pair-Coaching 235

Agile Pair-Coaching Canvas

The intent of the Canvas is to inspire conversations between the pair-coaches, to gain clarity around how you'll operate, and to establish your vision, mission, and environment.

Coach #1:	Last updated:
Coach #2:	

Coaching Stances, Agreements and Plans
How are we operating together? Why are we operating together?

The Sum Is Greater Than the Individuals *Both of our superpowers, strengths, challenges, 1+1=3 agreements.*	**Role: Driver** *Describe our Driver role in detail (expectations, boundaries).*
Client Goals *Clearly articulated outcomes for the client.*	**Role: Navigator** *Describe our Navigator role in detail (expectations, boundaries).*
Alignment *Principles, tactics, tools, and strategies for where we need to align. Both should sign off on this section.*	**Mentoring & Growing** *Mentoring, x-training, Dojo, role-playing, and strength-based strategies for our continuous growth.*

This work is licensed under CC BY-NC 4.0

FIGURE 34. Agile Pair-Coaching Canvas

This canvas is not intended to restrict your coaching sense-and-respond reactions, but to gain agreement within the pair about how you might be showing up to your client—and to each other for that matter.

Coaching Stances, Agreements, and Plans

This block is for your operating agreements. Beyond the roles, what sorts of models are you going to leverage? For example, I would recommend agreeing on using the Agile Coaching Growth Wheel as your model. This is where you would articulate any other tools you might agree to use; for example, Constellation, from ORSC, as a group-based tool.

Also, what is your specific *agreement* for your partnership and pairing? Think in terms of support, confidentiality, safety, candor, respect, and assuming positive intent.

The *plans*, in this case, reflect your personal plans to meet the client's goals. In other words, how will you as a pair support and focus on your client achieving their goals? Don't just think tactically here; think strategically too.

This might also be a place where you explore your primary coaching stances. For example, some clients might need or want more of a coaching stance, while others need more of a consulting or prescriptive stance. This is where you capture your thoughts and agreements around that balance.

Alignment

While you might think you're aligned, I often find that this is a critical area to explore. There is so much nuance in agile practices, tools, and tactics that differences of opinion and experience can easily create division in the pair. It's best to explore these areas in advance and then, one area at a time, agree on how you'll consistently handle them for your client. Consistency for *this* pair-coaching relationship is the key, not permanent agreement on the practice.

Common areas of contention could include estimation and planning, level of tasking, user story writing, coaching stances, the level of prescriptiveness, Shu Ha Ri situational coaching and the degree of coaching up, and the risk associated with each particular misalignment.

It's also a good practice to define a "safe word" or signal phrase that identifies when one member of the pair feels misaligned on something.

Roles

When pair-coaching, one of you will assume the role of *driver*. Think of it as being the lead coach, primary voice, or point-person for a particular coaching session, situation, or dialogue. The other coach will assume the role of *navigator* or *observer*.

In pair-coaching, we try to switch roles at points where it makes the most sense, for example:

- At the end of a coaching conversation.
- On closing a coaching goal with a particular client or person, team, or group.
- After a singular session, perhaps providing some sort of mentoring or teaching.

While the consistency of the situational coaching relationship is of paramount importance, you probably want to err on the side of switching roles too often rather than not often enough. To that point, you will want to establish some norms for how both individuals in the pair will behave and operate, and agree on your tactics for switching roles.

The role of driver is essentially that of a Badass Agile Coach. You are coaching as if the navigator isn't even there. In fact, you largely ignore the navigator unless they get your attention with some feedback. You will be engaging in your Coaching Arc and switching stances as appropriate with your client.

The role of navigator can be more interesting and more active than you might believe. Often, folks look at this role as being a passive observer, while I see the navigator as just as important and active as the driver. Here are a few activities that can fall to the navigator role:

- Actively listening to all channels of the conversation, paying particular attention to the emotional field.
- Taking detailed flow notes.
- Asking permission to interrupt to
  - make an observation, offer a suggestion, or propose a different strategy or stance;
  - point out something important that is being missed; or
  - suggest a pause or a switch of coaching roles.
- Observing the client, the coach, and the third entity (the system).
- Preparing to provide feedback to the lead coach after the coaching session, either verbally or (preferably) in a dojo session where you both role-play a different approach to the coaching.

Now, doesn't that sound more interesting than you thought? And remember, this isn't a passive role, and you'll want to establish pair norms for how you'll be operating as a navigator.

Mentoring and Growing

The discussion, agreements, and actions in this section include both sides of the learning, mentoring, and continuous development activity within the pair. I sometimes think of this section as being a bit selfish. That is, how will the pair develop and strengthen themselves as coaches during this pair-based coaching engagement? Note also that there is a strong connection between this section and the next.

Sum Is Greater Than the Individuals

As you fill in this canvas, you will have to do a fair amount of self-reflection about your superpowers, strengths, and weaknesses or challenges. Being transparent about your capabilities with your pair-partner only increases the strength and impact of your pair. Yes, there's a bit of vulnerability, transparency, and humility required here.

Superpowers are always interesting to me—that is, being aware of what they are and how to leverage them within your coaching pair. And it's important to understand the super side of these abilities, but also their shadow side.

One way to get at the heart of this is to reflect on feedback you've received from your other coaching pair partners. Most of us lack self-awareness, and what we perceive as our strengths and weaknesses often aren't. They're something else entirely. Gathering and reflecting on aggregate feedback is a wonderful way of getting closer to the truth.

Client Goals

Client goals are in the center of the canvas, front and center, as they should be in everything your pair is focused on. These goals aren't something that the coaching pair determines in a vacuum or on their own. No! These need to come directly (and indirectly) from your early conversations with your clients.

Keep these tips in mind when you're crafting goals with your clients:

- Try to make client goals outcome- and impact-based.
- Try to align them with the notion of acceptance criteria or doneness criteria—the clearer the better.
- Absolutely share them with the client for confirmation.
- Try to avoid coach-only goals.
- Establish a coaching plan and connect it to your client's goals.

Also, try to connect the goals to other areas of your canvas wherever appropriate so there is alignment and connection throughout.

I want you to leave this chapter with a renewed curiosity about and interest in pair-coaching. I believe it's a powerful model that helps you bring your best coaching to your clients. It's worth considering and experimenting with, and I hope you give it a try.

Further Reading

A complementary article to the focus of this chapter is the Agile42 post here: www.agile42.com/en/blog/2016/03/18/pair-coaching/.

I met Gerrit Lutter, from Berlin, at the Agile 2018 conference, where he presented an experiential talk focused on pair-coaching. Since then, he's published a wonderful set of articles as well. You can find them here:

- https://medium.com/@gerrit.lutter/pair-coaching-a-non-definitive-guide-part-1-a3e92d5b0191
- https://medium.com/@gerrit.lutter/pair-coaching-a-non-definitive-guide-part-2-29f7c0abf1ea

14

Badass Role-Based Coaching

One of the biggest threats to any organization is role confusion. It's caused by the disruption agile transformations create across a wide variety of traditional roles. Suddenly, people who knew what was expected of them in their job no longer have a clue. And often, the organization throws them into the fire of a new role with little to no training and even less coaching.

As a Badass Agile Coach, we want to be aware of and appreciate the different roles that we'll be typically coaching in agile contexts, including Scrum Masters, teams, product owners, and managers/leaders. Each needs unique things from us as coaches. We have to meet them where they are, individually and as a group, and then guide them to where they want to be.

And it sure helps if you've acted in one of those roles historically, so that you have high empathy and understanding.

In this chapter and the next, **Jennifer Fields** of Acklen Avenue will explore role-based and context-based coaching dynamics. I could think of no better person to write these two chapters than Jen—a dynamic coach with real-

> world experience—and I hope you learn from her experience and enjoy her powerful perspectives.

Introduction

In this chapter, we're going to do a bit of a deeper dive into the nuance of coaching specific roles in agile contexts. While there are a near-infinite number of roles in the real world, we're going to boil them down to the following three sets:

- Scrum Masters and coaches
- Product managers and product owners
- Leadership

You may have noticed that teams aren't in the list. Does that mean I don't care about coaching the team? Of course not. For the purposes of your agile coaching role, teams—agile teams, Scrum teams, Kanban teams, DevOps teams, all kinds of teams—are always potentially in play.

But there is contextual nuance to coaching practices, depending on the roles you are coaching. For example, if I'm coaching another coach, I'll be quite transparent about which stance I'm operating in and why. If I'm coaching a leader, senior leaders, or a critical organizational stakeholder, I'll probably spend less time in Coaching stance and more time in other stances.

When preparing for and navigating coaching sessions, it is imperative that you understand you have the freedom to flex and adjust based on feedback and interaction. If coaching were a dance, it wouldn't be choreographed; it would be a dance where both partners know all the steps but are free to move around the floor, creating and using patterns based on what they encounter on the dance floor and what brings them joy and feels right.

Scrum Masters and Coaches

I remember my first go at being a Scrum Master, fresh from a two-day Certified Scrum Master course where I had learned all the mechanics and even got to practice what I had learned during a very entertaining simulation. My enthusiasm faded quickly when the first daily Scrum was a tremendous failure. I remember thinking I hadn't asked the right questions during class, and on some days, I felt like sending my instructor a very pointed email about how the Scrum they spoke of in class didn't exist in the real world. No one was playing by the rules, there was *not* one product owner, the team wasn't dedicated, and the Iron Triangle[25] was very real.

I can still feel the anxiety and sense of failure when I think of those first few months. I didn't have an agile coach to partner with, so I moved from one failure to another, stumbling along, dragging the poor team with me. I lean on those lessons whenever I'm invited to coach Scrum Masters, always striving to be the coach I wish I'd had during that time.

Setting the Stage

The following scenario is an example of my time in the trenches coaching Scrum Masters. I, like many others, learn the most by doing the hands-on work, but I have found reading through Coaching Arcs and participating in discussions of them extremely helpful. They are like coaching case studies that you can break apart and experiment with.

This coaching conversation is with a Scrum Master you have been asked to coach. The team has made multiple complaints about this Scrum Master being too controlling. Questioning the validity of estimates and pushing for a faster pace were just a couple of the examples the team provided.

---

25. The Iron Triangle is often used to describe the triple constraint of project management—balancing time, cost, schedule, and sometimes quality dynamics.

You have scheduled your first session with the Scrum Master and, after two cancellations, are finally going to meet.

Opening Moves
- Set metaskills before the session: curiosity, courage, clarity, empathy.
- Turn up your emotional intelligence (EQ), listening intently to the emotional field.
- Establish a coaching agreement.
- Enter with Coaching stance.

Middle Game
- Explore:
  - Check their awareness of the behavior and the impact within the team.
  - Perhaps share an agile maturity model (Shu Ha Ri).
  - What do they feel they are responsible for vs. what the team is responsible for?
  - What are the driving forces for the behavior?
- Switch to Guiding Learning stance and discuss the role of the Scrum Master per the *Scrum Guide*, asking them to identify ways their actions align and do not align currently.
- Switch back to Coaching stance and ask what about the role as defined does not seem authentic to them.

Endgame
- Explore specific actions to take based on information obtained during session. (Get agreement to observe Scrum events; create what about the Scrum Master role is most challenging and least challenging for them and why?)
- Checkpoint in two weeks for feedback?

FIGURE 35. Role-based Coaching Arc: Scrum Master, first conversation

Preparation

It is always critical to enter with a genuine desire to build an authentic relationship with folks who have not sought out coaching but are being asked to submit to it. Providing a safe and respectful space that encourages open communication and sharing is like adding a spoonful of sugar to medicine—it makes it go down a little easier.

You'll want to keep the coaching agreement light but pointed, making sure to get the goals and rules of the engagement established. You also want to reinforce the client's shift away from being forced and toward owning the sessions and their own outcomes. One of my goals is to provide an environment that will move the person as quickly as possible to being a willing participant in their coaching journey.

Commentary

The key focus for this arc was to establish a coaching agreement and a shared understanding of what the role of Scrum Master is and is not. The shared understanding provides the foundation for subsequent sessions and lays the groundwork for a healthy coaching relationship. Agreeing on specific action items or homework promotes continued focus on areas discussed during the session.

Depending on how the conversation goes, if your client is being forced to attend a coaching session you may have to move to a more prescriptive or consultative stance in order to get established action items or next steps. It is helpful to think through possible pivots or side moves when entering this type of session.

We're going to explore two more possible arcs that could follow from this one: the first is a move to ongoing coaching and growth, and the second involves resistance or struggling to shift into the new role.

The Journey Continues

Two weeks have passed. The Scrum Master has realized that they are still largely operating within their previous role of project manager. They have asked for additional coaching to try and address this gap and to get more comfortable with their new role.

Preparation

You may want to re-establish the coaching agreement, or at the very least revisit the goals and desired outcomes for the engagement. You may want to take time before the session to gather supporting materials (blogs, articles, podcasts) related to the struggle of moving from command-and-control to servant leader. This will allow you to brush up on the topic and be prepared to make quality recommendations.

Above all, you need to enter as a cheerleader, aware and supportive of your client's willingness to change. It will be very tempting for them to fall back into old habits, especially in the beginning, so applauding any positive progress is vital.

Opening Moves
- Set metaskills before the session: curiosity, courage, empathy, positive intent.
- Refer to coaching agreement.
- Establish the goal for this coaching session. Where do we start?
- Enter with Coaching stance.

Middle Game
- Explore:
  - What parts of the Scrum Master role do you feel you are excelling at? Which parts bring you joy? Why?
  - What about the Scrum Master role do you find most challenging?
  - What are you hanging on to from your old role that you need to let go of? Why are you hanging on to it?
- What do you want to try, stop, start? What experiments might you want to run?

Endgame
- What action items do they want to commit to working on?
- What additional support, if any, do they need from your coaching?
- Checkpoint in two weeks?

FIGURE 36. Role-based Coaching Arc: Scrum Master, second conversation

Commentary

The key focus in this Coaching Arc was to establish goals for the long-term coaching engagement and applaud the courage it takes to ask for and accept coaching. Change is tremendously difficult, so it is important that you take every opportunity to encourage the effort and the decision to embrace it. This is a common situation that requires patience and time for folks to fail forward on their way to feeling comfortable in their new role.

An Alternate Journey

Two weeks have passed. You have observed several of the team's Scrum events and have witnessed firsthand the Scrum Master's command-and-control behavior. The Scrum Master is clearly resisting or struggling with the shift to the servant leader aspect of the new role, and shows no real concern for how the team is being affected, remaining sternly focused on managing the work and the team and on driving results.

The Scrum Master's manager, who first engaged you to change the Scrum Master's behavior in the team, is now putting pressure on you to "coach them up." To be honest, you feel a bit like you're doing their job in coaching the Scrum Master's performance, but you're willing to give it a go. Why? Well, because you're the organization's agile coach.

Preparation

The priority in this scenario is ensuring that you have clearly communicated your observations to the manager responsible for initiating the coaching engagement. Arriving at a clear strategy is imperative. You are now partnering with the leader to coach and mentor the Scrum Master, so arriving at an approach together will allow you to serve in the most authentic away. Things covered in this meeting may include whether the manager should join the session, whether the situation calls for continued exploration or you have enough evidence to be more direct and prescriptive, and what outcomes or options you want to coach toward.

In this scenario, the leader has decided they would like you to conduct another session with the Scrum Master. They also want you to be much more consultive and prescriptive about the expectations of the role. If you are new to having crucial conversations where real truth and candor are required, it may help to run through a coaching dojo with a fellow coach so you can practice moving in and out of different stances while communicating this tough message.[26] Experimenting with phrasing and with different ways to explain a point can be amazingly helpful and can set you up to coach through the minefield of high emotion and conflict more effectively.

Opening Moves
- Set metaskills before the session: curiosity, courage, empathy, positive intent.
- Refer to the coaching agreement.
- Establish the goal for this coaching session: Where do we start?
- Switch from Coaching stance to Advising stance.

Middle Game
- Explore:
  - How do you feel it has gone over the last two weeks?
  - What successes do you feel you have had? Failures?
  - Any aha moments since our last session about the role of Scrum Master as detailed in the Scrum Guide?
- What behaviors are not aligned with the Scrum Master role as it is defined by Scrum Guide?
- Are you interested in aligning with the Scrum Master Role? In other words, are you interested in changing the way you work with the team?

Endgame
- Switch back to Coaching stance.
- Define next steps together based on outcomes of Middle Game.
- What additional support, if any, do they need from the coach?
- Check point in two weeks?

FIGURE 37. Role-based Coaching Arc: Scrum Master, third conversation

You may also take some time to think through methods for calling a break if you feel emotions have gone beyond a productive level, so

---

26. We explore the notion of a coaching dojo for practice in chapter 18.

you don't have to stumble through calling for a cool-down break. Remember, you are ultimately serving your client (the Scrum Master) and are responsible for providing a productive and safe space. Therefore, you have every right to call a halt to sessions where that is no longer possible.

Commentary

As a coach, once you have determined the person you are coaching is not ready or interested in working on changes to their behavior, you must prepare to wrap up the engagement. This case is a bit more complicated because you are partnering with the Scrum Master's direct supervisor, but even in this situation you are responsible for deciding whether continued coaching is the right approach.

In this situation you may have a breakthrough that opens the door to a productive coaching engagement, or you might end with the Scrum Master having no desire to change or align with their role. You may discover that this Scrum Master might better serve themselves and the organization by pursuing agile project management and end up coaching them through that journey. You must be prepared to deal with all eventualities and realize that neither is good or bad; they are simply outcomes of a successful coaching session.

You also need to be prepared to have a crucial conversation with the manager. In this case, your role as coach needs to shift behind their role in coaching an employee's performance. In a way, they've used you to do their job for them. You'll need to shift them toward being the primary and responsible coach.

Product Managers and Product Owners

I have held every role on a Scrum team, including product owner, which gives me a unique perspective when coaching each role. My time as a product owner was not the most enjoyable. I didn't have any real passion for the job, and it showed. So, when I began coaching full time, my initial inclination was to avoid coaching product owners because I felt I didn't know enough or hadn't been good enough in the role to be an effective coach.

Fortunately, two folks who loved product ownership and had a real passion for it landed in my journey and asked me to coach them on some agile mindset areas they were struggling with. I shadowed them for several weeks, watching them do the job, acting as a second set of hands, and serving them. Over time, I became fascinated with the role, and before I knew it, I was coaching other product owners—all thanks to those two who had taught me to appreciate the joy and complexity of the role.

The New Product Owner

This is a conversation where I was asked to jump in and coach a brand-new product owner who was extremely enthusiastic but had zero agile or product ownership experience. You may ask why the Scrum Master was not assisting this poor person. As it often happens, I *was* the Scrum Master as well as the coach, and the only one at that point with any real agile experience. Yet more reason for us to coach and support Scrum Masters as the coaches and leaders they are and must be prepared to be.

Preparation

Knowing that you are going to start from ground zero and will most likely be in a Guiding Learning stance, dusting off your go-to training materials would be a good place to start. If teaching is not your favorite stance or one you feel most confident in, look for videos that cover some of the basic topics to support discussion and fill in gaps—or simply to provide you some space when covering topics.

When teaching someone from the beginning, I have found it is best not to overwhelm them, but rather to walk alongside them at a pace comfortable for them. Keep it simple and take your time, letting their curiosity or sense of exploration guide your teaching and mentoring.

Finally, I would spend a few moments reminding myself of why you are working in agile and why you feel it is the best way to work.

Badass Role-Based Coaching 251

When working with someone just beginning their agile journey, it is imperative that you ramp up your enthusiasm and that they feel your belief and passion for it. Change is hard and learning something new can be daunting when you're an adult with other responsibilities, so having someone excited about starting that journey goes a long way.

Opening Moves
- Set metaskills before the session: curiosity, courage, positive intent, empathy, active listening.
- Establish coaching agreement.
- Enter with Coaching stance.

Middle Game
- Explore:
  - What about this role excites you?
  - What about it makes you uneasy or concerned?
  - If you could get your arms around one thing, what would it be?
- Remaining in your Coaching stance, ask them to describe what success in their new role looks like to them.
- Moving to Guiding Learning stance, begin as simply as possible, talking through the one thing or area they feel is most important to learn or tackle.

Endgame
- Return to Coaching stance.
- Explore specific actions to take based on information obtained during session.
- Checkpoint interval determined and scheduled.

FIGURE 38. Role-based Coaching Arc: New Product Owner

Commentary

The key focus for this arc was to provide encouragement and support for the beginning of the product owner's agile journey. I would spend as little time as possible on the coaching agreement, scaling it down to a simple explanation of the stance you may use and how as a Scrum Master you will be partnering with them throughout. This allows more time for understanding fully what they feel is the most important thing for them to know or learn. If you begin to coach based on a training schedule or take a canned "how to start your agile journey" approach you may end up like I did, with a disinterested, frustrated audience.

Imagine that during this session the product owner says they would feel so much better if they simply had a way to get the ideas for the product out of their head and into some form of organized state. Voilà! We have story mapping for that right? Wait, don't we have to start with user stories and acceptance criteria? Nope, grab your stickies and begin with one of the many story mapping exercises[27] to explain the principle, and then let them write one-line descriptions of what how one type of user might use their product. Remember, this is their journey, and you are serving them; if they are stressed because they do not have an organized view of how a user might use the product, that is where you begin.

You will also notice that the checkpoint interval is up for discussion during this session. Be flexible, letting the action items and discussion guide you in recommending frequency. People react differently to stress, so where one newbie may gain confidence from daily interactions, another may feel even more inept and unprepared. In the end, it is a journey, and you can always adjust along the way.

The Experienced Product Owner

Now we will move on to an example of coaching a more experienced product owner, to demonstrate the need to move from one stance to another and the challenge and joy of joining folks on their journey.

This coaching conversation is with a product owner who has been in the role for a couple of years and has simply become overallocated. They have become almost totally focused on the outward aspects of the role and are struggling to find time with their team, especially on backlog refinement. Any time spent on the backlog leads to additional

---

27. www.agilesparks.com/blog/wake-up-in-the-morning-game/.

hours required to get their other jobs completed, which just digs the hole even deeper.

The problem is, this overallocation is drastically impacting the team, their results, and their morale. In an attempt to be all things to all people, the product owner is not only doing themselves a disservice but also their team and organization. Most worrying is that the team seems to be totally disengaging, which is becoming very visible to everyone.

Opening Moves
- Set metaskills before the session: curiosity, courage, positive intent, empathy, active listening.
- Establish coaching agreement.
- Enter with Coaching stance.

Middle Game
- Explore:
  - How did we get here? Talk through their journey over the last year.
  - What do they feel they are responsible for vs. what they feel was forced on them?
  - What activities bring joy to them at work? What drags them down?
- Remaining in your Coaching stance, ask them to describe their ideal day at work. What would the perfect balance be across their multiple responsibilities?
- Move to Guiding Learning (teaching) stance and cover work-in-progress techniques and prioritization approaches that are helpful for managing competing tasks.

Endgame
- Return to Coaching stance.
- Explore specific actions to take based on information obtained during session.
- Checkpoint in two weeks for feedback?

FIGURE 39. Role-based Coaching Arc: Experienced Product Owner

Preparation

If it has been a while since you have worked with product owners, you will want to brush up on all things related to this role before entering this coaching session. Understanding the role fully will help you to have empathy for what they deal with day-to-day. Knowing that this is potentially about time management or the ability to limit work in progress, I would probably spend some time focused on those areas as well—again, so you will have what you need to serve your client fresh and ready to go.

Finally, I would spend a few moments reminding myself to be open to whatever direction the session takes in service of the client, not holding on too tightly to any of the prep work.

Commentary

The key focus for this arc was to establish a coaching agreement and a shared understanding of what the client's day-to-day reality looks like. Understanding fully what a day in their life at work feels like allows you to better empathize and approach coaching the person and not the situation. If you begin to coach the situation, you will almost always fall into the trap of fixer. The key is providing space for the client to verbalize the problem and to continue with curiosity, peeling back layer after layer until they arrive at the aha moment, continuing to dig until they find the root of the problem.

This aha might not happen in the first session. In this situation, it took three sessions for the product owner to finally realize they struggled to say no to anything or anyone asking them for help. They had volunteered for committees, agreed to mentor junior employees, and taken on many other activities, leading to a full calendar and little to no time to do their real job.

After a couple sessions, we had a good understanding and visual of all the things taking up room on their calendar along with their assigned priority. While reflecting on the full days, I asked them to identify anything they had not willingly committed to. That question led to the realization that they were responsible for their own calendar nightmare. The actions defined at the end of that session began to offer real relief from the situation. They took steps to meet with their leadership and work with them to reduce their workload to a manageable amount and had tough conversations with various groups and teammates about their need to cut back on their volunteer services for a while.

It is always a balancing act deciding whether and when to move out of a pure coaching stance. In this case I realized during the first session that my client was willingly taking on too much, but I chose to remain in a coaching stance, allowing them to arrive at that realization through their own exploration and reflection. In other cases, you may deem it too risky or even irresponsible to remain in a coaching stance. There is no hard and fast rule. It takes intuition and experience, and sometimes you fail and make the wrong call. That is a part of being a human coach coaching humans.

Leaders

I spent a great deal of time complaining about and/or judging the decisions of those in leadership roles above me during the early days of my developer career. I still remember the first time I was moved into a leadership position and the tables were turned. I felt like I should send apology notes to all my previous managers, realizing I had in many cases judged them and their decisions unfairly.

This experience enables me to have greater empathy and a real passion for supporting leaders along their agile journey.

The Chief Financial Officer

This coaching conversation is with a chief financial officer that has requested time to discuss questions related to forecasting and estimation techniques that the organization is beginning to use. This is the first time you are meeting this leader and the meeting is scheduled for 30 minutes.

Preparation

Anytime you are going to coach someone in a leadership role, you need to do so with care. Leaders need empathy and safety as much as, if not more than, all the other roles. Our society normally doesn't reward leaders for admitting they don't know something, while in other roles there is much more acceptance of admitting ignorance or failure. Understanding that will help you to approach the Guiding Learning stance much more responsibly.

Still, I would think through clear, concise examples of how agile estimation and forecasting work and can be applied. I would also be prepared to discover the question behind the question—what isn't this leader hearing or getting that they need?

Also be mindful of the 30-minute time block. That can be a powerful indicator of style or of the priority this the leader places on this.

Opening Moves
- Set metaskills before the session: curiosity, courage, empathy.
- Enter with Coaching stance.

Middle Game
- Explore:
  - What brings us here today?
  - What questions do you have about agile estimation/forecasting?
  - Is there information you feel you are not getting? *[handwritten: Seems like a powerful question]*
  - Is there a better way to convey or present the teams' delivery information?
- Move to Guiding Learning (teaching) stance, providing examples of how agile estimation and forecasting can be effectively used.

Endgame
- Return to Coaching stance.
- Explore specific actions to take based on information obtained during the session.
- Checkpoint in two weeks for feedback?

FIGURE 40. Role-based Coaching Arc: Chief Financial Officer

Commentary

The key focus for this arc was to build some trust and establish the foundation for an ongoing relationship where coaching could be more productive. Notice that I didn't establish a coaching agreement. At this point the leader hasn't requested coaching, so it is appropriate to exclude that and simply use the brief time available to discover how you can best serve them. Trying to uncover the real reason for the meeting or the question behind the question is another key to this conversation. In this example, I discovered the leader truly didn't understand relative estimation and was sincerely interested in learning about it.

Moving to a Guiding Learning (teaching) stance and providing the appropriate level of detail here is key. You might offer more coaching or next steps, allowing the leader to decide whether they need further sessions or if they want to take any further action on this topic. It is crucial that you do not push but rather let them pull you into areas they are ready to or feel the need to work on.

The Chief Product Owner

This coaching conversation is tied to the overallocated product owner previously discussed. Often when coaching teams, it is necessary for you to reach out and work with the leadership directly involved to truly support their agile journey. In this case, you have met with the chief product owner (CPO) twice, established a coaching agreement, and established some measure of trust and partnership, but up until now the CPO has been reluctant to discuss anything related to solutions or action items.

Preparation

This being your third meeting with no real action items, you should be ready to revisit the coaching agreement, clearly communicating the need for acknowledgment of a problem or challenge that you will be attempting to focus on together. In the absence of that agreement, further coaching is a waste of time and money. Remember, coaching is meant to be a pull system, not a push system. No matter how clearly others see the challenge, if the CPO is not ready to acknowledge or deal with it there is nothing more to be done until they decide it's worth time and energy. The sooner you address this, the better. Remember, it doesn't mean they will never want to work on it, merely that they just aren't there yet.

Understanding that will help you to prepare for the discussion without emotion and with empathy for and understanding of the CPO's feelings and current perspective. You may want to spend some time thinking of exploratory questions that might help them feel comfortable or encouraged to make the move and begin taking action, no matter how small, to effect some helpful change in the organization. Modeling this servant coaching stance is one of the ways we demonstrate true agile coaching hearts to our agile teams.

Opening Moves
- Set metaskills before the session: curiosity, courage, empathy.
- Enter with Coaching stance.

Middle Game
- Explore:
    - What challenge or problem do you want to tackle today?
    - Do you think this challenge is something needing your attention and time right now?
- Revisit the coaching agreement based on what is discovered from above.

Endgame
- Explore specific actions to take based on information obtained during the session.
- Checkpoint in two weeks for feedback?

FIGURE 41. Role-based Coaching Arc: Chief Product Officer

Commentary

The key focus for this arc was to determine what, if anything, the CPO wanted to tackle. Notice that the coaching agreement discussion was held until after we did some exploration. Normally we would do this in the beginning, but in this instance, we needed more information first.

During this discussion, the CPO communicated a need to understand agile better to be able to properly lead the product owners. This leader admitted struggling to understand what product owners did and why, since their own front-line experience didn't involve agile ways of working. This led to action items as well as a new coaching agreement with more frequent check-ins.

Notice also that I didn't move out of coaching stance during the session. Although we discussed that training was needed, the real need for this session was clarity around the actions the CPO was truly ready to take—meeting them where they are. Not pushing but adjusting alongside them at their pace.

The nugget here is that we have a glimpse of how, as coaches of leaders, we get to create agile coaching leaders and partners. Our goal with leaders should always be for them to be able to provide agile coaching and leadership independent of us.

Wrapping Up

When practicing role-based coaching, possessing a keen understanding of the role and a true empathy for its complexity is crucial. I make it a point to spend time revisiting the specific role definition and to think through my own experiences in that role before entering a coaching session. This exercise allows me to settle in beside them as a partner on their journey, and I believe it makes me more effective in serving them.

If you have never served in the particular role you are being asked to coach, I would recommend that you find ways to gain some firsthand experience before attempting to coach this role. Following are a few ways I've used to gain experience and feel more qualified to do role-based coaching:

- **Pair.** Actively pair with someone doing that role throughout the day. I call this "dynamic duo" style.

- **Observe and shadow.** Follow someone around, actively taking notes that you review and discuss with the person each day.
- **Volunteer.** I have volunteered to lead training, facilitate executive meetings, scribe for committees and product owners, and so on, simply to gain experience.

In the end, experiment to find what ways feel authentic and give you the confidence to coach the roles within your coaching sphere. Remember, it is a journey, and failures are always an option to learn and grow your competency.

15

Badass Context-Based Coaching

Coaching is like a dance where the coach leads by choosing the appropriate stance and then begins moving seamlessly through the session, pivoting and changing directions in rhythm with the music and the other dancers. Context is to coaching what music is to dance. Context can quickly alter which stance you take, much like a dancer ready to waltz would have to adjust if the band began to play a salsa or select a different pattern or step if the music tempo changes during a song. In dancing, the more experience you have, the more comfortable you get with navigating different rhythms and musical styles. Similarly, the more you get comfortable with context changes, gaps, and nuances as a coach, the more effective and enjoyable your coaching will be.

Coaching without context is a lot like dancing without music. You can certainly coach with little to no context, and must do it sometimes, but it is important to quickly begin to gather context for our coaching to best serve our clients. Jennifer is now going to lead us through an exploration of context and

> how to adapt and smoothly move through our coaching sessions as context changes or evolves.

Introduction

You can't pay attention to everything while you're coaching, but one of the things that separates a mediocre coach from a Badass Agile Coach is their system awareness and ability to handle multiple contexts in a very rhythmic, fluid way.

In this chapter, we're going to explore contexts that may be relevant in your client coaching.

- **Client Maturity.** How skilled is the client, and how much experience do they have? What role do they play, and what is their overall personal or social maturity?
- **History with the Client.** Consider your history with the client and their history with you. How often and how long have you been coaching them? What has the journey been like so far?
- **Client Self-Awareness and Comfort Zone.** What is the client's level of self-awareness? Where are their comfort zones when it comes to specific topics, actions, and issues? The client's level of emotional intelligence (EQ) is also part of the equation here.
- **Client Stressors and Risks (Safety).** It's important to listen for and understand specific stresses and risks the client is experiencing, both real and perceived.
- **Levels of Self-Care (Yours and Your Client's).** Have you taken care of yourself lately? Are you fully charged and ready to coach? And what is the client's level of self-care? Are they in a position to be coached effectively?
- **Organizational and Business Visibility and Impact.** Where is the client in the organizational hierarchy? What is their overall influence and impact? (This can be two separate things.)
- **Culture and Norms.** Consider the client's ecosystem, from the more direct influences such as their boss or team to the overall organizational culture. Has anything happened within the ecosystem that might impact your coaching?

- **Personal.** Finally, and probably most importantly, consider the client's personal ecosystem. What season are they in? Have they had any significant life changes recently? How much change have they been experiencing? Where are they in the Satir Change Model? Lean heavily into your EQ for these answers.

This isn't a complete list, of course. Your coaching context is affected by a myriad of factors. But this can easily become a list you quickly review before beginning a coaching session. I strongly recommended that you develop or adopt a checklist like this one to activate your contextual radar to begin searching the landscape before each client coaching conversation. You'll notice immediately how it helps broaden your awareness. You can begin with the list in this chapter and add others you uncover or find helpful. Reviewing this list before a session and considering possible scenarios or directions the session may take allows me to move more seamlessly between stances and better serve my clients. Spending time familiarizing yourself with your client in this way will help to ensure you enter the session with authentic empathy and seeking positive intent.

Many times, especially early on, you may not know very much about your client, so entering with little to no context should become familiar territory. Being prepared with exploratory questions when you begin the opening moves of your Coaching Arc allows you to discover and explore context that future coaching sessions can build on. I will often leave my clients with self-reflection homework after the first session, to encourage them to be active partners in creating a shared context as it relates to the topics covered.

I review every session as soon as possible, filling in any pertinent information related to the context categories we covered in the session as well as any new discoveries I might want to explore next time. Doing this immediately after the session is best, but even if you do it hours or days later, don't skip this post-arc activity. Often, the smallest nugget captured produces the greatest returns in the future.

First, Know Thyself

Before we enter your client's context, we need to explore one other very important context—yours.

As a Badass Agile Coach, you will start any coaching session, with either an individual or group, by asking yourself a few questions:

- What happened to me today that might influence my coaching mindset with this client? How might I release that before I begin?
- What is my current mindset with respect to coaching? Am I energized or exhausted? Am I frustrated or balanced? Am I open or closed? (Remember, how we show up impacts our coaching presence.)
- How ready am I for this coaching session? Are there blind spots or biases I need to address? (Perhaps ask another coach or a trusted colleague how ready they think you are, as a self-awareness check.)
- What are my motivations for this coaching engagement? Am I in a client-first mindset? One of service, being present, and courage?

This is best done privately, as self-reflection, and should become a part of your coaching routine.

Now let's try walking through some of our previous arcs, taking into consideration the context categories.

Team Lead Troubles (Scenario 1)

Let's begin with a coaching conversation with the team lead from chapter 4. This person is overly protective of their knowledge and experience and unwilling to work well with the team. In other words, they're incredibly dominant.

You've had three coaching conversations to date, but there hasn't been a significant change in his behavior. The team brought it up as an impediment (#1) in the last retrospective, and the team lead walked out, upset about being "called out." This is your follow-up arc to that.

When preparing for the session, you review your checklist and choose a few context categories that will help you enter with a more well-rounded picture of the client. As you move through sessions you will return to the context list and add information. Below are the results of your current review:

- **History with the Client.** After three previous coaching sessions, observed team events and had conversations with Scrum Master. Witnessed client walking out of a highly charged retro after team complained about his actions and attitude.
- **Client Stressors and Risks (Safety).** Seems unable to let go of control—may be something there related to fear of failure or not meeting expectations of his leadership.
- **Culture and Norms.** May be helpful to better understand his functional manager's view of the lead role, as up to this point, I have been coaching the team and have little interaction with his functional manager.
- **Personal.** Has been extremely guarded in past sessions and still does not appear to be on board with coaching or discussing anything even remotely personal. May explore this some as well.

With this context, we can now enter the Coaching Arc with an idea of what questions we want to focus on and which areas we want to explore to best serve the client. Notice that we are not entering focused on the complaints but rather on helping him communicate his perceptions and feelings about his current work environment. We are not ignoring the information we received from our previous sessions or the team, but we are giving the client the benefit of assuming positive intent, respecting his journey, and allowing him space to voice his views and feelings without judgment. Here are a few questions that might accomplish this:

- What do you enjoy about your current role?
- How do you feel you serve your team?
- Do you feel your manager's expectations align with working in an agile way?

Armed with these questions, you make your opening moves. His answer to the first question is, "I like leading and being the final decision maker. I like figuring out how best to organize the work and assign it to team members in a way that gets the most done." Now, that is some real context, isn't it?

You follow up with your next question, about serving the team, and he takes a moment, seeming a bit stumped. Now you're getting some richer data. Could it be he does not understand that his behavior violates a major principle of working on an agile team? He finally answers, "I'm leading and directing the team because I need to help them deliver on time."

Got it. Time to pivot to a more advisory stance and ask how that aligns with agile principles and working on a self-managing, self-organized team.

This being your third session, you should be prepared to clearly speak to what about his behavior is negatively affecting the team, with the hope being he participates in the discussion. Once you have identified what about his current approach needs to change, you switch back to the coaching stance and ask your final question for the session: Does he feel his leadership's expectations of him are in alignment with the way of working you have discussed during the session?

How you end the session would depend on the answer to that question. If he says, "No, my manager has instructed me to make sure we deliver on time," your next moves would be different than if you get a simple "Yes." If he feels his manager's expectations are not in alignment with working on an agile team, you may simply end with an action item to schedule a session where the three of you can discuss this and arrive at a go forward plan. Otherwise, you would work to identify changes he would need to begin working on to effectively work with his team, making it clear that doing nothing would no longer be acceptable.

With the session over, you return to your context notes and make updates accordingly. You may schedule time with his immediate manager to verify whether the manager is aligned with working in an agile way. Once you have established the manager's perspective you will be able to plan your next moves. Remember to jot down questions you may want to ask in the next session, as well as any hunches or observations made during this session.

This may seem like a lot of unnecessary work, but I assure you it is worth the effort and will add a great deal to the quality of your coaching. After you've done it a few times, you will arrive at your own kind of shorthand and your own context list, falling into a rhythm that no longer feels like additional work.

Team Lead Troubles (Scenario 2)

Just for fun, let's rewind and look at the same scenario from above, where the context categories reveal a different picture, resulting in an entirely different coaching session and outcomes.

In preparing for your session, you spend some time filling in as much context as you can.

- **History with the Client.** After three previous coaching sessions, observed team events and had conversations with Scrum Master. Witnessed client walking out of a highly charged retro where team complained about his actions and attitude.
- **Client Stressors and Risks (Safety).** Client has a new boss who, based on feedback from others, is extremely agile minded.
- **Culture and Norms.** A quick break room conversation with the new boss confirms that he enthusiastically supports agile leadership and wants to meet to discuss how he can better coach his team members.
- **Personal.** Has been extremely guarded in past sessions and still does not appear to be on board with coaching or discussing anything even remotely personal. May explore this some as well.

Notice how a little context can have a huge effect on how we prepare for and approach a session. The information that the client has a new boss that is extremely agile minded leads to our altering the questions we enter with. What does not change is the fact that you enter without forming an opinion or having judgment; rather, you are simply better prepared, with a richer understanding of the situation. Considering all of this, you adjust your questions to explore the impact of the new highly agile boss:

- What do you enjoy about your current role?
- How do you feel you serve your team?
- Do you enjoy working on an agile team and working in alignment with agile principles?
- Do you think you are in alignment with your leadership?

Let's assume the first two questions are answered the same as in the previous scenario: He likes to be in charge, to be the brains for the team, and he sees driving the team to deliver on time as serving them. If the session ended at that point, you would probably be looking at either having a very candid discussion around how that doesn't align with working on an agile team, or at the very least discussing action items for him to spend some time thinking about how his actions are not aligned and what impact that might be having on the team.

The real change comes with the new questions.

If you ask whether he enjoys the agile approach and the lead says, "No, I think agile is a waste of time and not the best way to get things done," you would at the very least need to confront the fact that he is not aligned with the organizational direction. You may also suggest he reach out to his leadership to discuss this further, and you would let him know you would be discussing the outcome with his leadership. If he says, "Yes, I think agile is great, but not the way we are doing it," then you would need to pivot to explore the disconnect and determine whether training and or additional coaching could close the gap. Again, it is all about context and your ability to seamlessly change direction based on what is discovered during the session.

What happens if you move on to the final question, about alignment, and he says, "No, I'm not in alignment with my manager"? This is a real scenario I have encountered. It's a tricky one. You need to tread carefully, ensuring you are supporting the client you are coaching as well as the agile leader he works for. I find adopting a strong coaching stance with very open questions can be extremely helpful in this situation. It allows the client to feel safe to share as much or little as they want about their current relationship with their leadership without your opinions or judgment getting in the way.

When I encountered this scenario, the question I asked that led to the discovery was "What does your new boss expect from you?" His answer was, "He expects me to know everything about agile and how to lead agile teams." In this case, the lack of real agile experience and knowledge was stressing out the lead, who felt his new boss expected him to be further along and better at the job, with more agile experience and mindset then he possessed. Interestingly, his resistance did not arise from lack of support or lack of desire to work in an agile way, but rather from having a very experienced agile leader who made him feel like a failure. We co-created action items that the lead agreed to, and future coaching session were scheduled. And my next stop was—you guessed it—the office of the client's boss, where, as promised during our earlier break room conversation, I joined him on his journey.

This session ended completely differently than the first scenario and required different pivots and stances, all due to some differences in context. I find it useful sometimes to play with context and run exercises or coaching dojos by changing real-life scenarios to practice pivots and strategies. But to do this effectively, you must do the work of jotting down context notes and maintaining them throughout the coaching engagement.

Overallocated Product Owner

Let's move to another scenario and explore some additional context categories.

This coaching conversation is tied to the overallocated product owner we coached in chapter 14. You have met twice with the product owner's direct supervisor, the chief product owner (CPO), and have established a coaching agreement and some measure of trust and partnership, but the CPO has been reluctant to discuss anything related to solutions or action items. Meanwhile, the product owner you are coaching is still completely overallocated and unable to effectively support their team. You have coached the product owner to better manage their calendar, but in order for real, lasting change to occur the CPO will need to get actively involved in leading and coaching the product owner.

Preparing for the next conversation, you pull up your context categories, reviewing and updating to better ensure you leave the session with real tangible action items or an agreement to discontinue the coaching. After some digging, you find out new details about the CPO's tenure and work habits that you feel might need further exploration.

- **History with the Client.** Two previous 30-minute sessions, very friendly and agreeable but reluctant to act or even truly acknowledge the problem.
- **Levels of Self-Care.** Works 80+ hours a week routinely. Known for being first in and last out of the office.
- **Culture and Norms.** New to this company and role. Although the overall culture is agile, is the CPO's only exposure to an agile culture his present position?
- **Personal.** Empty nester with freedom to work many hours. Enjoys time at the office and loves new challenge?
- **Organizational and Business Visibility and Impact.** C-level, high visibility, new hire and role (within the last year).

Having this additional context, you craft the following questions:

- What about working with agile teams are you enjoying? What do you find challenging?
- What about the agile culture do you enjoy most? What is concerning?
- How do you feel you serve your product owners and their teams?

You ask the first question, and the CPO surprises you by enthusiastically stating he loves working with agile teams and, so far, it has not been challenging at all. Hmm, let's keep going with the follow-up question about the culture. Once again, he raves about how great the culture is. So you ask your third question, about how he serves his product owners and their teams. He appears confused. "What do you mean, 'How do I serve the product owners and teams?' They work for me."

Your work has paid off and allowed you to use the context to focus in on a possible reason the CPO continues to ignore the product owner's overallocation. You quickly ruled out that he was opposed to agile so, without being obvious, you discover he simply does not understand how the role of an agile leader is different from that of a traditional leader. This is a huge discovery that, coupled with what you know about his work hours and love of spending time at the office, explains how he would not pick up on others' overallocation being his issue—or even an issue at all.

Did you catch that? This is something else to explore, but in another session.

For now, you must pivot but tread lightly because, as discussed before, leaders do not always feel comfortable admitting they do not know something. Keep it simple and explain that agile teams see their leaders as folks who actively support and lead them to greater productivity. Then let it sit and give him space to absorb and think through that before asking your next question. Sometimes the silence can feel excruciating but as a coach it is vital that you get comfortable with silence and allow space for folks to think and process.

You ask the question again: "How do you feel you serve your product owners and their teams?"

I know it sounds strange, but this might be a good time to move on to action items where he can focus on what he can begin doing, without having to openly discuss what he needs to stop doing. I believe that keeping the focus on positive actions, especially early on, is the best approach. You may even suggest shadowing him over a couple days so you can gain greater context and understanding of his needs and how you can better serve him.

And now—you guessed it! —you need to go back and update the context sheet. And remember to loop back to your curiosity around the possible tie between his hours and time spent at the office and his lack of awareness that others' situations may be different.

Assuming Positive Intent

One of the most important contexts for entering *any* Coaching Arc is assuming positive intent on the part of your client.

I don't know about you, but I can often bring in baggage around what I've heard or been told about a client. Or what I've observed myself and used to assume some intent on their part. It's incredibly important to clear this out before you coach. I often leverage my metaskills to do that. Here's a story that illustrates the importance of maintaining your assumption of positive intent.

I once got a request to coach someone who, according to his manager and the several complaints in his file, was a lost cause. This person's performance had dropped considerably in recent months, and he was completely unable to work with others. Looking back, I think that I was brought in as a formality to satisfy an HR checkbox before firing him. I knew little about this person so when I went through the context activity prior to his session there was little information. Based on that, I assumed positive intent, curious to unpack the why behind his behavior. I prepared some questions to explore whether he understood how negatively his performance and actions were being perceived, as well as questions geared toward trying to figure out if there was something else going on that might provide answers.

The question that changed everything was, "Over the last few months, what have you done that brought you pure joy or happiness, either at home or work?" His answer was simply, "Nothing."

Think about that. What must be going on with this person that would lead to several months of no joy? I dug deeper, prefacing my next question by saying that if he didn't feel comfortable answering that was fine. Then I asked what, either at home or work, was contributing to a lack of joy. He again said one word.

"Cancer."

I was so thankful that day that I had properly prepared and had entered seeking positive intent and without judgment or an opinion about what had led to his performance drop. The context uncovered during this session moved him from the "lost cause" category to someone who needed support and care. Months later I received an email from him thanking me for my time and for asking the questions he was willing to answer, although he couldn't bring himself to volunteer the same information. I kept that email and read it every now and then to make sure I don't forget how much what I do can matter and how easy it would have been to not enter seeking positive intent.

Wrapping Up

I hope this chapter helped you realize three critical things:

1. Context matters. In the absence of context, seek positive intent.
2. Preparation matters.
3. Post-processing and learning from each coaching conversation matter.

We must remember we are coaching *people* first—not employees, or leaders, or clients, or roles. Spending time painting the full picture of our clients, playing out scenarios and tweaking contexts, running dojos, and so on makes us better coaches, allowing us to more effectively pivot in ways that protect and serve the people entrusted to us. And until we have gained context, we must enter seeking positive intent and without judgment. Remember, being invited to join someone on their journey is a great privilege.

16

Situational Awareness as a Badass Agile Coach

When we explore situational awareness, typically we think of the situation *around* the client—their role, skills, and experience, for example. We rarely think of situational awareness as being what's on the inside of the client, but that is often the most complex and important part of the situation.

For example, where have they come from culturally, what biases have they encountered professionally, and what are their significant life experiences? These can be even more important to understand than what appears around the client. And that's just scratching the service.

Fundamentally, we must treat every client as what they are: a unique person. We need to avoid stereotyping or false groupings or mirroring our own experiences. In order to do this at all levels, we must support increasing our client's self-awareness, while also increasing our own.

> In this chapter, I've invited my daughter Rhiannon Galen-Personick to share on diversity. Rhiannon has spent over 15 years in social work and has a deep and broad understanding of the subject as it relates to employee development, coaching, and leadership. I couldn't think of a better guide to explore the nuance of diversity in your badass agile coaching journey.

Introduction

We've mentioned before in the book that agile coaching is a situational game that requires broad and deep situational awareness. But there are some situations in coaching that I am, and I'm guessing you might be, situationally blind to. Consider this the inside-out view to our increased awareness, where we explore the nature of our clients—what has personally shaped them and their perspectives.

This awareness helps us to achieve badassery in our coaching because it increases our understanding and ability to meet our clients where they are. Now that we have developed our foundation of self-awareness, we are better equipped to assist those that we coach toward their own self-awareness.

So, this chapter is intended to explore the following areas:

- SOGI (sexual orientation and gender/gender identity)
- Neurodiversity
- Generational awareness
- Race, culture, and ethnicity

We can all agree that there are many more areas to understand. We have chosen these diversity aspects to support the coaching relationship and to start you on your own diversity exploration journey.

Breadth of Diversity Experiment

But first, what do you think about diversity? Where are your thoughts and experiences in relation to this broad and deep topic? Let's run a personal experiment.

Get out your journal. If you don't have one, or haven't been journaling, then this is a great opportunity to start. When you think about the word *diversity*, we are often limited by our own world view; our understanding of ourselves and those that we are closest to.

Take a second to write down everything that defines who *you* are as a person. Consider the following as a guide:

- SOGI (sexual orientation and gender/gender identity)
- Neurodiversity
- Generational awareness
- Race, culture, and ethnicity

Which on the list did you immediately consider? Which on the list have you either not heard of or never had to consider before? We will be coming back to these questions.

Now that we have defined who we are, let's dive into some of these characteristics and connect them from your personal self-awareness to how they might be reflected and considered in your client coaching.

Sexual Orientation and Gender/Gender Identity

SOGI is an expansive acronym that expresses a view of each term as a spectrum, versus the traditional binary view. For example, we have traditionally understood sexual orientation to mean gay or heterosexual; it's so important to stretch this to be more inclusive, especially when building relationships. When we see individuals for their whole selves, we can connect on deeper level. Therefore, SOGI includes biological sex, sexual orientation, gender, and gender identity.

Individual Coaching

Let's consider the following scenario: You are a cisgender female coach working with someone that you assume to identify as cisgender male. As your client introduces themselves, they ask that you use they, them, their pronouns. How do you respond?

When connecting to an individual as it relates to SOGI, as always, start with yourself. Think back to your reactions to our earlier activity on capturing your diversity reactions in your journals. What did you write down that fit into SOGI? If you did NOT identify your SOGI, this directly ties to your privilege. When connecting with someone as a coach, it can be terrifying to acknowledge your privilege.

I remember the first time I said "cisgender" to describe myself, along with my pronouns, "she/her/hers." I could feel my cheeks heating up and getting that redness that happens when I feel uncomfortable. However, it was exactly what needed to happen. I needed to sit with my discomfort, sit with the awareness of my privilege. Once we can sit in an uncomfortable place and connect with our privilege, we allow ourselves the chance to grow; growth is the ultimate goal we want to support our clients in achieving, and what better way to do that than by role modeling it.

Team Coaching

Let's consider the following scenario: You are working with a team that consists of seven members, and only one of them identifies as a female. The female team member approaches you one day complaining that there is one team member who continues to be chauvinistic toward them. How do you respond?

First, explore your own bias toward gender and gender expectations. How does your culture and your own gender play a part? Next, don't be afraid to provide transparency toward your bias. This is especially important for those in a position of privilege, such as a male coach working with a female client. If you brush off their complaint, or even redirect their concerns, it will completely invalidate them and your relationship with them.

Last, take time to hear and empathize with the team members' perspective; validation can go a long way in this scenario. I also encourage a good role-play. Remember, when coaching a team, it is not our job to go in and fix the problem, but to do what we can to empower the team member to address it directly.

Explore the following questions in your journal.

Self-Awareness Questions

- What, if any, privilege may I have as it relates to SOGI?
- How might my privilege impact the coaching relationship?
- How prepared am I to speak on my privilege with my client?
- What do I need to be prepared?

Client Questions

Please take note, be flexible and adaptable about when and how you ask these questions, to fit the relationship that you have with your client. Your client may have already answered these questions for you, or you may assess the need to ask based on working with your client for some time.

- What SOGI aspects do you feel are an important part of our coaching relationship?
- How can I support you in the area of SOGI?

Neurodiversity

Neurodiversity doesn't receive enough attention, especially in terms of the workforce and, of course, coaching. All of us have different ways of viewing the world, processing information, and communicating. The technology-driven workplace and the agile community have been a welcoming place for people with neurodiversity, so as a coach we need to become more aware and adept at navigating it during our coaching. It is important to add that the term *neurodiversity* helps destigmatize the various diagnoses that fit into that term.

Following are some of the terms related to neurodiversity. Take some time in your journal to write down the ones that you are *not* aware of, so you can dive into them later. For those that you *are* aware of, write down your initial thoughts/reactions to those terms to build your self-awareness related to potential bias.

- Autism spectrum conditions
- Attention Deficit Hyperactivity/Inattentive Disorder
- General Anxiety Disorder
- Dyslexia

I'm bringing these up solely to increase your self-awareness, and not to ask you to act as a therapist instead of a coach. Awareness here is the first goal, and then bringing that awareness into your coaching relationship with your client. It's important, though, that you don't step too far into an area where you are, respectfully, not qualified.

Individual Coaching

Let's consider the following scenario: You are working with a client that continues to bring concerns to the table that you feel are related to inattentive behaviors. They have not discussed or disclosed anything to you, but you feel that their inattentive behaviors are having an impact on their work.

Before anything, when working with someone who is neurodiverse, we must first understand how they want to be seen by their coach. Often, because of stigma, people are seen first as their diagnosis and second as a person. Some neurodivergent individuals will want their differences to be discussed, and others will not want this a part of the coaching relationship. Allow the individual to let you know who they are and what they want your coaching focus to be as it relates to their diagnosis.

We must also check on our own biases and how they will impact connecting with someone who may struggle to process information in a way that we as a coach are more comfortable with. This means we must adapt even more—our style, our messaging, even our tempo will need to change in order to create a supportive coaching environment.

Team Coaching

Let's consider the following scenario: You are working with a new team and your goal is to dive into some fun initial team building. Your first activity is asking each person to disclose things about themselves that the team needs to know, including what helps you work well within a team.

If your first thought is that the team must know all about each other, then stop for a second and check your privilege. When it comes to something that carries a heavy weight, it is important to allow neurodiverse individuals the space to connect and feel safe, which is the foundation for creating an effective team, before we encourage full disclosure.

Similar to individual coaching, it is important that we allow each person to share what they feel matters to them and what they deem important to share with the team. Focus more on creating strong connections and safety; dive into building empathy for the needs of each individual member to create the space that allows for neurodiversity to thrive.

Self-Awareness Questions

- What are my own cultural/cognitive biases that may exist related to neurodiversity?
- How do I feel about working with someone who is neurodiverse? What positive or negative work experiences have I had that may impact me?
- What knowledge do I have and what more do I need to learn?

Client Questions

Please take note, be flexible and adaptable about when and how you ask these questions, to fit the relationship that you have with your client. Your client may have already answered these questions for you, or you may assess the need to ask based on working with your client for some time.

- How do you need me to see you?
- Do you want for me to provide support in the area of neurodiversity? And how can I do this for you?

Generational Awareness

When I think of generational awareness, the first picture that comes to mind is a newly formed Scrum team with eight members. Two are brand-new to the field, most have a few years of experience, and then there are the so-called veterans, who have been in the field for at least 10 years.

What we are not addressing is the space that exists between the different generations. There are different expectations of work culture, expectations, and of working within each generation that can create conflict. With that being said, often, having various generations working together can create a much richer work experience and help to create beautiful products. We'll consider these generational boundaries:

- Baby boomers (born 1945–1964)
- Generation X (1965–1979)
- Generation Y/Millennials (1980–1994)
- Generation Z (1995–2010)

Individual Coaching

Let's consider the following scenario: You are a boomer coach that just began working with a Gen Zer.

The most interesting thing in terms of working across generations is first understanding how you feel toward each. Think about the leadership culture that each generation connects with; as a leader and coach, how will you adapt to what each generation expects?

There is so much adaptation that will be required here, so much empathy, that we must understand our own style first. Recognize your style, and have an open dialogue with your client about that style and how they might need you to show up. This may sound simple, but it will require a lot of self-disclosure and openness to feedback and adaptation.

Team Coaching

Let's consider the following scenario: You are a millennial coach working with a team that is mostly Gen Zers (and one person who is a boomer).

Working with a team that has various generations can be a gift. Bringing all that knowledge and passion together will be amazing. With that being said, where to start? In the case of generations, I suggest putting it all on the table. The best analogy I have is astrology: Some people are all over their astrological sign, and others are not. Have an open dialogue regarding the definitions of each generation, general characteristics, leadership needs, and so on, and allow the team to dive into what matters to them as individuals and what matters to them as a team.

Self-Awareness Questions

- How do I feel regarding my own generation?
- How do I feel regarding the other generations, specifically their leadership and cultural needs?
- What impacts may I have working with each generation, positive and negative?

Client Questions

Please take note, be flexible and adaptable about when and how you ask these questions, to fit the relationship that you have with your client. Your client may have already answered these questions for you, or you may assess the need to ask based on working with your client for some time.

- How do you see yourself in relation to your generation?
- What do you agree with or disagree with, in terms of the characteristics usually assigned to your generation?

- How do you want generational conversations to show up in our coaching?

Race, Culture, and Ethnicity

Take a second and go back to the list of diversity aspects that you wrote down during your self-awareness check. What areas, if any, did you identify related to race, culture, and ethnicity? Below are some terms to consider. After reviewing the list, consider creating a to-do list as a way to continue gaining self-awareness.

- Racial equity
- Racism
- Intersectionality
- Privilege
- White privilege
- White fragility
- Anti-racism
- Bias (implicit/explicit/social)
- Microaggressions (micro-insults, micro-invalidations, micro-assaults)

Individual Coaching

Let's consider the following scenario: You are a white woman coaching a Black woman, and have been tasked by your manager to address her negative attitude and how she shows up at various meetings.

Yes, you read that right, you are being asked to tell a Black woman that she is being "too angry" during meetings. There is *no* good way to say this without it being a microaggression and having a negative impact on the relationship.

Instead of giving feedback at our next one-to-one, I decided to do a general check-in.

Team Coaching

Let's consider the following scenario: You are working with a group of seven people, one of whom identifies as Black, and one as Latinx. The rest of the team identifies as white.

There are several factors to consider when it comes to team coaching around race, culture, and ethnicity. Let us take a second to reflect by thinking of either your current team or your most recent team. Reflect for a minute on the various members of your team. How do you feel your own race, culture, and ethnicity impacted the work of the team and the teamwork? What may have been the impact of your race on your team members?

The goal of any team is to create a safe culture, one that allows each member to be their authentic self without fear. Facilitate the team in creating a safe space, perhaps beginning with the daily stand-up, where each team member is fully embraced in the event.

For example, when forming a new team, allowing members to share how they identify themselves and/or want to be identified can begin the process of recognizing just how significant race, culture, and ethnicity are for each person.

In terms of the coaching relationship, consider the following questions to gain more self-awareness.

Self-Awareness Questions

- What privilege do you have or not have based on your race, culture, and ethnicity?
- What impact do you have on others that do not have the same privileges you have?
- How do your race, culture, and ethnicity impact those that you coach?
- How does your privilege impact those that you coach?

Client Questions

Please take note, be flexible and adaptable about when and how you ask these questions, to fit the relationship that you have with your client. Your client may have already answered these questions for you, or you may assess the need to ask based on working with your client for some time.

- As your coach, how can I best support you?
- Would you like race to be discussed in our coaching? How would you like it to be discussed?
- What privilege exists for you?
- How do you see race, culture, and ethnicity impacting you in your current role?
- How do your race, culture, and ethnicity impact others?

Wrapping Things Up

As I've said quite a few times throughout this chapter, this has by no means been an exhaustive treatment of diversity as it relates to your coaching. Then why add it, you might ask? Because it's an incredibly important topic for you to weave into your coaching mindset, from two critical perspectives.

The first is increasing your own self-awareness. That's something we perhaps haven't emphasized often enough in this book: looking at yourself honestly and openly and evaluating your own understanding and gaps when it comes to specific coaching situations. I hope that in allowing yourself to reflect on the many questions asked in this chapter, you may also think of other areas of growth to continue to explore!

The second important perspective is bringing that self-awareness to bear in meeting your clients where they are—not where you are or where you are comfortable or where your biases focus you. This will create a container within your coaching sessions that feels safe and allows you and your client to bring your whole selves to each session.

And as a final point, remember that diversity is individual. For example, if you've met one autistic Black woman, then you've met … just one autistic Black woman. When you're coaching, meet each individual and team as the unique and special entities that they are.

Further Reading

I cannot recommend this book enough, along with *all* of Kendi's books: *How to Be an Antiracist* by Ibram X. Kendi (New York: Random House, 2019).

I have this book sitting on my desk now; it was the first book that I read in my own journey toward self-awareness of my privilege: *Why Are All the Black Kids Sitting Together in the Cafeteria?* by Beverly Daniel Tatum (Basic Books, 1997)

If you are looking to really go there with how white privilege looks, then this is a must read: *White Fragility* by Robin DiAngelo (Boston: Beacon Press, 2018)

This is a newer book, but a wonderful read that provides the perspective from a person-centered approach: *Disability Visibility: First-Person Stories from the Twenty-First Century* by Alice Wong (New York: Vintage, 2020)

Here's a wonderful online resource for exploring race, culture, and ethnicity: www.racialequitytools.org/glossary.

Reflections

I want to encourage you to stop and reflect at the end of each section of the book—going back and reviewing to answer these questions.

This section focused on adding and broadening nuance within your coaching. Yes, it might raise the complexity of each coaching conversation, but realize the complexity is already there.

- What were your broader takeaways?
- What might you try as an experiment?

Jennifer spent a great deal of time exploring role-based and context-based coaching scenarios to broaden your awareness in these areas.

- How did that sit with you?
- What adjustments might you make to broaden your situational awareness?

Rhiannon spent some time focusing on adding diversity-based situational awareness to your coaching.

- How did that sit with you?

- What adjustments might you make to broaden your situational awareness?

Take a look at the Wheel-based learning references in our Badass Agile Coaching Repo (registration link in the afterword) and pick two or three books or articles that you're willing to commit to exploring.

Explore some of the ideas and inspiration from this section with your coach. Use them as a sounding board for your growth, experimentation, and learning.

Visualization

I want you to close your eyes and get quiet. Center your attention on the notion of a Badass Agile Coach. That's you. Envision what that looks and feels like.

Think about your typical coaching conversations, stances, and approaches. Now reflect deeply on this section of the book. What adjustments might you want to make in your overall coaching style and approach? Think of it as adding depth and breadth to your coaching, not reinventing it. Another metaphor might be adding seasoning to the recipes of your coaching. You want to spice up your situational awareness just a bit, but not over-season.

And just for fun, run through a few of your own real-world coaching conversations in your mind using these newfound ideas and tactics.

Now open your eyes and jot down those ideas, aspirations, insights, plans, hopes, and dreams in your journal.

Haven't started journaling yet?

Well then, read this: www.agile-moose.com/blog/2019/6/23/journaling-how-to-get-started, and consider using our Agile Coach Journaling Canvas, which you can find in the repo.

IV • Continuous Learning

A Badass Agile Coach's Guide to Starting Your Day

Dojo Practice for the Badass Agile Coach

Setting Up a Badass Agile Coaching Community of Practice

Sharpening Your Badass Saw

17

The Badass Agile Coach's Guide to Starting Your Day

WHAT ARE THE MOST IMPORTANT THINGS FOR ME TO FOCUS ON TODAY?

A lot of coaches consider their day complete when they spend the entire time coaching. A packed schedule full of coaching session after coaching session creates perceived value through, well, coaching. Particularly if you're a consultant or outside coach focusing on billable time.

But just staying busy coaching isn't the point. Nor does staying busy always serve your clients and their goals. Sometimes the most important thing you can do is spend some time reading a book or giving your client more space for reflection by not coaching them.

Every day you need to start your day by asking yourself, What are the most important things for me to focus on today to

- serve or invest in myself and my self-care,
- serve my clients, and
- help my clients best achieve their goals and outcomes?

> It's not about the hours! It's about your service-oriented mindset, your impact, and walking your talk.

Introduction

To be honest, this chapter wasn't in the original plan for the book. But as we were developing and writing the book, I decided it might be helpful to describe how to build an "ideal" day in the life of an agile coach. I realize that this is dependent on your client's goals and your skills, but I do think the topic is worth exploring.

Let's start with what I mean by an ideal day. Or, more importantly, what I don't mean by it:

- Checking or following your schedule or plan for the day
- Deciding how long you'll take for breaks or when to stop for lunch
- Deciding on what book, article, or blog to read
- Setting up a to-do list for the day

These sorts of tactical, day-to-day, rote decisions are not what I'm trying to influence you toward. Instead, I'm hoping that this chapter takes you on a bit of a journey through activities that enhance your overall effectiveness as a Badass Agile Coach.

Here, I'd like to explore balance a bit more, and discuss why "just coaching" is rarely a good daily focus. I want to inspire you to reflect more, to show up strategically more, and to coach less toward what your clients ask for and more toward what your clients need.

Scrum Master Shepherds

I often use the metaphor of Scrum Masters as shepherds when describing the coaching nuance I expect to see from them. It's common for Scrum Masters to adopt a stance of protecting their teams from outside influences, diversions, interruptions, and impediments to keep them focused on their sprint goals and on effectively collaborating as a team.

The Badass Agile Coach's Guide to Starting Your Day 295

I sometimes call it a shepherd's mindset, where protecting the team is their prime directive.

This metaphor is often only outwardly focused; that is, protecting the teams from harsh outside influences. But I often coach Scrum Masters to augment that thinking—to focus on the internal distractions as well. They should be protecting the team from themselves, from doing major self-harm, or from making the same mistakes over and over again, reminding the team (and the Scrum Master) that danger can come from all directions.

I firmly believe that a Badass Agile Coach has a similar responsibility. It's challenging to strike the right balance, but sometimes one of the most responsible things you can do is step in and stop your clients from making huge mistakes. Of course, it's situational and nuanced, but to never do it is malpractice as far as I'm concerned. You're essentially feeding your client to the wolves. Metaphorically speaking, of course.

[Margin note: Protect from external + internal]

Check In

[Margin note: I do this every morning]

Each day, I'd suggest you check in with yourself first. I like to do this early. Since I'm an early riser, this usually happens at around 6:00 a.m.

I'll check my calendar to see if things are still relevant for the day. I'm trying to create as much free time as I can, so I ask myself if I still need to attend that meeting or have that coaching conversation. Is it still the most important thing I can do today, or has something more important supplanted it?

Next, I think about the agreements and goals I've created with my clients (the organization, the teams, and the individuals). I try to envision what they need from me today versus just doing what I'd already planned to do. Of course, sometimes I'll follow my plan, because it's still meaningful and relevant. But more times than not, I need to make real-time adjustments. My morning check-in is a place to explore those opportunities for realignment to higher-level goals.

Invest in Yourself

I don't want a day to go by where I'm not significantly investing in myself. This aligns with the self-care ideas we explore in chapter 20. In that chapter, there is a general sense of *reviewing* self-care, but here I want you to focus intentionally on *doing* it.

So, each day, right after your daily check-in, I want you to consider what you're going to do for yourself today. Capture it and commit to doing it. Better yet, consider your schedule and create sufficient space for your self-care activities.

Reflect

Now I'd like to explore the "meat and potatoes" of starting your day: creating the space for reflection. We're going to review a series of reflections that I've found helpful in guiding my coaching activity; I hope it helps you as well. I recommend you start every day by reflecting on the following considerations.

Your Daily Strategy

Begin by reflecting on your daily strategy, particularly these questions:

- What progress has your client made over the last month, the last week, and yesterday?
- Are they on track to meet their goals?
- How have you been showing up as a coach (stances, EQ, sensing, meeting the clients where they are)?

Given your answers to these questions, what adjustments do you need to make today, tomorrow, over the next week, and over the next month?

Importantly, what experiments can or should you be running in your coaching activity? Remember, experiments aren't just for your agile teams or organization; they're for you as well. What risks might you take? What new stances might you try in specific situations? What new facilitative techniques might you employ?

A big part of your strategy-setting should be focused inwardly, as part of your efforts to sharpen your saw (continuous learning and improvement). Part of this reflection is avoiding rote activity—just going through the motions or staying too much in your comfort zone. Put on the mindset of disrupting and challenging yourself.

Am I Coaching the Right People, at the Right Level, with the Right Focus?

Another important part of your daily strategy check is determining whether you've been coaching at the right level organizationally. First, check in with the following questions:

- What is your client's overarching organizational coaching goal?
- What is your client asking for?
- Most importantly, what does your client need today?
- And, in this case, is the client more team-centric, management-centric, or leadership-centric?

The last point is important. And yes, my advice here is moving beyond your Coaching stance. If you were solely in Coaching stance, then you would 100% adhere to and focus on your client's stated goals. There would be very little interpretation around what they need versus what they're asking for. But in this reflection, I want you to go beyond that. Just a wee bit perhaps, but go beyond. Put on your Agile/Lean Practitioner and Advising stances and see if all of your client's goals are aligned with their overarching organizational goals. If not, you might want to make some strategic adjustments in your focus.

Many years ago, I was in a senior technical leadership role at a company called iContact. I was also their agile transformation leader and often operated across the enterprise as an agile coach. I was part of their agile journey for over three years, and we sustained a wonderful level of organizational maturity in our agile practices and mindset at all levels of the organization.

Coaching Focus

- Leadership 10%
- Teams 30%
- Management 60%

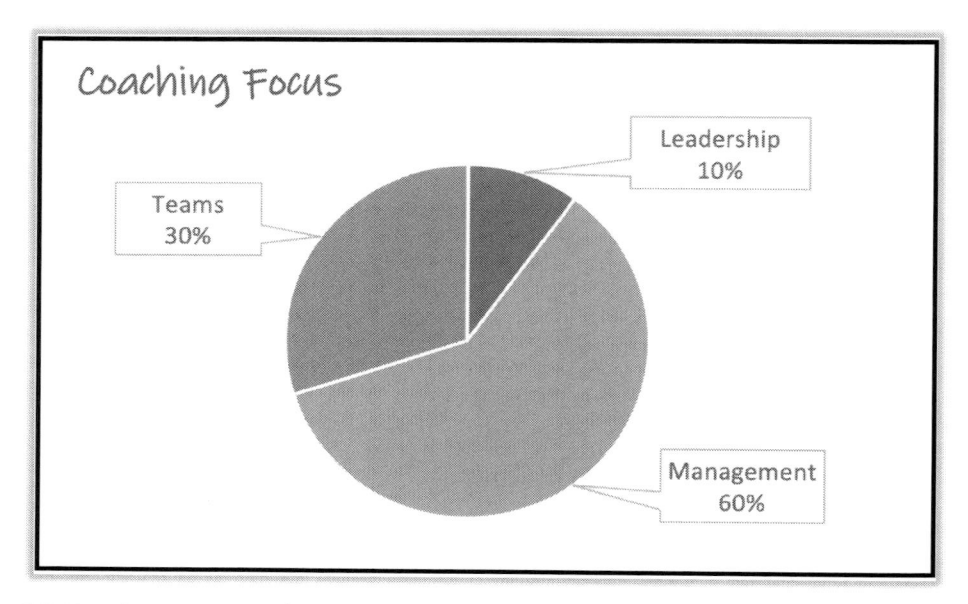

FIGURE 42. iContact Coaching Focus Across Organizational Tiers

If you had asked me back then where I spent most of my time coaching, I probably would have guessed it was at the team level, with a smattering of coaching at the management and senior leadership levels. It just felt correct. But it wasn't.

A year after leaving iContact, I sat down and reflected on where I spent my coaching time there. The reality turned out to be quite different from what I'd perceived during my tenure. Figure 42 represents the truth of my focus. As you can see, I spent the vast majority of my time coaching the management and leadership tiers within the organization.

I'm sharing this here so that you reflect not only on who you're coaching, but where within the organization and what your balance might be. I've found these percentages to be about right if I want to effectively coach the whole organization in their agile transformation.

Am I Allowing for Sufficient "Pull" from My Clients?

As you're planning your day, you might want to plan some "pull time" for your client coaching. What is pull time? Well, from your perspective, it's open coaching time, when you're available but not booked. It's time you can spend reading a good book or catching up on a new coaching technique or preparing for your next coaching session. Its time spent waiting for a client to come pull you into a coaching conversation.

The advantage of taking a "pull me in" posture more often in your coaching day is that it places the onus on your clients across the teams and the organization to take the initiative to ask you for help. You're not "inflicting" coaching on them; they're reaching out for it. My experience is that this creates a better balance and greater receptiveness to your coaching.

Often, the problem is that we as coaches are uncomfortable establishing a pull model for coaching. Particularly if we're getting paid to coach. That's why I recommend making it a part of your daily reflections. That will help you be more intentional about it and become more comfortable with the practice.

When I'm Coaching Leaders Today, What Will I Consider?

Quite often in agile coaching we're asked to coach leaders at different levels, or, we discover the need for this coaching. But many agile coaches don't have experience in leadership roles, which affects the empathy, focus, and effectiveness of their coaching. As a coach, I think we need to put ourselves in a solid position to determine the following when coaching leaders:

- **Their overall leadership maturity.** I often use Shu Ha Ri as a metaphor for identifying a leader's experience level.
- **Where they are coming from.** We need to have empathy by walking beside them or in their shoes.
- **Where they are in their journey.** Ensure you're meeting leaders where they are in their agile leadership journey rather than where you'd like them to be.

- **Where they are on the Leadership Agility continuum.** Is the client an Expert, an Achiever, or a Catalyst (discussed below)?
- **Their stressors and risks.** Be sure you understand their stressors, particularly within the organizational hierarchy and the culture.

It's important to have all of these factors in the back of your mind as you reflect on coaching leaders. I've found Bill Joiner's *Leadership Agility*[28] particularly helpful in my leadership coaching. In his book, Bill defines a series of leadership levels that characterize the evolution of modern leaders. In the middle of the progression are the three central levels previously mentioned:

1. **Expert** (I know what to do; let me tell you …)
   - Leadership style: Tactical, problem-solving orientation. Believes a leader's power depends upon expertise and positional authority.
   - Leading teams: More of a supervisor than a manager. Creates a group of individuals rather than a team. Usually too caught up in details to lead in a strategic manner.

2. **Achiever** (Here are our goals, strategies, and outcomes; now go …)
   - Leadership style: Strategic, outcome orientation. Believes that power comes not only from authority and expertise but also from motivating others.
   - Leading teams: Operates like a full-fledged manager. Meetings to discuss important issues are often orchestrated to try to gain buy-in to the leader's own views.

3. **Catalyst** (Let's co-create our vision; now I need to grow the capabilities of my teams …)
   - Leadership style: Visionary, facilitative orientation. Believes

---

28. Bill Joiner and Stephen Josephs' book *Leadership Agility* provides helpful thinking and a model that fosters helpful coaching conversations with leaders. While the title focuses on leaders and leadership, it can also be applied to teams and within organizations: https://changewise.biz/.

that leaders articulate an innovative, inspiring vision to empower people to transform the vision into reality.
- Leading teams: Acts as a team leader and facilitator to create a highly participative team. Welcomes open exchange of views on difficult issues. Empowers direct reports and uses team development as a vehicle for leadership development.

An important aspect of leadership agility is that these levels are not mutually exclusive. In fact, all leaders operate from each level. The question is, where is your default, primary, or most comfortable space? If a leader spends 80% of their time as an Expert, then they are leading via that primary stance, which strongly influences the culture they are creating.

As agile coaches, we want agile leaders to migrate to more of a Catalyst stance in order to support the healthy agile culture that they aspire to.

One of the more powerful aspects of this model for the coach is that it gives us a framework and a model to enable awareness and conversations with our leadership clients. You don't want to use it for judgment, but as an evolutionary guide and model for each leader.

How Will I Enter Each Coaching Space?

As you cast your reflective net out across the planned and unplanned possibilities for your day, consider the conditions of entry for your coaching conversations. For example, lightly consider:

- **Metaskills**. Determine what metaskills you might want to leverage in each session and throughout the day.
- **Presence, and being present**. How will you focus on showing up as present *and* amplifying your presence in each of your coaching conversations?
- **Being sufficiently unprepared**. Are you effectively underplanning and leaving your baggage behind each day? I know this is counterintuitive, given the nature of this whole chapter. I do want you to reflect and prepare for your day, but I don't want you to overprepare or bring too many assumptions to bear.

- **Emptying your cup.** Release your assumptions, baggage, and biases. Just being self-aware of these is often enough to clean things up a bit.
- **Humility and service to your client.** Again, this is simply a check and a reminder of your client orientation.

This is all part of the agile coaching mindset that we discussed in chapter 2, but a conscious, focused reminder of key aspects of how we'll show up is always a good idea.

Do You Need Help, or Do You Need to Provide Help?

I believe one of the most important reflective exercises each day is *helping*. Consider whether and when you might need or extend help during the day. This could take many forms:

- Bouncing an idea off a colleague, or letting them bounce an idea off you.
- Running through a coaching dojo (see chapter 18) before you dive into a coaching session, or helping someone run a dojo to prepare.
- Looking for someone to pair-coach with you for a variety of reasons—support, learning, new perspectives, reflection—or offering to pair-coach with a colleague.
- Reviewing your coaching plans and strategies with a colleague to see if your ideas are sound and to get another viewpoint, or offering to review other coach's plans and strategies.

All of these come to mind as helping patterns you might want to reflect on and consider. I believe that an individual coach can't get too much help, or give too much help, during their coaching journey. It's an attribute of coaching experience and maturity as far as I'm concerned.

What If ...?

Finally, reflect on possible what ifs that you might encounter during the day. For example, what if ...

- ... my client stakeholder asks me about individual, team, group, organization, or other leader performance levels? How would I ethically answer that question?
- ... I observe a situation with a powerful client in action that might require me to take immediate or near immediate intervention?
- ... I find myself over my head situationally as a coach? What will I do? Can I anticipate it first? Who can help me?
- ... I encounter Four Horsemen-style toxins throughout my day? How should I prepare for that? Do I have antidotes in the back of my mind and ready to use?
- ... I encounter any serious issues throughout the day; for example, emotional, dangerous, or potentially volatile encounters? Am I prepared for them? Have I established HR partnerships to leverage?

You get the idea. It's important not to get stuck here trying to envision everything that can possibly go wrong—or everything that could go right, for that matter. But thoughtfully considering potential extenuating events can help prepare you if and when they occur.

Head On Straight

After all of this preparation, I want you to energize yourself to walk out into your day. You've got your head on straight and are prepared for whatever you might encounter. Certainly not everything, but you've got a solid picture of the day. And while the day will emerge in front of you, you've been decisive about guiding your actions and activity.

I guess what I'm saying is that I don't want you to walk out each day and be or play a victim to what unfolds. I want you to decide and take some responsibility for the unfolding. I believe you'll find your coaching will greatly benefit from your daily preparatory regimen.

And as an additional guide for your preparation, I offer the Agile Coaching Daily Prep Canvas in figure 43 as a way of helping you prepare and focus yourself.

Agile Coaching Daily Prep Canvas

The intent of the Canvas is to strike a balance between planning and reacting, preparation and going where the needs are, and meeting your client's goals.

Coach:	Last updated:
Reflect - Daily Strategy & Entry *What's my overall strategy today? How am I entering each session?*	**Daily Check-in** *Checking in on your plans & schedule. Do you need to pivot?*
Reflect - Enough *Pull* Today? *Are you providing enough space to be pulled in today? How?*	**Reflect - What Ifs?** *This is a space for considering what emerges and the unexpected.*
Reflect - Am I Coaching the *Right* People? *Are you balanced across individuals, teams, and systems? Leadership, management, and teams?*	**Reflect - When I'm Coaching Leaders...** *Being decisive and balanced in how you're showing up to coach leaders today. Situational awareness!*

This work is licensed under CC BY-NC 4.0

FIGURE 43. Agile Coaching Daily Prep Canvas

Further Reading

Anthony Mersino has written a wonderful blog that focuses on "walking in the shoes of leaders" as coaches. I highly recommend it: https://vitalitychicago.com/blog/empathy-for-technology-managers-in-agile/.

This is a relatively up-to-date article that explores the Leadership Agility levels of leadership: www.amanet.org/articles/the-five-levels-of-leadership-agility/.

And a wonderful podcast that explores Leadership Agility as well: https://agileuprising.libsyn.com/leadership-agility-with-bill-joiner.

18

Dojo Practice for the Badass Agile Coach

Alan Iverson, a former basketball star, did an infamous post-game interview in 2002 where he dismissed the value of practice. He kept making the distinction between performance in the game and participation in practice. He clearly didn't value practice time as much as game time. But his outstanding performance was surely rooted in countless hours of historical practice.

As agile coaches, we also have to spend an inordinate amount of time practicing our art and craft. That is, we do if we want to master it and become badass. And there are very few better and more impactful ways to improve than participating with our peers in agile coaching dojos.

Introduction

I've been using the notion of a dojo for the past 10 or more years to practice coaching scenarios. The term *dojo* makes sense to me, as coaching dojos emulate many of the characteristics and benefits of a traditional martial arts dojo:

- A safe place to practice your craft.
- A place to run through your katas (scenarios) until you are proficient.
- A place where a "master" helps you to learn from your mistakes (and successes) and grow your skills.
- A place where students learn from each other and mentor each other.

In the agile community, I think the notion originated as coding dojos where folks worked on their development skills by practicing coding katas. Sometimes this was done in pairs, and often by focusing on design patterns, refactoring, unit test design, and other aspects of modern software development.

Around 2010, I heard of dojos being applied to agile coaching practice and thought it was a unique modification of the concept. Only after I attended some alternative classes around positive psychology, leadership agility, and the Leadership Circle Profile did I realize that many professions use the dojo concept to sharpen their skills.

For example, my daughter Rhiannon is a child social worker. She is a practice director of a larger children's social work firm in the New York City area, and she's responsible for the training and development of the staff. We think agile coaching is a challenging area of practice, and it is, but there is no comparison between it and the high-stakes world of family and child social work, where they often have to enter families and remove children to safer situations. So, I wasn't too surprised when I learned that Rhiannon's colleagues used dojos to sharpen their communication, conflict resolution, system entry, and negotiation skills on a regular basis. It gave the concept even more real-world value for me.

In this chapter, I will explore the various aspects of an agile coaching dojo so you can put this practice to work with your colleagues in your Communities of Practice, which we explore in chapter 19.

Dojo Scenarios

The centerpiece of the coaching dojo session is the *scenario*. Essentially, we're role-playing, so we need a script or a scene in which to play our roles.

Here's an example scenario:

> You have observed the chief product owner (CPO) influencing estimates in more than one backlog refinement session. The good news is that she is very interested and engaged in these team meetings. The bad news is that she is influencing the estimates, and more importantly, the conversations. You've brought this to her attention several times, but, if anything, the behavior has only gotten worse. What to do?

The dojo members could adopt several roles to initiate the discussion. You could be:

- A Scrum Master initiating a discussion with the CPO to try to improve this situation for your team.
- A functional manager initiating the discussion with the CPO based on an impediment raised by one of the Scrum Masters.
- An organizational agile coach initiating the discussion with the CPO based on an impediment raised by the Scrum Master.

The scenario changes quite a bit based on your role and other context elements—for example, how many times you've had this conversation.

One of the most important aspects of the scene is your getting into the role, so dojos require a bit of acting and improvisation. The more you know the individual or individuals in the scenario, the more you should act as they would act, trying to emulate them to the best of your abilities. For example, in this case, if you know the CPO is a bit controlling and a micromanager, then you'll want to factor those characteristics into your role-playing.

Here's another example scenario from a leadership perspective:

> You've been coaching at your client for a number of sprints/weeks. You've noticed a horrible pattern where members of the senior staff interrupt individual team members with emergency customer requests or repairs. What's insidious is that the entire culture is tolerant of this behavior, so the teams, product owners, and Scrum Master simply acquiesce to it. Then, these very leaders berate the teams for missing their sprint goals and commitments in the sprint demos.

Again, you could adopt several roles to initiate the discussion. You could be:

- A functional manager initiating the discussion with their boss, based on an impediment raised by many of the Scrum Masters.
- An organizational agile coach initiating a discussion with the CEO (or another C-level leader), trying to initiate more systemic change.
- A senior leader initiating a discussion with one of their leadership peers, pointing out their interrupt-driven behavior within the agile teams.

Several scenarios are highlighted throughout the book to give you a sense of how to setup this powerful practice technique. But now I want to share the three roles essential to every agile coaching dojo.

Dojo Roles

A dojo is composed of three interacting roles:

1. **The coach.** Sometimes I call this person the *conversation initiator* (as in the arc of the coaching conversation). They might have the actual role of coach, or they might be a leader or manager in an organization who is coaching an individual or group. No matter

their organizational role, in the dojo format we'll refer to them as the coach.
2. **The client.** I also sometimes refer to this person as the *receiver* or *coachee*. This role is the heart of the role-play in the dojo. It's this person who is trying their best to represent the personality, style, attitude, and overall persona at the core of the scenario. I think it's useful to spend a few minutes before the dojo for the three participants to paint a picture of the persona the client will assume.
3. **The facilitator.** The facilitator does not actively participate in the conversation. Instead, they observe, take notes, and prepare to facilitate a short retrospective after the conversation closes. A big part of the facilitator role is paying close attention to the conversation arc—the words, the body language, the strategy, and so on.

The dojo format is designed for these three roles and, usually, for a triad of people occupying them. If you have more than three people, I normally recommend overloading the facilitator role with two people—but no more than that. An effective dojo needs no less than three and no more than four people participating, with a strong bias toward three.

Typical Dojo Practice Sessions

There are a few common ways to implement or leverage agile coaching dojos in your skill-strengthening journey.

Regular Practice

I normally recommend dojo practice sessions as part of an ongoing Community of Practice (CoP). For example, if you have established an Agile Coaching CoP, making dojos a part of your monthly rituals might be a great way to continuously sharpen your coaching skills.

Often, you'll want to pick a focus or theme for your dojo sessions. For example, one month you might focus on coaching leaders, and the next, product management.

You can mine the organization for scenarios that would be useful for everyone to practice. Examples could include:

- Situations that folks have already encountered that they want to run through again, to see if they could learn from that past coaching conversation.
- Situations that folks are in the middle of right now that they want to practice some coaching conversational arcs for—past, present, and future.
- Scenarios that folks have coming up that they want to practice beforehand, to boost their confidence and preparation.

The more the scenarios map to real-world coaching challenges, the more impactful they are to the coaches and for your clients.

Emergency Practice

There are often situations (scenarios) where we need to initiate a coaching conversation before the next dojo. In these cases, I've seen organizations implement the notion of an emergency dojo, where anyone can call on two other colleagues and run a dojo session for a particular high-risk, high-stakes coaching conversation. The focus of emergency dojo sessions is very specific, but the dynamics of the format are exactly the same.

Rotating Roles

It's a good practice to rotate the roles in between scenarios. I personally like to run dojo sessions for about an hour. Within that format, each scenario gets about 10 minutes for the conversation and about 5 for the retrospective, or about 15 minutes to explore each scenario. In an hour, you can usually explore three scenarios, which gives all three participants the opportunity to "put on" each of the roles. This maximizes the learning for the dojo triad.

Keys to Dojo Effectiveness

I want to share the elephant in the room right away: Most people really don't like to role-play. I think part of it is that many in technology are introverts and it's really not a comfortable thing to do if you're an introvert. But it's a bit like public speaking as well, in that nobody seems to really like doing it, but practice does lead to improvement.

Playing the persona effectively—role-playing effectively—is a primary key to the effectiveness and value of the dojo. So, we have to get over any reluctance we might have and simply dive in, try it, and motivate ourselves by helping our colleagues.

Taking the Dojos Seriously

Dojos are about practice. For the dojos to really be effective, you need to commit to them and participate regularly. If you don't, they won't help upgrade and refine your skills.

That's why I propose making dojos a part of your CoPs. And not just your Agile Coaching CoP, but your Scrum Mastery, Product Ownership, and Agile Leadership CoP too. Tailor the scenarios and personas to fit your role and the common conversational situations that you find yourself in for each of these roles.

Avoid Under- and Overacting

A common mistake in dojos is that the scenario client either underacts or overacts, and I see both equally often. In the case of underacting, everything seems to be going fine. It's like having a conversation with your best friend. There is no conflict and it's the perfect sunny-day conversation. While certainly pleasant, this rarely reflects the real-world tensions. But an equally common case is overacting, where the scenario client goes way overboard in embellishing the role—far beyond the reality of the real client they're intending to role-play.

You'll want to be aware of both of these cases and try—really try—to target the essence of the persona. A good facilitator will detect these extremes and pause the role-play to influence adjustments in the focus.

It's as simple as pausing, giving the pair the feedback, and then stepping back out of the scene.

Varying the Scenario Strategy or Persona

One of the things I like about the dojo format is you can rerun a scenario in a variety of ways to sharpen your situation awareness and nimbleness in your coaching. I can't think of any other way, other than longer-term experience, to get this sort of awareness.

I like to talk about three ways to run any scenario. They are:

- **Normal state.** This is running the scenario as the parties expect the client persona to usually react. It's closest to how you anticipate the real-world conversation going.
- **Sunny-day state.** This is running the scenario in the best case. Everything goes along swimmingly. While perhaps this doesn't happen very often, it *can* happen, and it's useful for everyone to see what "sunny" might feel like.
- **Rainy-day state.** This is running the scenario in the worst case, where nothing you try works, triggering occurs, and the outcome is unpredictable.

In a dojo, you could take a single scenario, and then run it through all three states in a single one-hour session. As a triad, you could experience a wide variety of tools, techniques, arcs, approaches, strategies, and so on surrounding a singular coaching conversation.

Active Facilitator

As I alluded to in the discussion of under- and overacting, the facilitator should be a somewhat active role in the dojo. Quite often, inexperienced facilitators will only engage during the retrospective; but I encourage them to understand the scenario and tune into how the coaching simulation is unfolding to see if they need to interrupt and provide real-time guidance.

For example, here are some actions that the facilitator might take during the dojo:

- Point out under- or overacting and suggest an appropriate shift in the role-play.
- Suggest a different Coaching Arc strategy or shift.
- Suggest the use of a different tool or approach.
- Point out that one party or the other is talking too much, not listening, etc.
- Suggest an amping-up or amping-down of the emotional field.
- Step into the role-play on either side and demonstrate a different approach.

Of course, these suggestions need to be made quickly and surgically, so as to not dominate the dojo. But I encourage facilitators to be as active as they need to be in order to increase the value of the triad's learning.

Retrospectives

Using the term *retrospective* for closing a dojo really doesn't do the value proposition justice. Like the facilitator role, the retrospective is a fundamental key to your learning and continuous improvement.

But the dojo retrospective is not just a place to review the conversation. In many ways, that's the easy part. More importantly, you can talk about tools, tactics, stance variety, and technique alternatives that could have been used instead, playing back alternative strategies and how they might have flexed the entire conversation in a new direction. Also, the triad can share their own experiences (stories) of handling similar situations—how they prepared, how they approached it, and what the ultimate outcomes were.

The retrospective is a place for rich, shared learnings that can you can take forward in the next scenario, future dojos, and your practice of agile coaching.

And don't be afraid to rinse and repeat the scenario based on retrospective feedback. It's a wonderful way to land new learnings.

A Few More Scenarios

I thought I'd close this chapter with a couple more scenarios, to help you understand what they typically look like.

> Your key leadership sponsor pulls you aside and tells you that they are a little unsettled by your coaching style, and more importantly, by the lack of results. She explains that of the 20+ teams in the organization, only three have consistent and increasing velocity. These same three teams seem to be working the hardest as well. She's challenging you that you only have two or three more sprints to get the remaining 15+ teams "up to speed" with the other teams; otherwise, they'll have to find a coach who can drive the results the senior leadership team is after.

> We all know that a Scrum Master's job is to put themselves "out of a job." That also applies to agile coaches. You feel that your coaching influence at your current client has run its course. Your ability to influence things in the beginning was strong, but lately you (and the organization) seem to be going through the motions. You've even heard this from a wide variety of leaders and team members. You have at least six months left on your contract and you've scheduled a crucial conversation with the CEO.

Each of these scenarios sets the stage for both the client and the coach. Scenarios should provide enough context and emotional nuance for you to have a real-world conversation.

But the very best scenarios are mined from your organization's actual experience. The more they align with your culture, roles, challenges, and situations, the better the dojo learning. And to be frank, the more fun the dojo participants will have.

Further Reading

This is an example from Carlton Nettleton at Applied Frameworks describing a coaching dojo: https://appliedframeworks.com/how-to-run-a-coaching-dojo/. You should notice that he amplifies only the coaching stance as a viable way to interact as a coach. While you can certainly focus on developing your coaching stance in a dojo, I recommend using the approach to practice and sharpen all of your stances and to smoothly transition between them.

19

Setting Up a Badass Agile Coaching Community of Practice

There is nothing sadder in the world than a bunch of coaches going it alone. Coaching by themselves, never collaborating, and trying to figure everything out by themselves. Repeating their mistakes and never getting actionable feedback. Never having someone who has their back in support and partnership.

These coaches are choosing to be lone wolves. But there is a better way.

By establishing a Community of Practice, both within your company and outside of it, you can create a place where like-minded agile coaches get together to discuss, explore, and refine their craft.

> A Community of Practice is a place of powerful learning, powerful insights, and powerful feedback. It's a safe place to mentor and coach each other. And it's a place to practice, practice, and practice your craft by coaching. The title says it all—establishing a Community (of coaches) of Practice (sharpening our craft).

Introduction

I've been facilitating a lean-coffee-style meeting twice a week called the Agile Moose Herd.[29] I've been doing it off and on for the last five years or so. I think of it as a way for like-minded agilists to benefit from each other's experiences.

We do this in a number of different ways:

- We share our real-world challenges and get help.
- We talk about our learning journeys and share new approaches, lessons, and tools.
- We trade war stories.
- We often talk about interviewing and how to represent solid agile coaching in interviews.
- Sometimes we role-play scenarios where we practice the craft of coaching.

All of this is done in a safe, peer-to-peer environment where everyone is an equal participant and has an equal voice. It really is a *community*, and when asked, many of the coaches talk about it as a highlight of their day—something they look forward to and that recharges their batteries.

I share this because the Herd represents some of the very best characteristics of an Agile Coaching CoP.

Defining a CoP

A coaching CoP is, at its heart, a group (the community) of similar

---

29. www.agile-moose.com/moose-herd.

roles (the practice) getting together periodically to share, learn, and grow as a group. This group also generates value for their company by increasing their role's impact within the organizational context. It's as simple as that—group growth and business impact.

The CoP aligns well with the Spotify notion of a Guild, where folks in similar roles get together periodically to learn and grow within a functional skill set and discipline. Both CoPs and Guilds have the additional goal of trying to align everyone so that they develop a common mindset and use consistent tools, approaches, and practices.

Contrasting the CoP and CoE

When discussing this kind of community skill development, you'll often come across the notion of a Center of Excellence, or CoE. While they sound similar, a CoE serves a very different function and may not always be appropriate. My bias is going to shine through a bit here, but please bear with me.

A CoE is a more formal, top-down mechanism whose primary goal is consistency of practice. That is, it's focused on regulation and governance. Agile performance metrics are often tied to a CoE as well. A good example of this idea is the Scaled Agile Framework's Lean Agile Center of Excellence, or LACE. You can also see the idea marketed or aligned with the Agile PMO or with PMI's Disciplined Agile.

I've already alluded to the two problems I have with generic CoEs. The first is the prescriptive, top-down nature of these groups—where the organization tries to mandate practices. I think that's a non-starter in agile contexts and certainly not aligned with the agile mindset. Implementing a CoE can actually harm the culture you're trying to instill or support.

My second problem with the CoE concept is that it disengages the initiative strategy from the people doing the actual work—the very people who are part of the "center" you're trying to create. Typically, the teams and individuals only engage with the CoE because they're told to, not because they're inspired to or are invited to participate.

You don't create an agile culture by top-down mandate. It just doesn't work. The organic nature of building a community of practitioners aligns so much better with our agile mindsets.

Keep It Opt-In or Invitation

Speaking of the organic nature being best, and taking a page from Dan Mezick's Open Space Agility work, I recommend you adopt an opt-in approach, inviting others to help set up your Agile Coaching CoP.

That is, don't demand that folks join or come. Instead, create a compelling charter and vision, and then invite your coaches to co-create something that excites them. Setting up an Open Space event is a great way to do this.

Setting Up an Agile Coaching CoP

Setting up an Agile Coaching CoP is simple. You only need a few things:

- The **intent**, or desire for group collaboration
- A **group** of agile coaches
- A **place** to meet
- A **charter** of sorts (vision, mission, purpose, why)
- Optionally, an **Open Space** event

Then, simply **start** meeting.

The hard part is gaining momentum, showing value, continuing to grow, and keeping the energy level and engagement consistently high. To help you with that, here are a handful of critical success factors that I've learned over the years. You don't need to meet all of these conditions initially, but keep them in the back of your mind as your momentum builds and your community grows.

Sparkplug Leader. Creating a successful CoP requires an energetic leader who can maintain energy and commitment, and who can focus on the growth and value of the CoP. This sounds easier than it is. Many folks try to find the most seasoned or experienced coach to lead the

CoP, and that often fails. Instead, look for someone with passion and energy around the craft of coaching. While experience is nice, I'll take a passionate, committed, and doggedly persistent coach every time. I call them "sparkplugs," and I think finding the right person (or people) is crucial.

Leadership Engagement, Priority, and Support. Another huge factor in CoP success is for your organizational leadership team to make growth and learning a priority. This means ensuring that everyone is empowered to invest their time and energy into the CoP, and making professional growth a clear goal within the organization. Of course, this includes providing budget and engaging with the CoP in real time. One of the best things a leadership team can do to support the CoP is to leverage the CoP's capabilities (wisdom, insights, ideas, recommendations) whenever possible.

Many CoPs, or CoPs as a Silo-Buster. CoPs aren't just for coaches. You can (and perhaps should) create them for Scrum Masters, product owners, DevOps, UX, security and performance, leaders, and coaches in agile contexts. The more the merrier, because you create a broader sense of community and collaboration across all roles and tiers of the organization. And the additional CoPs give you multiple systems to enter as a coach, which makes your coaching opportunities broader and richer.

Other Perspectives and Varied Focus. Bring in outside voices (speakers, videos, panels, etc.) to share with your CoP. Don't be too internally focused. Success emerges from the convergence of your internal ideas with external insights. Also, vary the focus as much as possible; use books, presentations, teach-backs, dojos, lean coffees, panel discussions, fish bowls, fireside chats, vision setting, and anything else you think might expand perspectives and broaden viewpoints.

Frequent Reflection on the CoP Dynamics. Listen to your "customers" and endeavor to always be increasing the value, energy, and impact of the CoP. The Agile Coaching CoP is a place for individual reflection, peer coaching group reflection, service-oriented and customer reflection, and organizational impact reflection. And then, there's the opportunity to *do something*, with the reflection focused on continuous improvement.

Remembering Self-Care. The CoP can play a role in emphasizing self-care and balance across your entire organization. This is a place where the agile coaches can lead the way by showing everyone how they take care of themselves first, no matter what challenges they are facing.

The Service-Oriented Agile Coaching CoP

One way to define or instantiate your CoP is to have it focus on offering a series of services to the organization.[30] You can fairly easily split them into community-based services (internal to the group) and organizational-based services (external to the group).

Another way of thinking about this is that the group gives back to themselves and provides value to the organization, all in the name of growing in their agile mindset and practices.

Community (Internal) Services

Internal services are focused more toward the teams within the organization. Consider this the informal collaborative setting, where CoP members get together to collaborate, share, learn, and grow. You probably don't want to try to measure organizational impact here; instead, consider it part of the internal growth of your agile-centric skills.

Collaboration. Provide a safe space for like-minded agilists to gather and share. A big part of this focus is silo-busting and trying to create and grow an agile-supportive culture over time.

Training. The internal training provided by a CoP is more informal; for example, sponsoring a reading group, having group members share presentations, inviting outside parties to share, collaborating

---

30. I found this "service-oriented" idea at https://age-of-product.com/agile-community/ and really aligned with it.

around experience reports. It's focused less on formal classes and more on targeted learning in topics of value to the community.

Mentoring. One of the key internal services provided by a CoP is individuals mentoring one another—across members of the CoP, with others outside of the CoP, or both. A fundamental part of the service is identifying what mentoring is, establishing some guidelines, and creating a clearinghouse of sorts so that mentors and mentees can meet and connect.

Coaching. Coaching isn't just for the coaches or the Scrum Masters. Agile coaching is a skill that needs to be developed and grown across all of the change agents in (and out of) the community. The coaching in this sense can be related to coaching skills development, coaching practice, pair-coaching, and learning by doing. Of course, there is some synergy between mentoring and coaching, so the two often blend a bit.

Organizational (External) Services

Often, CoPs focus too much on the internal side and don't provide sufficient impact and value to the organization to warrant organizational support, funding, and excitement. Here are some externally facing service ideas that can generate some impact and buzz.

Recruiting and Onboarding. One of the ways a CoP can have the greatest impact on an organization is by helping to recruit, interview, and onboard individuals. This might start as a niche practice to help with finding Scrum Masters, and perhaps leads or architects. But over time it can become a pervasive service to ensure you're hiring the right folks and giving them a proper beginning.

Website: Visibility, Communication, and Transparency. I personally get excited when a CoP sets up a website and begins to activate their transparency by sharing the overall adoption strategy, early successes (and failures), learning, and goals and plans. This often involves a blog where individuals share their personal agile journey and learnings. It can be quite powerful.

Shared Practices. One of the more obvious services of the CoPs is sharing practices. This includes things like checklists, lessons learned, scripts and recipes, templates, guidelines, and tooling guidance. If you generate energy in this space, it becomes an organic place for participants to share what's working for them.

Modeling. One of the biggest challenges in agile transformations is determining what "good" looks like at the team level, at the management level, and at the senior leadership level. The coaches in the CoP, if they play it right, can become role models (modelers, exemplars) of what good agile looks like at all levels of the organization. In a way, they become active ambassadors of agile maturity, mindset, practice, and emergence.

Role Coaching. A huge way to accelerate agile adoption is for the Agile Coaching CoP to spending time coaching Scrum Masters, product owners, and managers—three critical roles in any agile transformation. I've often said that one of the biggest challenges in moving to agile is the inherent role confusion the transition creates. Actively coaching individuals through their personal transformation can pay huge dividends.

Events. Internal conferences and Open Space events are a wonderful way to share agility across the company and explain what it is, the impacts, the goals, and the successes—not only by telling, but more importantly, by sharing and showing.

I'm sure you can envision different service views in your own contexts, so feel free to build on mine or replace them with your own. But however you do it, creating an Agile Coaching CoP with a service-oriented mindset can be incredibly powerful.

The Danger of Maturity Assessments

Probably one of the most destructive anti-patterns that surfaces in many CoPs and CoEs is the incredible need to measure *everything* in your agile transformation ... starting with your coaches and your teams.

I simply want to encourage your Agile Coaching CoP to tread very carefully and very lightly when it comes to organizational maturity metrics.

Very lightly!

Tuckman Model

As a final point in the chapter, I want you to keep the Tuckman model in the back of your mind as you influence and guide the evolution of your Communities of Practice. The model speaks to the different stages of group development: forming, storming, norming, and performing; which can certainly be applied to starting an Agile Coaching CoP—or any CoP, for that matter.

One of the more interesting points in the model is the early energy and focus required in building relationships. If you want an elevator pitch for getting your CoP to a self-sustaining or high-performing level, most of your early energy needs to focus on gaining cross-organizational feedback and adapting to that feedback. Another key will be the CoP providing value to the individual participants and the organization in equal measure.

Further Reading

Tom Cagly shares a post by Anthony Mersino that explores why a CoE is a *bad* idea: https://tcagley.wordpress.com/2018/11/29/guest-post-why-an-agile-center-of-excellence-is-a-really-bad-idea/.

Guilds in general are wonderfully explored in this *Communications of the ACM* article: https://cacm.acm.org/magazines/2020/3/243029-spotify-guilds/. It's worth reviewing this piece and mapping some of the ideas back to your Agile Coaching CoP.

20

Sharpening Your Badass Saw

We are all works in progress who are never complete, as we are always learning and growing. One of the greatest gifts the universe has bestowed on us is its beautiful, ever-changing nature and incredible complexity—something that none of us, as humans, can ever fully grasp or master.

But we can be curious and we can explore. We can be relentless in our personal learning and development. And we can be generous in our teaching and mentoring of others.

In the end, to stay static or satisfied is anathema. To continuously learn and grow is a celebration of the universal mystery.

Introduction

Stephen Covey published the book *7 Habits of Highly Effective People* in 1989. In it, his seventh habit was "Sharpening the Saw." That is, creating a habit of continuously learning, adapting, and growing your skills. Nothing can be more important for the professional Badass Agile Coach than a laser focus on this habit. I would also argue that there are many aspects to your learning, growing, and improving.

That's one of the reasons I like the Agile Coaching Growth Wheel described in chapter 7. Not only is it a capabilities matrix for all of the skills required, it also helps to clarify the depth of skill you currently have within each capability and where you might want to focus your strengthening efforts.

Strength-Based Learning and Growth

I want to share an important lesson I've discovered over the years: It's not the best strategy for your personal improvement to focus on improving your weaknesses. A much better approach is identifying your strengths and working hard to improve and leverage them in your coaching (and life).

My learning around the importance of strengths has been strongly influenced by three factors.

The first is the strengths-based movement. You see it recognized in *CliftonStrengths* by Don Clifton and *StrengthsFinders 2.0* by Tom Rath, both published by Gallup, and in the later *StandOut 2.0* by Marcus Buckingham. In each of these systems, the focus is on discovering your strengths and then leveraging them to your advantage.

The next factor is my discovery of Appreciative Inquiry, or AI. When you focus on AI in your coaching, you're focusing on understanding, uncovering, and appreciating the strengths of your client. When you're focusing it on yourself, it's the same—identifying your strengths and exploring strategies for leveraging them more.

Finally, I see strengths-based learning reflected in the area of positive psychology. This runs the gamut from assuming positive intent when I'm coaching clients to maintaining a positive attitude when facing challenges and adversity.

Far too many of us focus on the wrong things in our journeys to become a better coach. Instead of worrying about weaknesses, I would recommend working with your own coach to discover your strengths in coaching and work to grow them. You could even align this strengths-finding effort to the Agile Coaching Growth Wheel and map your strengths to its competencies.

But now, let's focus on another counterintuitive area of sharpening your saw—sharpening from the inside.

Self-Care

I can't tell you how many coaches I've met who talk a good game about self-care to others, but who don't walk their talk when it comes to themselves. I want you to reflect on that statement to see if you might be one of those coaches. I know I was, and still am from time to time.

We all need to stop doing that and invest first in our own self-care and growth. This also aligns with our servant leader selves, in that in order to serve others, we first need to serve ourselves. Or, put our own oxygen masks on first before helping others, if you like that metaphor better.

Agile Coaching Self-Care Canvas

One of the best ways I've found to practice self-care is via the Agile Coaching Self-Care Canvas in figure 44. While I'll explain the intent of each section, I want to first explain the intent of the overall canvas.

First and foremost, this is a reflective device. I want you to use it to explore yourself, your care needs, and your current context, and then envision a future context where you invest more in you and your care. I want the canvas to become an active component of your personal reflection and part of your sharpening the saw habit.

Now let's explore each of the focus areas in more detail.

Agile Coaching Self-Care Canvas

The intent of the Canvas is to meet yourself where you are, to pursue relentless, incremental (baby) step improvement, to model your future state, and to find the courage to care for yourself first.

Coach:	Last updated:
Ecosystem How are you operating? What's the environment?	**Goals** What are your self-care goals? Include WIP and focus goals.
Mindfulness Quiet reflection, observations, experiments, spider-sense?	**Energy** What are the opportunities for recharging your battery?
Partners Mentors, pairing partners, your coach, and role models?	**Growth & Learning** What areas should you focus on next?

This work is licensed under CC BY-NC 4.0

FIGURE 44. Agile Coaching Self-Care Canvas

- **Ecosystem**. This is where you reflect on and capture your current coaching (professional) ecosystem. Where are your joys? Your stressors? Articulate as many factors as you can to envision your current space. You shouldn't be judging or evaluating. Instead, just try to capture a snapshot of your coaching world — the ecosystem where you operate. Using a Kanban principle, this is starting from where you are.
- **Mindfulness**. This area is for identifying what you're doing with respect to mindfulness and capturing ideas to become more mindful. This is also the reflection and experimentation area of the canvas, where you do your dreaming around possibilities. If there's an area of the canvas intended to connect with your "inner coach" and inspire you, then this is it.
- **Energy**. There's a reason this area is next to mindfulness. This is an expansion of a metaphor where you focus on managing your energy levels. I want you to think of yourself as a battery and your self-care (or lack thereof) as having positive, neutral, or negative impacts on your energy levels. Extending the metaphor, you need to spend sufficient time charging yourself to an optimal level of effectiveness. Explore what energizes you.
- **Partners**. This area is beside your ecosystem because they're so closely coupled. Your partners are your mentors and mentees, your coaches and coachees, your role models, and your trusted colleagues. If you don't have many names here, then you have some work to do to expand the list. Any professional Badass Agile Coach must have at least one coach actively coaching them at all times.
- **Growth and Learning**. One of the major reasons I appreciate the Agile Coaching Growth Wheel is its connection to growing each of your competency areas. As we discussed in chapter 7, each area progresses from Beginner to Catalyst. Any Badass Agile Coach should at least be active as an Advanced Beginner, but needs to have their sights set on Guide (just below Catalyst). The guidance for the Wheel gives you hints and ideas for what this looks like so you can capture it within the canvas.

- **Goals**. I recommend that each time you visit your canvas you begin and end with your goals. To start, check in with your goals to reflect on what you've accomplished. Are they all still relevant? What, if anything, needs to be changed, added, or removed? Then, after your journey through the canvas, come back to your goals and do the same thing again. When you leave your goals, they should be prioritized, of high value to you, and something you're committing time to accomplish. If you're feeling particularly "agile," you might want to define acceptance criteria and/or clear outcomes for each goal.

Being Coachable

Here's an example of a coaching team that wasn't very coachable.

I have some coaching colleagues who have joined a relatively large firm. They're tasked with being the internal agile coaches and leading the organization's agile transformation.

Several times, members of the organization's leadership team have reached out to me to come in and discuss various aspects of high-performance agility. Topics like culture-shaping, scaling, and leadership agility were of heavy interest. I think they were simply looking to get an outside, experienced coach to come in and provide additional insights. They certainly were not looking to undermine the internal coaches.

Each time this happened, the internal coaching team squashed the inquiry and insisted that *they* do the information session. In some cases, they wanted to go over "talking points" with me to ensure that I wouldn't say something that differed from their guidance or perspectives. Given that level of scrutiny and insecurity, I respectfully withdrew any interest in sharing my experience with this organization.

This is an actual example. I've seen and heard it repeated many times in my own agile journey.

Let me be clear: These were not bad or inexperienced coaches. They had loads of experience in a wide variety of business domains and across a variety of agile scaling models and frameworks. In other words, it was a solid coaching team.

But any coach or team of coaches clearly lacks some experience with something, somewhere. We all have weaknesses. We all have limited experience in specific business cultures. We all have difficulty with something. In other words, no one is perfect and all coaches can use and leverage help in their learning, growth, and ongoing coaching journey.

My real issue with this team is that they were closed off to any outside views. They viewed outside ideas as a threat instead of a gift. And fundamentally, I think that's a bad habit for any agile coach to get into.

Situations like this inspired me to share a set of guidelines that might help remind agile coaches—all of us—to receive as well as we give.

The First Rule: *Be open to all possibilities, not just your own.*

As an agile coach, you shouldn't be making decisions based on you. Your ego shouldn't be getting in the way. It's all about serving your coaching clients; and that goes for internal and external coaches.

If someone else can help your clients (and you) learn and grow, or provide a different perspective or approach, then why wouldn't you fully support them? It's about leveraging all of your tools and resources to help your client.

The Second Rule: *Be open to the wisdom of the crowd.*

Multiple viewpoints and approaches are always better than one. I'm always a better coach when I pair with someone, and the client outcomes are always better. They help me consider things I might miss and avoid my own baggage. My partner keeps me sharp, honest, open-minded, and observant.

The obvious extension to this rule is being open to learning from those you're coaching as well.

The Third Rule: *Be a sponge, intent on continuous learning from everyone and everywhere.*

You should be coachable. How can you expect to be effective in coaching when you don't walk your own talk and seek to be coached? What kind of a role model are you being?

What does being coachable look like? I immediately think of three key aspects:

1. **External coaching and mentorship**. You seek out external coaches who have experience and skills to share with you, and you're open to their ideas.
2. **Internal reflection**. You spend a lot of time reflecting in your journey, your strengths, your successes and failures, your experiments, your comfort zone, and so on, continually improving your self-awareness.
3. **Feedback**. You relentlessly look for and listen to feedback, while also improving your observational and listening skills.

The primary problem is that many coaches don't want to ask for help or to admit that they might not know something or that someone else might have more experience than they do. This happens a lot with internal coaches. Once people have the title "Agile Coach" they often feel that they have to provide all of the answers or that asking for help is a sign of weakness or incompetence.

I view it quite differently. When we're open to others—learning, growing, trying new things, and asking for help—we become much more skilled and capable coaches. Which is exactly how we sharpen our saws.

Finding Places to Coach

You'd be surprised at the number of opportunities you have to practice your craft beyond your own company, organization, or client coaching opportunities. I firmly believe that every Badass Agile Coach should sharpen their saw by coaching as much and as often as possible. There's no better way to grow within our craft.

Here are just a few coaching opportunity ideas for you:

- **The Agile Alliance's Annual Agile Conference.** Quite often, the Agile Alliance conferences have opportunities for coaching in clinics, in open space, even in hallways.
- **Scrum Alliance Global and Regional Gatherings.** Usually, the Scrum Alliance gatherings have an area reserved for coaching, often called a *coaching clinic*, where volunteer coaches can provide coaching to attendees. Often, the sessions are timeboxed to 15–30 minutes so you can practice a variety of coaching stances, and stance switches, in a relatively short time. You can also pair-coach if you choose to do so.
- **Scrum Alliance Coaching Retreats.** These are events designed for people on the CEC and CTC certification tracks and for aspiring coaches. Often there are open space, dojo, and training opportunities offered. And the relationships you build can be priceless.
- **Agile Coach Camps.** There is a loose group of volunteers who host and plan annual coach camps in a variety of locales globally.
    - www.agilealliance.org/up-your-agile-coaching-by-organizing-an-agile-coach-camp/
    - https://agilecoachcampus.com/
    - https://agilecoachcamp.net/about-acc-worldwide/
- **Local Agile Conferences and Coaching Clinics.** Almost every week, it seems there is an agile coaching conference somewhere in the world. These are great opportunities for you to reach out to the organizers and offer to set up a coaching clinic. It can be as small as just you or as large as the conference space will allow. All it takes is a few interested coaches. And there always seem to be more than enough "clients" among the attendees.
- **Virtual Coaching Circles.** There are online coaching circles that provide places to mentor, be mentored, and practice your craft. Usually these are in some sort of dojo format using breakout rooms. I'm fond of Agile Coaching Circles (www.agilecoachingcircles.com), but I would encourage you to look around for others.

Beyond opportunities like these, I've been known to put on my own "events" just to gain more coaching opportunities. So, I'm encouraging you to be creative here. I'll give you just two examples to get your creative juices flowing.

Our local Raleigh-Durham ALN group has established a once-a-month Agile Coach's Breakfast meetup where we often learn and grow as coaches. One of my favorite parts is the coaching dojo practice sessions that we sometimes conduct. It's a safe place to sharpen our saws by practicing.

Another idea is creating your own local coaching opportunity. A few years ago, I started a coaching group called the Agile Moose Herd. It's a lean-coffee-ish format where like-minded agilists get together in an intimate and safe environment and help one another. We're always having coaching conversations and occasionally we break out into dojo-based practice sessions. It's energizing for me to see that everyone, no matter their experience level, has something valuable to offer the group.

I hope I've inspired you to find opportunities to practice your craft in the wild. I know they're out there, but you might have to do a bit of discovery work and ideation to find or create them.

Sharing Is Caring

There's probably no better way to wrap up this chapter than to explore a critical growth focus that I've alluded to throughout the chapter.

I've come to understand that the universe will return to you what you give it. For example, I often offer to coach and mentor folks. As I think back, it's been very often. I usually do it freely as part of my effort to give back to this wonderful agile community that I love so dearly. I do it so often that it's not uncommon for folks to ask me why I'm doing it. What's in it for me?

My answer is that I always get more from a coaching or mentoring relationship—much more. For example, I might have received:

- Additional learning and practice of my craft.
- Personal insights, inspiration, and hope.
- Business referrals and recommendations.
- A simple and grateful "thank you."
- The joy of helping someone else.
- The chance to see people grow and help others, paying it forward.

I may not see the return on my investment immediately. Sometimes it has come months or even years afterward. Sometimes I might not notice it at all. Nevertheless, I believe there is always a return that makes me smile inside and inspires me to trust the universe and continue to give back.

I hope that you try applying this secret for yourself. It really amplifies the sharpening of your saw while you're helping others do the same.

Further Reading

Here's a link to StrengthsFinders 2.0: www.gallup.com/cliftonstrengths/en/253676/how-cliftonstrengths-works.aspx.

Here's a link to StandOut 2.0 and a free assessment they offer: https://mailchi.mp/marcusbuckingham.com/standout-assessment.

Reflections

I want to encourage you to stop and reflect at the end of each section of the book—going back and reviewing to answer these questions.

This section focused largely on your ongoing development and growth as a Badass Agile Coach. The good news is that you're never really finished with your personal development, modeling that development, and serving as a role model to others (individuals, teams, and organizations) for their ongoing growth. To that end:

- What were your broader takeaways?
- What learning experiments might you try?
- How balanced are you right now around the Wheel and where might you need strengthening?

Take a look at the Wheel-based learning references in our Badass Agile Coaching Repo (registration link in the afterword) and pick two or three books or articles that you're willing to commit to exploring.

What are your ideas around Communities of Practice? Are there experiments or things to try here that you can influence, either in your company contexts or in your agile communities?

Explore some of the ideas and inspiration from this section with your coach. Use them as a sounding board for your growth, experimentation, and learning.

Visualization

I want you to close your eyes and get quiet. Center your attention on the notion of a Badass Agile Coach. That's you. Envision what that looks and feels like. Now think back over your career and over the entire book.

Now open your eyes. Perhaps fire up a mind map application and start to visualize your coaching career journey.

- Start in the past, capturing the essence points of your journey.
- Next, capture where you are now: your successes, challenges and hopes.
- Finally, map out possibilities for your future. Dream about where you want to go and capture aspects to get you there. Have multiple paths if you like.

If you don't want to capture them in a mind map, then jot down those ideas, aspirations, insights, plans, hopes, and dreams in your journal.

Haven't started journaling yet?

Well then, read this: www.agilemoose.com/blog/2019/6/23/journaling-how-to-get-started, and consider using our Agile Coach Journaling Canvas, which you can find in the repo.

Afterword

Phew! I think we're done.

Every time I've published a book, I've quickly forgotten how much work it takes. I guess that's good, because if I kept it fresh in mind I might not ever write another one. So, when I near the end, there is utter joy in finishing it, but also sadness around the end of another writing journey.

This effort was a bit different in that I collaborated with Jennifer, Rhiannon, and Mark on the writing. I hope and believe that the book is so much richer because of their contributions, both in writing and in thought provocation. And again, I want to thank them for traveling on this journey with me.

Final Thought

I thought long and hard about how I might want to end this book. What would wrap up the essence of the book's ideas, messages, and intentions? It's a challenging question to ponder. Then it came to me.

I needed a quote from another book. Not just any book, but Lyssa Adkins's classic work on *Coaching Agile Teams*.

> Agile coaching is 40% doing and 60% being. The powerful (silent) influence you have because of who you are and how agile values shine through your every move should not be underestimated. It's potent stuff. Through your being, you exert a far-reaching and long-lasting impact on people, teams, and organizations.

And I believe this captures the essence of what we've been exploring. That what you ARE and what you DO are your most important coaching attributes. To become a truly Extraordinarily Badass Agile Coach, it's about developing and shining as YOU.

Grateful

If you've made it this far as a reader, the first thing we want to tell you is: Thank you. We're incredibly grateful that you took the time to read and consider our thoughts, ideas, and experiences around *Extraordinarily Badass Agile Coaching*.

Everyone who has contributed to this book is incredibly humble and grateful for the opportunity you've given us to share and explore with you.

Comparative Agility

During the process of writing the book, I re-discovered Comparative Agility. They are a company created by Mike Cohn and Kenny Rubin around 2010. They provide a family of surveys around a wide variety of agile skills, roles, and themes.

The aha moment for me was the synergy between the concept and intent of this book, the evolution of the Agile Coaching Growth Wheel, and the support of the Personal Improvement (PI) surveys within Comparative Agility to complement your continuous learning.

Mark Summers and I are working with Comparative Agility to create an Agile Coaching PI survey that is centered on the Wheel. It should be available in late 2021, so look for it at www.comparativeagility.com.

Additional Resources – Badass Agile Coaching Repo

I had originally planned on adding quite a few appendixes to the book around several topics:

1. The history and evolution of the Agile Coaching Growth Wheel.
2. Additional coaching dojo scenarios.
3. Coaching anti-patterns and advice for avoiding them.
4. A rich learning resource roadmap for the Wheel's various competencies.
5. Guidance for hiring Badass Agile Coaches.
6. More actual coaching stories.

But then I realized that these would be relatively volatile and subject to change. So, I've decided to make an online supplemental resource repository available instead: the **Badass Agile Coaching Repo**.

I will keep the repo up-to-date with all of the resources and stories mentioned above. It will also allow me to update things over time so that everything stays current. And we will also consider evolving the repo into a community of sorts for community-based collaboration, learning, and growth.

The repo will be particularly important, as the Agile Coaching Growth Wheel is undergoing a major update in a volunteer-based effort sponsored by the Scrum Alliance. So, things will be changing.

In other words, the repo will be a special place for readers of the book to continue their development into Extraordinarily Badass Agile Coaches.

Please join us here: www.agile-moose.com/repo-landing.

Feedback

Our hope is that this book provided some valuable insights and ideas on how you might become a Badass Agile Coach. However, it was never intended to be exhaustive or prescriptive in nature. If we've learned one thing in our agile experience and reading, it's that the learning primarily comes in the doing.

If in your doing you find things you want to add or change in the text, please send them to me at bob@rgalen.com. You can also connect with me via LinkedIn (www.linkedin.com/in/bobgalen) if you wish to stay in touch.

And please consider writing a review of the book, either on Amazon or elsewhere. It makes a huge difference in how others become aware of our work.

Stay agile my friends!
Bob

About the Author

Bob Galen is an agile methodologist, practitioner, and coach based in Cary, NC. In this role, he helps guide companies and teams in their pragmatic adoption and organizational shift toward Scrum and other agile methods and practices. He is currently President and Principal Consultant at RGalen Consulting Group, LLC.

Bob regularly speaks at international conferences and professional groups on topics related to software development, project management, software testing, and team leadership. He is a Certified Enterprise Coach (CEC), ORSC trained, SAFe and Scrum@Scale certified, a Certified Kanban Master Coach, and an active member of the Agile and Scrum Alliances.

His previous books include *Software Endgames: Eliminating Defects, Controlling Change, and the Countdown to On-time Delivery* (2004); *Agile Reflections: Musings Toward Becoming "Seriously Agile" in Software Development* (2012); and *The Three Pillars of Agile Quality & Testing* (2015).

He also is co-host (with Josh Anderson) of the Meta-Cast podcast.

Bob can be reached at bob@rgalen.com or through his websites at https://rgalen.com/ and www.agile-moose.com, where he maintains active blogs.

Index

A
acceptance criteria, 54, 56
active listening, 96–99, 201. *See also* empathy
Adkins, Lyssa, 39
Advising stance
    at heart of mindset, 44, 297
    demonstrated, 131–32, 137–38
    in the Wheel, 110–11, 117
    with leaders, 27, 194, 196, 202–5, 208, 210
age, 276, 282–84
agile coaching
    3 Rules, 335–36
    challenges of, 3–4, 108
    defined, 9, 13, 23, 36
    internal vs. external, 11–12
    vs. professional coaching, 9–11, 91–92, 219
Agile Coaching Competency Framework (ACCF), 36, 39–43, 48
Agile Coaching Growth Wheel
    development, 108–10
    domain knowledge, 112–13, 123
    ethical guidance, 64, 67
    for group reflection, 114–17
    mastery areas, 111–12, 120–23
    personal growth, 113–14, 123–24
    stances, 110–11, 117–20
Agile Coaching Institute, 36, 39, 48
Agile/Lean Practitioner mastery, 112, 122–23, 297
Agile Manifesto, 34, 44
Agile Moose Herd, 320, 338
alignment (coach), 225, 233, 236–37
Anderson, Josh, 223
Appreciative Inquiry (AI), 330
assuming positive intent (API), 206, 209–10, 265–66, 272–73
Attention Deficit Hyperactivity Disorder. *See* neurodiversity
autism. *See* neurodiversity

B
Badass Agile Coaches
    are coachable, 334–36
    are contextually aware, 261–62
    are shepherds, 294–95
    are situationally aware, 241
    have an ongoing coach, 333
    invest in themselves, 296
    speak mindfully, 220–22, 223–25
Badass Agile Coaching Operating System, 88–90
badass/badassery
    3 Rules, 335–36
    choice of word, 2–4
    defined, 3, 13–15
    need for, 35
Braden, Jeremy, 210, 212
Bubolz, Jeff, 223

C
Cagly, Tom, 328
Calabrese, Jake, 43, 48
canvases
    Entry-Prep, 61, 62
    Coaching Agreement, 55, 56
    Client, 79, 80
    Daily Prep, 303–4
    Self-Care, 331–34
    Pair-Coaching, 234–39
Center of Excellence (CoE), 321–22

change artistry (metaskill), 183–87
change fatigue, 186–87
check-in questions, 141, 151, 161
Clean Language, 93
client experience, 89–90, 99–100
client goals
 documenting, 55, 56, 239
 establishing, 51–53, 54, 77
 reviewing, 59–60, 295–97
clients
 Client Canvas, 79, 80
 contexts, 262–63
 defined, 13
 feedback from, 145
 meeting as individuals, 286
 personas, 220
 responsibilities of, 12, 99–100
 serving them, 20–21
 as whole and resourceful, 22–23
coachability, 334–36
coach entry. *See* entering coaches
coaching agreements
 canvas, 55, 56
 Coaching Arc examples, 128–34, 142, 171, 173, 257–59
 ending, 59–60, 83
 establishing, 50–56, 67
 updating, 52
Coaching Arcs
 ad hoc, 170–73
 Coaching Habit questions, 94–95
 context-based, 264–67
 cycle of, 81, 149, 177
 demonstrated, 151–58, 161–66, 170–73
 overview, 70, 76–79
 planning, 38–39, 74–76
 planning examples, 57–59, 244, 246, 251, 253, 256
 role-based, 243–60

The Coaching Habit, 93–95, 101
coaching level, 297–98
coaching life cycle, 83–84
coaching models
 Agile Coaching Competency Framework (ACCF), 39–43
 baseline model, 36–38
 GROW, 85, 174
 The Heart of Agile, 44–45, 47, 48
 Kanban, 45–46
 Modern Agile Wheel, 46–47
 See also Agile Coaching Growth Wheel
Coaching Questions (Stoltzfus), 101
Coaching stance
 danger of overuse, 10–11, 43–44
 demonstrated, 129–30, 135–37, 170–73, 265–66
 in the Wheel, 111, 117–18
Co-Active Coaching, 91
Co-Active Leadership, 200–201
Cockburn, Alistair, 44–45
Community of Practice (CoP)
 activities, 320, 324–26
 vs. Center of Excellence, 321–22
 critical success factors, 322–23, 326–27
 defined, 320–21
 setting up, 322, 327
Comparative Agility, 16
conferences, 337
contextual awareness
 Coaching Arc examples, 264–72
 factors, 70–71, 262–63, 264, 265, 267, 270
 when coaching leaders, 299–301
CRR Global, 91
crucial conversations, 201–2, 212
Cynefin, 73–74, 185, 207

D

Daily Prep Canvas, 303–4
dancing in the moment, 24, 72–73, 137, 242, 261
Death by a Thousand Questions, 95–96, 170–73
designed coaching alliance/partnership, 51–52
diversity self-assessment, 276–77
dojos
    overview, 307–9
    roles, 310–11, 312, 314–15
    running effective, 313–15
    scenarios, 269, 309–10, 316 (*see also* scenarios)
    session types, 211, 311–12
domain knowledge, 112
dyslexia. *See* neurodiversity

E

Emory, Dale, 32–33
emotional field, 28, 31–32
emotional intelligence (EQ), 29–31, 262–63
empathy
    building, 31, 218–19
    context-based, 263
    defined, 30–31
    role-based, 194–96, 259–60
    situational, 281, 282–83
entering coaches
    Coaching Arc example, 128–34
    Entry-Prep Canvas, 61, 62
    into the system, 27, 60–61, 67
    without baggage, 20–21
ethics, 61, 63–66, 67
ethnicity, 276, 284–86
even over statements, 143–44
executives. *See* leaders
experiment cards, 165–67
explaining coaching, 53–54
external v. internal coaching, 11–12

F

Facilitating stance
    demonstrated, 142–44, 151–58, 161–66
    in the Wheel, 111, 118–19
    with leaders, 194
feedback from clients, 145
Fields, Jennifer, 5, 7, 241, 261
A Fixer (poem), 21
frameworks. *See* coaching models

G

Galen-Personick, Rhiannon, 6, 7, 276, 308
gender. *See* SOGI
General Anxiety Disorder. *See* neurodiversity
generations, 276, 282–84
Goleman, Daniel, 29
Greenleaf, Robert K., 22, 34
GROW model, 85, 174
Guiding Learning stance
    examples, 151, 250–52, 256–57
    in the Wheel, 111, 119
    with leaders, 194

H–K

The Heart of Agile, 44–45, 47, 48
helping, 302
humility, 19–21
iContact, 297–98
inspiration (metaskill), 187–89
internal v. external coaching, 11–12
International Coaching Federation (ICF), 23, 51, 63–64, 67, 90–91
Joiner, Bill, 198, 300
journaling

developing the habit, 34
for dojos, 269
planning, 57
situational awareness, 277, 279–80, 281, 283, 284, 285
skill development, 28–29, 182
Kanban Mindset, 45–46, 48
Kerievsky, Joshua, 46
Kessel-Fell, Jonathan, 41–43
Kotter's 8 Steps of Change, 183, 192

L

Lagestee, Len, 70, 83
language
　and empathy, 218
　guidance for coaches, 220–23
　as a maturity measure, 223–25
leaders
　agile transformations, 128–32, 207–8, 210–11
　arc examples, 170–73, 255–59
　coaching, 25, 27, 201–3, 299–301
　coaching on language, 226
　empathy for, 194–97, 212
　partnering with, 197
　scenarios, 203–11
　styles, 198–201
　and successful CoP, 323
leadership (metaskill), 180–83
Leadership Agility, 198, 300–301, 305
Leadership Circle, 198–99, 308
Leadership Style Canvas, 199
Leading stance, 111, 119–20, 194, 202
Little, Todd, 48

M

Maleski, Jeff, 223
maturity (agile)
　as coaching context, 262
　measuring, 223–25, 326–27
　Shu Ha Ri levels, 70–71
mentoring, 238, 325, 338–39. *See also* pair-coaching
Mersino, Anthony, 195–96, 212, 305, 328
metaskills
　applying, 27–28, 134, 301
　for client, 99–100
　defined, 26
　demonstrated, 135, 206, 208, 210
　examples, 26, 180–90
　practicing, 190–91
　when coaching leaders, 203
　See also specific metaskills
Mezick, Dan, 322
micromanaging leaders, 204–5
mindfulness, 23–24, 30, 333
mindset, agile/lean, 122–23, 222–23, 321–22
mindset, coaching, 89–99, 122
mindset, personal
　and the coaching ecosystem, 89
　curiosity, 28
　emotional intelligence, 29–32
　mindfulness, 23–25, 170, 264, 301
　models, 44–48
　reframing triggers, 32–33
　respect for clients, 21–23
　serving, 20–21, 293–95, 302
　See also ethics
Modern Agile Wheel, 46–48
motivation, 30

N–O

Nettleton, Carlton, 317
neurodiversity, 276, 279–82
non-positive closure, 59–60

Open Space events, 322, 326
Organization and Relationship Systems Coaching (ORSC), 24, 26, 31, 51, 91, 203

P

pair-coaching
  alignment, 233
  canvas, 234–39
  examples, 134, 139, 147, 159–60, 169, 175
  overview, 229–33
  roles, 237–38
  types of, 234
  See also mentoring
Personal Improvement survey, 16
personalizing coaching, 53–54
personas, 220
planning a coaching session, 56–57
polling questions, 116
positive psychology, 330–31
post-arc conversation, 79, 145
post-arc reflection, 132–34, 138–39, 146–47, 158–60, 167–69, 174–75, 263
powerful questions, 92–93, 95–96, 101
pre-arc planning, 128, 135, 140, 150, 160–61
presence, 24–25
prime directive, 23
privilege, 11–12, 25, 34, 278–79, 281, 284–87
product owners, 249–55, 269–72
professional vs. agile coaching, 9–11, 91–92, 219
pronouns, 277–78
pull vs. push coaching
  encouraging pull, 197, 298–99
  examples, 247–49, 257–59

R

race, culture, and ethnicity, 276, 284–86
Razzetti, Gustavo, 199
reflection, 293–94, 296–303, 323–24
reframing, 32–33, 218
resistance, 33, 185, 218, 247–49, 267–69
role-based coaching, 241–60, 326
role clarity and confusion, 12, 241
role modeling (metaskill), 19, 120, 189–90, 202, 278
roles
  agile, 242
  coaching, 36–38 (*see also* stances)
  dojos, 309, 310–11, 312, 314–15
Rule of 3 (Weinberg), 204, 212

S

safety
  client, 46, 47, 119, 165, 262
  coach, 12, 25, 188, 201, 236–37
  leader, 256
  for learning, 308, 320, 324, 338
  providing as a coach, 249, 269, 281, 285, 286
Satir Change Model, 183–86, 192, 263
scenarios
  coaching up, 203–10
  for dojos, 309–10, 316
  overallocated PO, 269–72
  team-lead troubles, 264–69
Scrum Alliance, 109, 337
Scrum Masters, 243–49, 294–95, 325
self-awareness, 29–30, 203, 238–39, 286
self-care, 262, 296, 324
Self-Care Canvas, 331–34
Self-Mastery, 110, 120, 132, 176

self-regulation, 30
Senge, Peter, 161
sense-and-respond, 10, 38, 72, 207
servant leadership, 20, 22
Serving (mastery), 21, 111, 121
sexual orientation. *See* SOGI
sharpening your saw, 297, 329–40
shepherd's mindset, 294–95
Sheridan, Richard, 47
Shu Ha Ri, 70–71
situational awareness, 71, 276–87, 302–3
Snowden, Dave, 73
social skills, 31
SOGI (sexual orientation and gender/gender identity), 276, 277–79
Spayd, Michael, 39
speaking truth to power, 201–2
Spotify Guilds, 321, 328
stances
    and the coaching ecosystem, 89
    overview, 9–10, 36–38
    switching, 137, 140, 151, 176
    in the Wheel, 110–11
    when coaching leaders, 194
    See also individual stances
Stanier, Michael Bungay, 93–94
storytelling, 83, 202
strengths-based learning, 330–31
Summers, Mark, 6–7, 108, 149
superpowers, 238–39
systems thinking, 203, 262–63, 333

T

team working agreements, 142–45
tensions, 161–65
Transforming (mastery), 112, 121–22, 194, 196, 202–3

V–Z

virtual coaching circles, 337
Whitmore, John, 85, 118
working agreements, 142–45
X-wing coaching model. *See* Agile Coaching Competency Framework (ACCF)

Made in the USA
Columbia, SC
16 January 2024